Unemployment
Insurance
and
Active Labor
Market Policy

Labor Economics and Policy Series

Editor
John D. Owen
Wayne State University

Series Advisory Board

John T. Addison
University of South Carolina

Morley K. Gunderson
University of Toronto

Günther Schmid
Wissenschaftszentrum
Berlin and Free
University of Berlin

Masanori Hashimoto
Ohio State University

Books in this series

The Aging of the American Work Force: Problems, Programs, Policies,
edited by Irving Bluestone, Rhonda J. V. Montgomery, and John D.
Owen, 1990

Job Displacement: Consequences and Implications for Policy, edited by
John T. Addison, 1991

Unemployment Insurance and Active Labor Market Policy: An International Comparison of Financing Systems, by Günther Schmid, Bernd
Reissert, and Gert Bruche, 1992

Unemployment Insurance and Active Labor Market Policy

*An International Comparison
of Financing Systems*

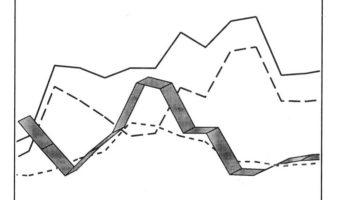

Günther Schmid, Bernd Reissert,
and Gert Bruche

 Wayne State University Press   Detroit

Manufactured in the United States of America.
96 95 94 93 92   5 4 3 2 1

Library of Congress Cataloging-in-Publication Data

Schmid, Günther, 1942–
    [Arbeitslosenversicherung und aktive Arbeitsmarktpolitik.
English]
    Unemployment insurance and active labor market policy : an
international comparison of financing systems / Günther
Schmid, Bernd Reissert, and Gert Bruche.
        p.   cm. — (Labor economics and policy series)
    "Revised version of Arbeitslosenversicherung und aktive
Arbeitsmarktpolitik"—
    Includes bibliographical references and index.
    ISBN 0-8143-2314-6 (alk. paper)
    1. Insurance, Unemployment—Finance—Case studies.
    2. Full employment policies—Case studies.
    I. Reissert, Bernd.   II. Bruche, Gert.
    III. Title.   IV. Series.
    HD7095.S35   1992
    368.4'401—dc20   91–19311

Designer: Mary Krzewinski

This book is a revised version of *Arbeitslosenversicherung und
aktive Arbeitsmarktpolitik* (Berlin: Edition Sigma, 1987).

Contents

5

Tables and Figures

FIGURES

Preface

This is an institutional study. Specifically, we investigate how impending or actual unemployment is processed by social institutions and, in particular, the role played by systems of financing for unemployment insurance and active labor market policy. Financing systems determine which institutions have to bear the financial burden of unemployment or benefit if unemployment is avoided; whether an unemployed person is eligible for any wage-replacement benefits and the amount and duration of the benefit entitlement; and whether societal resources will be used for financing measures to prevent or reduce unemployment (active labor market policy) instead of merely for benefits (passive labor market policy). These institutional conditions also affect the behavior of labor market actors: the job-search behavior of the unemployed, the mobility of the employed, the hiring practices of firms, wage negotiations between trade unions and employers, and the employment policies of different levels of government. Our thesis is that the same economic causes (price changes, technological rationalization, new products) can have very different labor market effects because of such institutional factors and their impact on the behavior of labor market actors.

Our study examines how public labor market policy has developed under different national financing systems and the extent to which differences in financing and organization have led to different patterns in the development of unemployment insurance and active

11

labor market policy. In this context a cross-national comparative analysis seems to be most appropriate because the question of whether financing systems "make a difference" can only be studied empirically through observation of actual differences in financing systems.

Labor market policy in the six countries investigated (Austria, France, Federal Republic of Germany, Great Britain, Sweden, and the United States) has existed under quite different institutional conditions during the last twenty years. The distribution of responsibility for labor market programs, responsibility for financing these programs, and procedures for determining revenues and expenditures all differ markedly from country to country. For example, in the German institutional system for labor market policy, unemployment insurance and active labor market policy are incorporated in a single administrative organization. The Federal Employment Institute, financed through contributions with federal government responsibility for covering any deficits, does not exist in the same form in any other country. The institutional systems of other countries are also quite varied. We are thus confronted with a situation in which similar disturbances in the employment system are processed by different organizational and financing systems. If—as we suppose—different institutional conditions are associated with different patterns of response to the employment problem, this will provide important insights into the challenging problem of redesigning institutions (institutional engineering), when existing arrangements exhibit clear and politically undesirable shortcomings.

While other comparative institutional studies have focused on systems of unemployment insurance in isolation, none has investigated the interrelationship between the financing of wage-replacement benefits and active labor market policy, which is central to our study. We think that spending billions annually for unproductive income maintenance—in particular for the long-term unemployed—is irrational not only economically but also from the point of view of social policy. Most unemployed persons, it should be emphasized, wish nothing more than to find satisfactory employment again as soon as possible, to earn their own keep and be productive members of society.

Separate consideration of unemployment insurance and active labor market policy tends to lead to isolated and, in our opinion, false solutions. A one-sided focus on unemployment insurance tends to regard wage-replacement benefits as mere cost or as a barrier to the downward flexibility of wages. When financing problems occur, this perspective—depending on the particular institutional tradition—

tends to recommend either that bad risks be excluded or that wage-replacement benefits be drastically curtailed. The productive functions of unemployment insurance are thereby overlooked—namely, that predictable and generous provision of social security in cases of unemployment inter alia increases the readiness of the unemployed not only to accept the occupational or regional mobility necessary to reintegrate them into the labor market but to do so willingly. The possibility that such a system can be abused—which is undeniable—obscures this insight. The danger of abuse—this is one of the key results of our analysis—can, however, be in part eliminated by coupling unemployment insurance with attractive active labor market policy offers.

The one-sided emphasis on the traditional instruments of active labor market policy can also lead to undesirable reactions: the expansion of programs merely in order to achieve a statistical effect (e.g., a reduction in registered unemployment), the use of labor market measures to shift fiscal burdens (e.g., the substitution of job creation measures for regular public tasks), or even oppressive forms of work discipline (e.g., employment programs that border on compulsory work). Only a well-developed system of unemployment insurance based on entitlements can prevent such abuse of the instruments of active labor market policy.

In order to avoid both of these one-sided approaches, suitable financing institutions are needed. What form they might take is the object of the following study. Our principal results can be summarized as follows: the promotion of labor market flexibility requires not less but a comprehensive social security for the unemployed consisting of a basic income security provision for all and the maintenance of an appropriate standard of living for regular wage and salary earners. Such a system of unemployment insurance is financially feasible if it is closely tied to active labor market policy and if flexible forms of financing are institutionalized. The financial basis for unemployment benefits and active measures in the future should be contributions, supplemented, however, by a state (tax-financed) subsidy and by special-purpose funds.

This comparative study would not have been possible without the assistance of numerous persons and institutions. Special thanks are due to our foreign collaborators, friends, and experts who assisted us in the production of country reports. We would like to thank in particular those colleagues who played a major role in the production of national case studies by contributing their expertise and comprehensive background materials: Stefan Potmesil, Helmut Höpflinger, Georg Waller, Michael Wagner (Austria); Jean François Colin and

Jocelyne Gaudin (France); Richard Disney and David Metcalf (Great Britain); Jan Johannesson and Eskil Wadensjö (Sweden); and William Mirengoff (U.S.A.).

Fortunately, cross-national comparative research is not a one-sided transfer of knowledge and experience. Travels in other countries not only educate the visitor but also provoke the host to see things in new ways or even take notice of them for the first time when confronted with intensive questioning or a different perspective. Whether we have been able to offer an equivalent exchange through our work contacts, country reports, and the present study must, of course, be left to our foreign colleagues to judge. Special thanks are also due to the Federal Minister for Labor and Social Affairs, who provided financial support in the project's initial phase. We are, of course, solely responsible for the contents of the study, which in no way represents the opinion of the Labor Ministry. Finally, we would like to thank all those colleagues at the Wissenschaftszentrum Berlin, Labor Market and Employment Unit, who frequently provided substantive or moral support. Thanks go especially to Brigitte Freihoff, who typed many versions of the study and the related country reports and who also had to cope with the change from typewriter to word-processing technology. We would like to thank Christoph Büchtemann and Egon Matzner for reading and commenting on the entire manuscript. Thanks also to Susanne Jahn, Lothar Linke, Holger Peinemann, Winnetou Sosa, and Gerold Kirchner for untiring and skillful assistance in the collection, analysis, and presentation of statistical data. Last but not least, we are very much indebted to Hugh Mosley who has translated the German text. In our view, he has done an extremely good job and has often helped to clarify our arguments.

PART ONE

Introduction

CHAPTER 1

Financing Problems of
Labor Market Policy

> Thus a problem, if it is to be solved, must be formulated
> in quantitative terms or at least expressed in terms of
> "more" or "less"—which may not be possible. Econo-
> mists are often not even able to give approximate values:
> this imprecision can also be intentionally imprecise for
> political reasons. As in every exact science, the formula-
> tion of the problem itself can be such a difficult task that
> it already entails a solution.
>
> (Morgenstern 1966:19)

1.1 THE DIFFICULTY OF FORMULATING THE PROBLEM

At first sight the problem seems to be clear: How much should
the unemployed receive in wage-replacement benefits and for how
long; how much public funding should go (instead) for manpower programs, invested in "active" labor market policy; and, finally, how
should the necessary financial resources be made available? Or, from
the point of view of the citizen: How are my financial needs to be provided for in case of unemployment, what does the state do, what do
the trade unions and employers do about it, and who pays for it?

The above quotation from the economist and game theorist
Oskar Morgenstern suggests the difficulties inherent in formulating the
problem more precisely. More than twenty years ago Morgenstern
considered the economic and social sciences to be so under developed
that it was usually impossible even to clearly define a problem, much
less to solve it (Morgenstern 1966:12). The examination of financing
unemployment insurance and active labor market policy appears to
prove him right: under in-depth observation the topic disintegrates

into a multiplicity of viewpoints and problems each of which appears to be plausible in itself.

1. The financing of labor market policy and unemployment insurance is, from the point of view of finance ministries, above all a problem of avoiding deficits in public budgets. If unemployment does not result in any deficits, then the problem is solved.

2. From the point of view of ministers of trade and industry, the problem is frequently reduced to the displacement of private investment by excessive expenditures for labor market policy, which results in a natural coalition with the finance ministry. If there is enough private investment, there will not be any unemployment and thus no problem of financing labor market policy.

3. Ministers for labor and social affairs are, as a rule, interested in the mobilization of additional resources for unemployment insurance and active labor market policy, either out of sheer necessity caused by increasing unemployment and deficits in the unemployment insurance system, or in order to prevent the deficits in the pension and health insurance systems that result from higher levels of unemployment, or because they feel committed to support the interests of employees, or merely in order to enhance the importance of their own ministry.

4. Local governments fear high and persistent unemployment because in most countries they will have to finance public assistance outlays for those who are not covered by social insurance, the primary safety net of the social security system.

5. Employers complain about the growing burden of nonwage labor costs that results from the financing of unemployment benefits or active labor market policy, employees' lack of motivation and lack of interest in mobility as a supposed result of excessively generous social benefits, as well as the inefficiency of the labor market authority.

6. Trade unions demand the rechanneling of public resources into labor market and employment programs and defend high wage-replacement levels as a brake against the downward pressure of unemployment on wages.

7. Employees, insofar as they are fortunate enough to have a job, are sensitive to the increasing burden of social security contributions, and their solidarity with the unemployed is strained.
8. A growing number of unemployed persons who receive no benefits or only reduced benefits resent having been abandoned by labor market policy.

This (in no way exhaustive) enumeration of problem perspectives is evidently a reflection of different interests. The formulation of problems in the social sciences and economics requires consideration of interests, both overlapping and conflicting, and the formulation of constraints under which problems have to be solved largely depends on how these interests are weighted. Lack of clarity in the formulation of the problems is thus in no way an expression of the analytic and theoretical underdevelopment of the social sciences but rather is indicative of the complexity of the subject matter *and* of the political implications of problem definitions, as the quotation from Morgenstern suggests.

The strategy of the "hard" sciences—of which mathematics is the model—of achieving clarity in the formulation of problems through the elimination of complexity and the reduction of constraints to a minimum can only be pursued to a limited extent in the "soft" social sciences. The latter cannot afford to eliminate by definition essential interrelationships *and* essential political interests in complex causal constellations. "The decisive question in light of the greater complexity of problems of economic policy is: What is permissible in order to solve a problem?" (Morgenstern 1966:14). Another quote from Morgenstern further clarifies this point:

> The history of mankind manifests frequent changes in the means that society regards as being permissible for solving its problems. For example, one could eliminate unemployment very easily if enslavement of the unemployed, simply shooting them, confining them to a labor camp, or drafting them into military service were regarded as being suitable methods. On the other hand, in the present state of economic theory it is almost impossible to employ the unemployed if neither a temporary reduction in wages nor an allocation of workers to industries or to other geographic districts is permissible. There may possibly be solutions given these constraints, but clearly the situation is fundamentally more compli-

cated and only distantly resembles the "purely theoretical" situation in which wage reductions and labor mobility are unrestrictedly permissible. (Morgenstern 1966:18)

The message here is clear: "Limitations on the means employed reflect in many respects an advance in civilization" (Morgenstern 1966:19). This, however, puts the social sciences in a much more difficult situation than is the case for the (exact) natural sciences. The object of investigation is more complex and the constraints are greater because of established institutions and norms. Just as the demand for simplicity has promoted progress in mathematics, the demand for due consideration of societal complexity—existing institutions, diversity of interests, and high normative standards—leads to advance in the social sciences.

The problem of financing social security for the unemployed and combating unemployment by "active" policy measures is thus neither exhausted nor adequately defined by asking how much is to be spent on labor market policy and who should pay for it. On the one hand, solutions to the problem are already in place in the form of historically evolved financing institutions, and, on the other hand, the multiplicity of interest-oriented problem perceptions complicates assessment of their adequacy in the light of changed economic, social, and political conditions. We must first elucidate the significance of "institutional filters" as historically evolved responses to problems and then order the complexity generated by the multiplicity of problem perspectives into analyzable subproblems. The first task, therefore, is to specify more precisely the goals of this study. After this preliminary analysis we will not have obtained a "quantitative" formulation of the problem—in Morgenstern's sense—but at least we will have surveyed the terrain and identified those points requiring further information and explanation.

1.2 FINANCING SYSTEMS DETERMINE POLICY

During his travels, as Odysseus anticipated coming into the vicinity of the sirens, he had himself bound to the mast of his ship in order to protect himself against this dangerous temptation. He thus resolved a decision-making problem prospectively in a rational way, which would not have been possible if he had waited until the problem itself occurred (Elster 1979:36).

This function of self-binding and prospective decision making is performed in social life by institutions. Through norms, regulations, and the allocation of tasks and responsibilities, institutions determine how one is to behave in future decision-making situations or—where it is not possible to formulate a rule in advance—who decides what and when.

Institutions may be based on Odysseus's clever foresight that—because of weakness, confusion, or magical powers—one's own decisions in a critical moment can be false. "Fore-sight" thus becomes "pre-caution" (self-binding function of norms). Such precautionary measures can also be taken to protect oneself against the erroneous decisions of others (other-binding function of norms).

Institutions may also arise from a desire to reduce the transaction costs of decision making (efficiency function) in similar and recurring decision-making situations by means of fixed responses (in the form of rules and regulations) or by specifying the locus of authority and responsibility in order to make behavior predictable for others (the function of stabilizing expectations).

Finally, institutions may be established in order to regulate the settlement of future conflicts and cleavages that cannot be rationally resolved in advance. The necessary consensus for future decision-making situations with an uncertain outcome can be attained by establishing procedures and conditions that are perceived as being fair (negotiating or bargaining function).

Institutions may develop that are specialized in one of the above goals. Usually, however, they fulfill a number of the functions. Financing systems also represent a complex of institutions that are derived from different motives and fulfill different functions. Thus, financing institutions for labor market policy are precautionary measures in light of the risk of unemployment (e.g., compulsory contributions to unemployment insurance), routinizing and economizing mechanisms for deciding recurring problems of resource allocation (e.g., determination of the amount and duration of unemployment benefits), or procedural rules for settling conflicts in decision-making situations (e.g., decisions about the level of contributions to unemployment insurance to be made by parliament in case of changed economic and financial conditions and not, for example, through collective bargaining).

Whatever the form of these institutions, they always act as a filter for information and interests, as incentives for individual or collective decison makers, or as norms for individual or collective behavior, so that they delimit the spectrum of possible decisions and actions and, as a consequence of their selective impact, favor certain solutions and impede or exclude others entirely.

Institutions are, therefore, not politically neutral: they reflect power relations, represent a congealed form of political will. As such, they are in principle changeable when political will changes. Nevertheless, once established, they acquire their own dynamics and display unanticipated effects. Because of their steering function, which is in part indirect ("hidden hand"), and their own institutional momentum, they may come into conflict with new socioeconomic constellations and policy goals.

From an institutional point of view, it is, therefore, interesting to observe how public labor market policy has developed under different financing systems and the extent to which they have led to different patterns of policy. The next section discusses such possible issues in financing systems for labor market policy.

1.3 PRINCIPAL ISSUES INVESTIGATED

The original impetus for this study was the observed fiscal functionalization of the labor market budget in the German system of financing, that is, that expenditures for active labor market policy depend more on the short-term constraints affecting the federal government budget than on the actual requirements of the labor market situation. In the Federal Republic of Germany funding for both branches of labor market policy—unemployment benefits, or "passive" labor market policy, and "active" labor market policy (training, mobility promotion, temporary public job creation)—comes from the same source: contributions of employers and employees to the Federal Employment Institute. As a consequence, expenditures for passive and active labor market policy compete, especially during a recession when contributions fall and expenditures for passive labor market policy rise almost automatically because of increasing unemployment. When the Federal Employment Institute runs a deficit, the federal government is obligated to cover the shortfall with a grant from its own general government budget. With increasing deficits, the political pressure to reduce the FEI's deficit also increases. In such a situation, two fiscal rules of thumb are usually applied: cut expenditures where they arise, and cut expenditure items with the highest costs. Because expenditures for labor market training, for example, are higher per person than are expenditures for unemployment benefits, it is plausible to cut the first type of expenditure. Another reason is that

it is easier for the government to reduce expenditures for general purposes (as is the case with most expenditures for active labor market
policy) than expenditures for specific benefits based on legal entitlements. It is, therefore, reasonable to expect that passive labor market
policy will crowd out active measures. This is exactly what has happened: expenditures for active labor market policy were cut when unemployment increased after the first oil crisis, and disadvantaged
groups on the labor market were especially hard hit by the cuts. The
second test of the German system for financing labor market policy,
the 1981–82 recession induced by the second oil price increase, led to
even larger cuts in active labor market policy. How can this fiscal
functionalization of the labor market budget be avoided? Do countries
with different financing systems exhibit different patterns of spending
for labor market policy?

An examination of the current system for financing labor market policy is also necessary for a number of other reasons related to the
above considerations. They can be described in terms of the following
questions and hypotheses:

1. Does the fiscal functionalization of the labor market budget—that is, the subordination of labor market policy to the
   fiscal constraints of the federal budget—not itself lead to a
   decline in the significance and efficiency of labor market
   policy, which is then used to justify even further reductions
   in active measures? How can labor market policy fulfill its
   preventive tasks when its financing and personnel resources are increasingly committed to the urgent task of
   providing wage-replacement benefits for the unemployed
   (administration of unemployment)? How can a policy instrument function efficiently when its financing and regulations are continually being changed? A stop-and-go policy
   prevents systematic learning at the operational level and
   creates uncertainty among both the target groups and the
   sponsors of labor market policy measures.

2. To what extent is it correct to assume that the conflict
   between federal budgetary constraint and the financial
   requirements of manpower programs is based on assumptions that are false from a broader societal perspective? Active labor market policy might be beneficial even from a
   fiscal point of view if the different government budgets and
   specialized funding institutions were viewed as a whole.
   From this perspective the financing of labor market policy

is less a problem of overcoming budgetary restrictions by developing additional funding resources than a question of political-institutional reform: the need for a greater institutional congruence in the cost and benefit flows of labor market policy in order to eliminate the apparent conflict between it and fiscal policy (incongruence thesis).

3. What influence does the financing system for labor market policy have on the frequently praised built-in stabilizer function of labor market policy? According to the new macroeconomic employment theory (Malinvaud 1977, 1984), this operates less through the multiplier effect of investments than through the greater demand stimulation resulting from transfer payments to the unemployed, whose marginal propensity to consume is on the average higher than that of those still employed. Is this stabilizer function not weakened when an increasing percentage of the unemployed no longer receive unemployment insurance benefits, as a consequence either of the increasing duration of unemployment (exhaustion of benefits) or of the changing structure of unemployment (an increasing percentage of the unemployed who have never been entitled to benefits)? What impact do reductions in benefits (wage-replacement rate) resulting from efforts to reduce deficits have on the demand-stabilizer function?

4. The stabilizer function is also affected by the revenue side. Sources of financing vary in their sensitivity to the business cycle. Financing through contributions makes labor market policy dependent on the level of covered employment, which is more sensitive to fluctuations in the business cycle than are general tax revenues. Financing both active and passive labor market policy out of the same fund based on revenues from contributions can, under conditions of increasing unemployment, lead to a "crowding out" of active labor market policy by wage-replacement benefits. The consequence would be procyclical variation in active labor market policy and thus a diminution of its preventive and countercyclical function. There is also the contrasting thesis that adherence to insurance principles and financing through contributions protect active labor market policy from intervention by the treasury and thus for this reason form a suitable basis for long-term financing of permanent tasks.

5. A further problem is the effect of increases in contributions to finance increased benefits on the profitability and hence investment and employment behavior of firms. Do increases in contributions—where the labor market budget is (predominantly) financed by employers—deter investment or constitute a positive incentive for accelerated rationalization such that this procyclical effect offsets the above-mentioned demand-side built-in stabilizer effect?

6. In addition, there is also the question of the indirect demand-stabilizing effect of labor market policy. Is it true that a well-developed social security system and active labor market policy reduce both the objective and subjective risk of loss of income and status in times of crisis and hence prevent procyclical psychological reactions, such as an overcautious savings response—and hence loss of demand—because of fear of unemployment?

7. Unemployment, as a rule, is unequally distributed across regions and economic sectors. The financing system influences the regional and sectoral impact of labor market policy on both the revenue and expenditure sides. Is our supposition correct that tax-financed systems—as opposed to those financed through contributions—are more likely to display a regional or sectoral selectivity in expenditures corresponding to the intensity of labor market problems? This supposition is based on the fact that the incidence of burdens (payment of contributions) and program benefits have to be related; they may not diverge too much (insurance or equivalence principle) in a system financed through contributions. In other words, to what extent do systems based on contributions limit the application of the principle of solidarity, and how do other types of financing systems function in this regard?

8. An analogous problem results from the interpersonal distribution of unemployment. Is it true, as sometimes supposed, that—as a result of insurance principle—systems based on contributions concentrate program benefits more on those who pay contributions—that is, on "core workers"—to the neglect of marginal groups in the labor force? Can tax-financed systems better perform functions of interpersonal redistribution to the benefit of problem and marginal groups? What is the relationship between financing systems and the generosity of benefits? Is it true

that contribution-based systems are more generous than tax-financed systems, with, however, the consequence that certain groups among the unemployed are increasingly excluded from receipt of benefits?

9. A general problem of collective financing systems is also applicable to labor market policy: How do the various types of financing structures affect the behavior of those who benefit from programs? Is it true that certain types of systems encourage abuse (moral hazard or free rider problem)? To what extent is it reasonable to strengthen insurance principles (different benefit and contribution rates, discounts, waiting periods)?

10. Numerous other problems and questions might also be mentioned. For example, it is unclear how political-administrative decision-making structures affect the level and composition of revenues (resource mobilization mix) and the expenditure side (policy mix) of the labor market budget. Of great political and practical importance also is the question of the extent to which the financing system promotes or hinders the transferability of unemployment insurance entitlements into productive labor market programs, such as subsidies for entering self-employment, subsidies for workplace alterations so that jobs can be performed by disabled persons, or subsidies for employer-based training in case of restructuring measures.

1.4 OBJECTIVES AND ORGANIZATION OF THE STUDY

In summary, we investigate the relationship between the financing system and revenues and expenditures for labor market policy, the role played by labor market policy in employment policy as a whole, and the impact of the financing system for labor market policy on the classical goals of the welfare state. The study's findings should contribute to the redeployment of financial resources from those currently being used to finance unemployment (unemployment benefit, unemployment assistance, public assistance) to financing employment.

There are three basic reasons for this policy preference. First, unemployment is more than a question of income. Only those who earn their own living can feel like full members of society and experience self-fulfillment. Second, the long-term payment of the unemployed who want to work is economically irrational and socially undesirable. Third, those who pay taxes and contributions to financing a large number of involuntarily unemployed persons can hardly be expected to finance additional meaningful public tasks. Deficiencies in labor market policy financing diminish the resources available for other purposes.

Figure 1 depicts schematically the objectives of our investigation. The thickness of the connecting lines indicates the relative importance of different topics.

The comparative analysis of the financing systems of several countries should contribute to answering the questions and problems discussed above. It should yield knowledge about the interrelationship between financing structures and the dynamics of revenues and expenditures as well as their impact on the efficiency and redistributional effects of labor market policy. It should also provide useful information for the current discussion of institutional engineering, the improvement of the financing systems for labor market policy.

The selection of the six countries included in the study was based on various characteristics: differences in the organization and financing of labor market policy and in the role of labor market policy within the total system of employment policy, as well as differences in the level, structure, and development of unemployment. The Federal Republic of Germany is the only country in which unemployment (passive labor market policy) and manpower programs (active labor market policy) are organizationally and financially integrated in a single institution, which is financed through contributions and for which the state covers any deficits. Labor market policy plays an important role in the employment system, and the labor market administration that implements it is institutionally well developed. Unemployment remained limited in the 1970s, and the financing system was first seriously tested as a result of the rapid increase in unemployment in the 1980s.

France was selected because both the institutional system of labor market policy and the financing system are highly fragmented, which raises the question of how in such a system the interdependence of active and passive labor market policy and other instruments of employment policy are coordinated. Active labor market policy played initially a modest role and then an increasingly important one. Unemployment had already increased strongly in the mid-1970s and is above all characterized by a high rate of youth unemployment.

Great Britain is interesting as a country that experienced chronic and high levels of unemployment early. Moreover, it is also

Figure 1

A Contextural Model of Financing Labor Market Policy

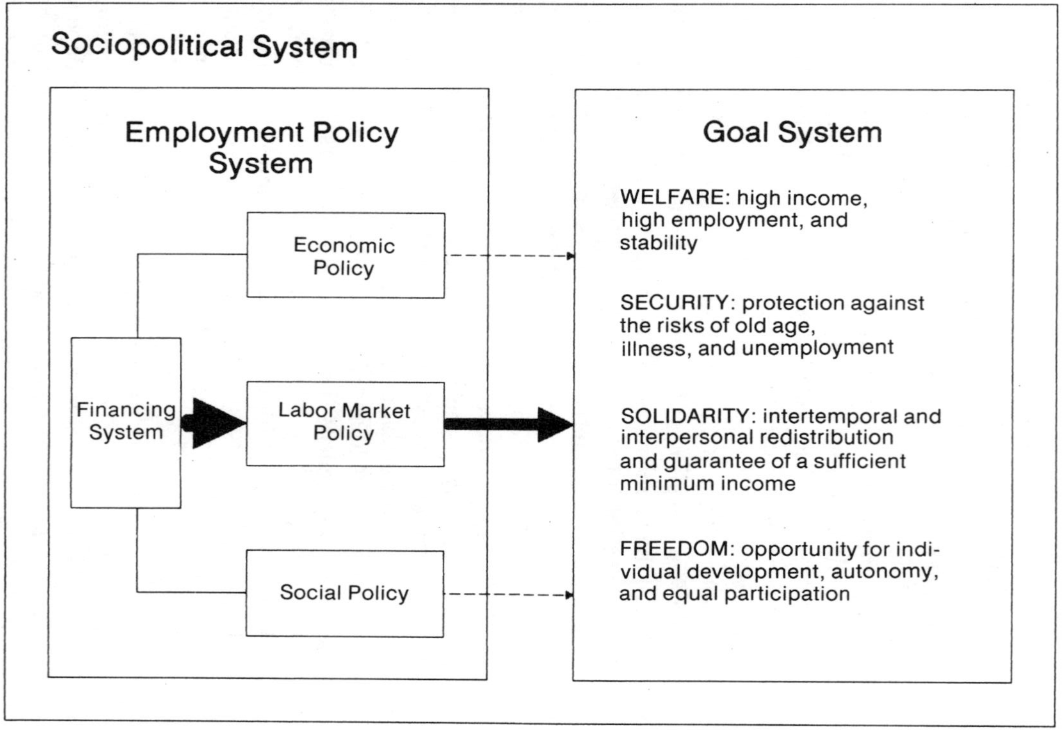

Sociopolitical System

Employment Policy System

Economic Policy

Labor Market Policy

Social Policy

Financing System

Goal System

WELFARE: high income, high employment, and stability

SECURITY: protection against the risks of old age, illness, and unemployment

SOLIDARITY: intertemporal and interpersonal redistribution and guarantee of a sufficient minimum income

FREEDOM: opportunity for individual development, autonomy, and equal participation interesting because of the policies of the Thatcher government, which have attempted to combat unemployment with monetarist and strictly market-oriented means. Although labor market policy plays in principle no significant role in this economic strategy, its actual importance has increased continuously. Moreover, labor market policy financing is highly integrated in the general social security system, and active labor market policy is financed from general revenues rather than from social insurance contributions.

Austria and Sweden both have low unemployment rates in contrast to most other OECD countries, but their labor market policies play quite different roles. The financing systems are also very different: Austria has a system based on contributions which is comparable with that in West Germany (although labor market policy plays a very small role), whereas Sweden has a more tax-financed system of labor market policy which—in contrast to all other countries—plays a central role in employment policy.

The United States was selected because it is the only OECD country that considerably reduced active labor market policy in the 1980s after a strong expansive phase at the end of the 1970s. This is indicative of a low degree of institutionalization and a high degree of flexibility in the financing system. As in Great Britain, the financing system is characterized by a strict separation between active and passive labor market policy, and by financing through general revenues for the former and through contributions for the latter. The United States is also the only country in which unemployment insurance is largely decentralized and contributions to unemployment insurance are almost exclusively paid by employers. Although the United States in the middle of the 1970s had one of the highest rates of unemployment—heavily concentrated among youth and ethnic minorities—its relative position improved in comparison to most European countries as a result of an impressive expansion of employment.

In addition to these selection criteria, a number of pragmatic considerations also played a role; international comparison requires intimate knowledge of the countries studied. The number of countries must remain limited, and we chose countries that we are familiar with from earlier studies and in which we have good institutional and personal contacts.

The study focuses on those policy areas in which public expenditures are used to directly influence supply and demand on the labor market or to provide benefits for the unemployed: active labor market policy in the sense of job placement and counseling, measures of vocational training and retraining, job creation measures, measures to promote employment for certain target groups, vocational rehabilitation and sheltered employment, measures to preserve jobs (e.g., short-time compensation); passive labor market policy in the sense of wage-replacement benefits in case of unemployment, bankruptcy, and (insofar as it is considered to be part of the national labor market budget) early retirement.[1] This definition of labor market policy is roughly congruent with the tasks that are carried out by the Federal Employment Institute in West Germany.

In Chapter 2, we start with a description of the basic features of the organization and financing of labor market policy in the countries studied. This brief sketch of the six national systems is based on detailed country reports which have already been published elsewhere separately (Bruche and Reissert 1985; Bruche 1984a, 1984b; Schmid 1984; Reissert 1985).

The comparative analysis begins in Part II. We consider the theoretical foundations and the historical development of the institutions of unemployment insurance, their organizational forms and financing regulations prior to the beginning of the first great recession in 1974–75, and then the changes that have taken place in reaction to the growing labor market crisis up to the mid-1980s. Next we analyze the effects of the financing systems on social security for the unemployed, on public budgets, and on supply and demand in the labor market.

Part III is the empirical complement to Part II. First a historical overview of the development of active labor market policy as an institution is presented. Then the organization and financing of active labor market policy are described in relationship to the development of the labor market situation. The comparative analysis focuses on the effects of the financing systems on the level and composition of active labor market policy measures; the incentives (or disincentives) that result from the institutional distribution of the costs and benefits of these measures; their impact on the business cycle; and regional, sectoral, and interpersonal patterns of distribution.

In Part IV we summarize what we have learned through our survey of six countries and the conclusions that can be drawn for the design of institutions (institutional engineering) for labor market policy financing.

In addition to an extensive bibliography, this study also includes comprehensive comparative data in tabular form in an appendix, which can be used either to recapitulate our comparative findings or for further secondary analysis.

Because the original German version of our study was completed in 1987, most of our descriptions of labor market policy organizations and financing systems refer to the mid-1980s and do not take into account such recent changes as the abolition of the Manpower Services Commission in Great Britain. However, our empirical analyses of labor market policy expenditures in Parts II and III have been updated to 1988.

CHAPTER **2**

Financing Systems for Labor Market Policy in Six Countries: An Overview

This chapter briefly describes the most important characteristics of the financing systems in the six countries[1] studied: the role of labor market policy in employment policy as a whole, the administrative structure of labor market policy, the sources of financing for passive and active labor market policy, the rules and procedures for budget making and implementation. A diagram of labor market policy financing is included for each national system.

2.1 AUSTRIA

Until the beginning of the 1980s, Austrian labor market policy —despite a considerable increase in expenditures—was not a significant factor in federal government finances. This was a consequence of the priority given to the creation and protection of employment in fiscal policy, which limited expenditures for income security for the unemployed and gave no role to active labor market policy with regard to the *level* of employment. The crisis of 1981–83 appears to have led to the temporary end of this division of labor: expenditures for the income security of the unemployed increased dramatically, active labor market policy measures to maintain employment were expanded, and an "alternative labor market" began to come into being—even though at a modest level—in the form of public job creation measures.

Labor market policy in Austria is conducted by a three-tiered federal administration (Arbeitsmarktverwaltung), whose highest administrative level is one of the six divisions of the Federal Ministry for Social Administration (BMS). In the 1950s, this labor market authority was primarily responsible for unemployment insurance. It was only in the 1970s that it was made responsible for active labor market policy measures. Until then only special measures for the construction industry and short-time benefits had been of some importance in Austria. The Austrian labor market authority is a traditional administrative agency without any special autonomy, which administers both entitlements (unemployment insurance) and active programs (active labor market policy). It represents one of the policy areas in which the federal government has its own administration at the regional and local levels. At the intermediate level the nine *Land* labor offices (one for each region) are actually responsible for deciding and implementing manpower programs, while the ninety-five local labor offices are largely confined to the tasks of processing of applications for unemployment benefits and job placement and usually play no role in decisions with regard to financial measures.

Input from the organizational environment of the labor market authority takes place through formal committees, which are attached to the various levels of administrative hierarchy. At the central level general policy and annual priorities in active labor market policy are coordinated in an advisory council for labor market policy, which includes representatives of employers, employees, and other federal ministries. This council also coordinates assistance to individual firms, which is largely determined at the federal level. Similar councils exist on the level of the *Land* labor offices. Comparable committees of the local labor offices, which are primarily concerned with questions of unemployment insurance, are of lesser importance, corresponding to the low level of development of the cooperation between local labor market offices and local governments.

Labor market policy is financed essentially through unemployment insurance contributions. The contributions of employers and employees flow into a fund that is part of the federal budget and is administered by the BMS. The most important expenditures for active and passive labor market policy are financed from this "unemployment insurance fund." If revenues exceed expenditures, the surplus can be accumulated in the form of a reserve fund up to a maximum amount equivalent to one year's revenues; deficits in the fund have to be covered from general revenues in the federal budget. However, permanent financing of deficits from general revenues is only permissible up to the level of expenditures for unemployment assistance (*Notstandshilfe*, the means-tested level of the unemployment benefit system); any deficits in excess of this amount may only be temporarily covered through general government revenues and must be subsequently repaid out of income from contributions.

There are a number of special regulations and exceptions within this financing system. Only a fixed percentage of expenditures for early retirement pensions, which are granted by the labor market authority, are financed from the unemployment insurance fund with the balance being borne by the federal government budget. Fifty percent of the administrative costs of the labor market authority are financed through the unemployment insurance fund and the rest by the federal government. Finally, a temporary program to preserve employment, which was initiated in 1983 and subsequently extended, is financed directly by the federal government.

Three additional sources of financing for special types of benefits should also be mentioned. Apart from labor market policy expenditures in a narrow sense, the unemployment insurance fund also covers 50 percent of the costs of maternity benefits; the rest is covered by the "family assistance fund," which is itself financed through employer contributions and a specifically earmarked share of tax revenues (the fund is also used to finance other benefits in the area of family policy). Employers and employees in the construction industry pay special "bad weather" contributions, which are used to (partially) finance weather-related loss of earnings in this industry (bad weather benefits). If expenditures for bad weather benefits exceed revenues from contributions, then the resources of the unemployment insurance fund can be used, up to a certain limit, to finance these benefits. Finally, there is also a special levy on employers to finance bankruptcy wage benefits for employees.

This structure of financing has remained stable with only slight changes because the fiscal pressure has been limited. Total expenditures for labor market policy, excluding maternity benefits, increased 3.1 times between 1973 and 1980; revenues from contributions increased 2.6 times over the same period without any significant increases in contribution rates. Pressure on the financing system increased only with the rapid rise in unemployment after 1981 as labor market policy grew in importance relative to employment policy.

The existence of a separately administered fund from which both income security and active labor market policy measures for the unemployed are financed has implications for decision making and budgeting in labor market policy. Whereas the unemployment insurance fund's favorable financial situation at the end of the 1960s and the beginning of the 1970s certainly eased the expansion of active labor market policy, this financial room for maneuver was used to improve unemployment benefits in the latter part of the 1970s (also after 1978 for payments to the pension system to offset the loss of contributions by the unemployed). During this period, expenditures for active labor market policy increased considerably more slowly than did spending for passive measures. This was not, however, the result of any shortage of funds caused, for example, by the crowding out of active labor market policy by increasing expenditures for passive measures. On the contrary, the resources available for active labor market policy between 1975 and 1981 could not even be fully spent, primarily because of the limited capacities of the labor market authority for implementing such programs. The total system of Austrian labor market financing is presented in Figure 2.

2.2 FEDERAL REPUBLIC OF GERMANY

Until the end of the 1960s, labor market policy in the Federal Republic of Germany was primarily limited to the classic functions of unemployment insurance, job placement, and counseling. In addition, seasonal measures for assistance to the construction industry traditionally played an important role (bad weather benefits, winter allowances). Vocational training, job creation measures, and short-time compensation existed as instruments but were hardly utilized during the period of full employment up to the passage of the 1969 Employment Promotion Act (AFG). Together with the new law, the small 1966–67 recession, which signaled a need for regional and sectoral adjustments (crisis in mining and steel), and the anticipation (until the mid-1970s) of continued labor shortages led, however, to a changed definition of the role of labor market policy: prospective labor market policy was supposed to play an active role in the formation of economic policy, to promote structural change and mobilize additional labor resources (e.g., women). The central element of this reform was a considerable expansion of vocational training and retraining and vocational rehabilitation. Thus, even before the unexpected crisis in unemployment in the mid-1970s, a comprehensive set of instruments had been created, which could also be used for a considerable absorption of the unemployed in manpower programs under the changed labor market conditions after 1974.

The budgeting and implementation of labor market policy measures in the Federal Republic are tasks of the Federal Employment Institute (FEI), an independent public agency. It was established in 1969 as the successor to the Federal Institute for Job Placement and

Figure 2

The Financing System for Labor Market Policy in Austria

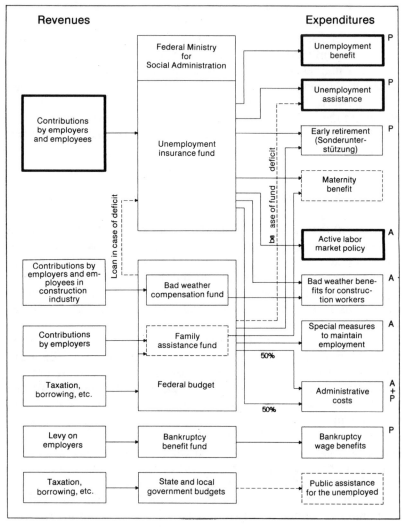

P = Passive labor market policy; A = Active labor market policy (LMP)

Blocks with heavy shading denote the quantitatively most important types of revenues and expenditures.

Unemployment Insurance, established in 1952 and its predecessor, the National Office for Placement and Unemployment Insurance, established in 1927. As an independent public authority, the FEI is not part of the regular federal administration. It is, however, subject to legal supervision by the Federal Ministry for Labor and Social Affairs, which in a number of individual matters must also approve its decisions or can direct its actions. The FEI's tasks are set down in and regulated by the AFG.

The FEI is governed by two central bodies: the board of directors and the executive committee. The board has primarily legislative functions (adoption of its charter, approval of the budget, issuance of regulations for carrying out individual tasks); the executive committee has managerial functions (e.g., external representation of the FEI, preparation of its budget, issuance of guidelines for the conduct of administration by the president). There is tripartite representation of employers, employees, and public governments in both governing bodies and at all levels of the FEI's self-governing administration. In addition to the central office in Nuremberg, the FEI has 9 *Land* labor offices at the regional level and 146 local labor offices. They likewise operate under the oversight of tripartite administrative committees. Labor offices in the Federal Republic of Germany have a monopoly of placement functions; commercial placement services are—with few exceptions—prohibited.

Active and passive labor market policy are largely financed through the FEI's budget, which is funded mainly through contributions (i.e., a payroll tax) paid by employers and employees. Any surpluses are accumulated in a reserve fund, which is used to cover any subsequent deficits. If the annual deficit cannot be covered by drawing on available reserves, then it is covered by a subsidy from general funds in the federal budget, which does not have to be repaid.

Although the preparation of the budget is in principle a task of the FEI itself and its self-governing bodies, decisions with regard to revenues (changes in the contribution rate, changes in the definition of covered earnings) usually require parliamentary action. The expenditure side is also largely determined through benefit entitlements prescribed by law. The FEI's budget is subject to the approval of the federal government.

There are also a number of special financing provisions in addition to the general rule of financing through contributions with governmental responsibility for covering any deficits. From 1967 until 1980, unemployment assistance (i.e., the means-tested level of unemployment benefits) was almost entirely financed through the FEI's budget; since 1981, this benefit has again been financed completely through the federal budget—as foreseen by the AFG. Funds for bankruptcy wage benefits administered by the FEI are raised through a levy on employers. Unemployed persons who are entitled to neither unemployment benefits nor unemployment assistance (about one-third of all unemployed) may be eligible for means-tested public assistance, which is financed by local governments. Subsidies to promote winter construction, which are likewise administered by the FEI, are largely financed through a special winter construction levy on employers in the construction industry. Finally, there are a number of special active and passive labor market policy measures administered by the FEI but financed directly from the federal budget, which have been financially significant only in relatively few years.

The federal government's responsibility for deficits, determination of revenues by Parliament, the fact that the FEI's activities and hence also expenditures are primarily determined by entitlement legislation, and the requirement that its budget be approved by the federal cabinet are among the factors that make labor market policy in the Federal Republic highly susceptible to politically and fiscally motivated interventions. For example, the deep recessions in 1974–75 and 1981–82 led to large deficits in the FEI's budget, which—because of the obligation of the federal government to cover its deficits—led parliament to adopt more restrictive terms and conditions and reduce benefits. As a result, the FEI's budget was even able to show surpluses in 1984 and 1985, although the number of unemployed remained greater than 2 million. Conversely, under favorable fiscal conditions the integrated financing of active and passive labor market policy facilitates, as in Austria, an expansion of both wage-replacement benefits and active labor market policy measures. Figure 3 presents an overview of labor market policy financing in the Federal Republic of Germany.

2.3 FRANCE

In contrast to Austria and the Federal Republic of Germany, the organization of French labor market policy is highly fragmented. The unemployment insurance system, which is an autonomous body under bipartite administration, is institutionally fully separate from the state-administered active labor market policy. Responsibility for active labor market policy itself is divided among a number of large organizations, which is the source of considerable difficulties in coor-

Figure 3

The Financing System for Labor Market Policy in the Federal Republic of Germany

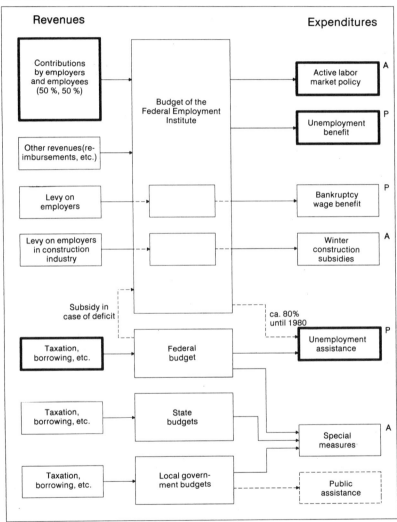

dination at all levels. A particular characteristic of the French system is a strong concentration on early retirement measures, whereas the classical tasks of active labor market policy—training and retraining, job creation measures—have only recently become more important. A further characteristic is that training programs have to a large extent the function of compensating for deficiencies in the system of primary vocational education, which is evident, for example, in the disproportionately high number of unemployed youth in training and measures to promote integration into the labor market.

Three (separate) organizations are primarily responsible for the regional and local implementation of active labor market policy: (1) the external services of the labor ministry (labor directorates), (2) a National Employment Service (ANPE), and (3) the National Office for Adult Vocational Education (AFPA).

The 23 regional and 122 departmental labor directorates are the territorial organizations of the earlier labor ministry. They were originally concerned with questions of working conditions and industrial relations, and their labor inspectorates were principally engaged in enforcement activities, but they also became responsible for labor market policy tasks in the 1960s and the 1970s. Today the directorates are responsible for the implementation of most subsidy programs in active labor market policy.

The employment service (ANPE), which was established in 1967, is an autonomous body subject to the oversight of the employment ministry. In addition to placement activities, the ANPE is also responsible for vocational counseling and information services and provides administrative support for training programs (e.g., processing applications). ANPE has 25 regional labor offices, 102 departmental offices, and a total of 650 local placement offices. The third large state organization involved in labor market policy is the National Office for Adult Education (AFPA) with 7 regional offices, 125 local training centers, and 19 so-called psychotechnical centers.

The fragmented organization of French labor market policy is also reflected in the relatively complicated financing system. We shall describe passive and active labor market policy separately, because they are in fact largely separately financed and administered. There is a linkage between the financing and budgeting systems for passive and active measures only in two respects. The unemployment insurance fund receives grants from the central government budget, which is also the source of funding for a large share of active labor market policy. On the other hand, two measures of active labor market policy, which are financially not very significant, are financed through the unemployment insurance fund: stipends for recipients of the special unemployment benefit (*allocation speciale*) who participate in retraining programs, and the "capitalized" lump-sum payment of unemployment benefits as start capital for the unemployed who enter self-employment. Our account of the financing system for passive labor market policy does not include these programs.

The institutional carrier of French unemployment insurance is a bipartite independent authority (UNEDIC/ASSEDIC) financed through its own special-purpose fund. Until 1979, there was essentially a dual structure of financing: UNEDIC/ASSEDIC financed out of its fund benefits with an insurance character, while a form of public assistance for the unemployed (*aide publique*) was financed through the government budget but also administered by UNEDIC/ASSEDIC. As a result of reforms in 1979–80, this financing system was replaced by an integrated one with a regular government subsidy according to a fixed formula; this changed again as a result of another reform of unemployment benefits in mid-1984, which reintroduced a dual system of benefits and financing. The following description refers to the financing system for passive labor market policy that was in force from 1980 to mid-1984, including the extensive early retirement measures, which were organized as part of labor market policy in France during this period.

UNEDIC/ASSEDIC receives payroll contributions from employers and employees. Furthermore, an agreement between UNEDIC/ASSEDIC and the government provides for a regular state subsidy. The size of the state subsidy is adjusted to reflect changes in expenditures but may not be less than 24 percent or exceed about one-third of program expenditures. The government has no obligation to cover any deficits, which means that the social partners must react to changes in the financial situation of the fund by agreeing on changes in contributions (or benefits). These collective agreements are then made binding through legislation. In 1981–82, as a result of the enormous increase in expenditures for early retirement and the rapid increase in unemployment, employer and union representatives were not able to adjust contributions or expenditures fast enough, which resulted in a deficit.

In order to finance this deficit, more financial sources were developed for UNEDIC/ASSEDIC in addition to contributions and the regular government grant: a one-time loan from banks and insurance companies with a government guarantee of repayment; a supplementary government grant financed through a temporary income tax surcharge (*impot de solidarité*); a temporary solidarity contribution (*contribution de solidarité*) applicable to public employees; and an additional contribution for pensioners in higher income brackets with supplementary sources of income (*cumul emploi-retraite*). In addition to benefits financed through the UNEDIC/ASSEDIC fund, there are also a number of benefits directly financed through the state budget. The government budget (in a special budget item, the National

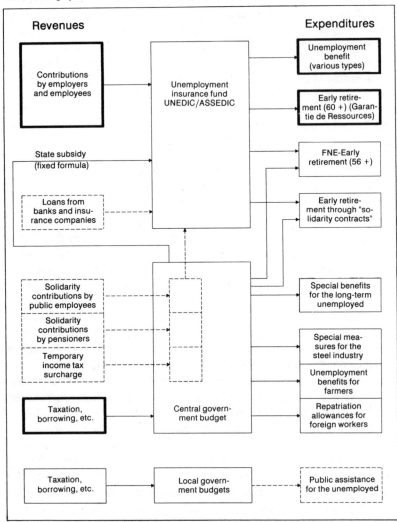

Employment Fund) assumes financial responsibility for a certain percentage of two forms of early retirement for those less than sixty years of age. A number of other benefits of less financial significance are wholly financed through the government budget (see Figure 4).

For active labor market policy three different forms of financing can be distinguished: (1) direct financing through the government budget, (2) financing through levies and deductible expenditures, and (3) financing through funds of the UNEDIC/ASSEDIC (contributions/state grant). The last financing source for a number of active labor market policy measures (the capitalized lump-sum unemployment benefit, stipends for recipients of the special unemployment benefit) is of less importance. By contrast, approximately half of all expenditures for active labor market policy are financed through the government budget (largely through the employment ministry), covering the entire spectrum of active measures; the single most important budget item here is the National Employment Fund, which also finances part of the costs of some early retirement measures.

The most important special type of financing in addition to government and UNEDIC/ASSEDIC funds is in the area of vocational education and training. Since 1971, firms are required to pay a levy for further training, which at present amounts to 1.1 percent of payroll; funds from this levy flow in part into the government budget, but firms can also deduct the costs incurred for their own training measures from the amount they are required to pay or finance qualification measures in joint training centers set by collective agreements (see Figure 5). Another levy, which has existed for decades, regulates the financing of apprenticeship training: firms must pay 0.5 percent of their gross payroll in the form of a levy for apprenticeship training; their own expenditures for vocational education and the financing of joint apprenticeship training institutions can be deducted from this amount to a limited extent. The contributions remitted are not earmarked for special purposes but are part of general revenues.

On the whole, the financing system for active labor market policy is quite complicated as a result of the multiplicity of funds and budget items and the various forms of special financing; even the collection of comprehensive data on expenditures in this area requires special efforts by the responsible offices (see *Bilan physico-financier de l'emploi*). On the other hand, the institutional fragmentation of financing and responsibility also guarantees a certain stability above all in active labor market policy. The number and the complicated network of institutional vested interests are obstacles to drastic budget cuts that are politically or fiscally motivated.

2.4 GREAT BRITAIN

Labor market policy is an unfamiliar concept in Great Britain. The idea of a comprehensive policy area, including both economic

Figure 5

Financing for Training and Retraining Measures in France through the Training Levy

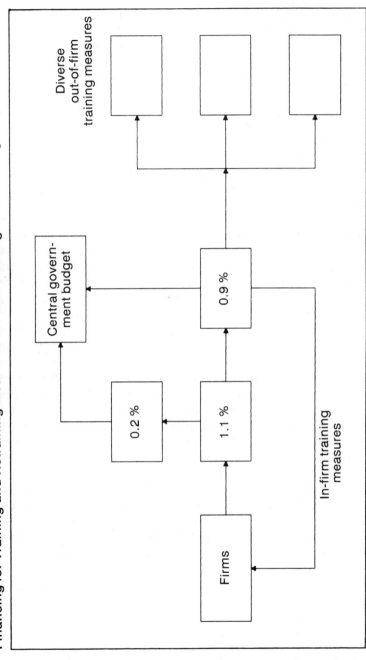

security for the unemployed (passive labor market policy) and public measures and programs to influence the level and structure of the supply and demand for labor (active labor market policy), is seldom encountered. This concept is also at odds with the institutional system in which both functions are almost completely separated and in which there are hardly any institutional linkages between unemployment benefits and active labor market policy.

The only institutional connection between active and passive labor market policy is the Department of Employment (DE), which is primarily responsible for three tasks: (1) the disbursement of unemployment benefit and supplementary benefit for the unemployed through 8 regional and about 900 local unemployment benefit offices (the legislative basis of unemployment benefit and supplementary benefit and their financing is the responsibility of the Department of Health and Social Security rather than the DE); (2) the design and implementation of wage-subsidy programs within active labor market policy (through the 8 regional offices); (3) the supervision and financing of the independent labor market authority.

The Department of Health and Social Security (DHSS) is responsible for the legal regulation of unemployment benefit and its financing within the social security system. It is also responsible for the regulation and financing of supplementary benefit, which is a means-tested benefit that may be claimed by the unemployed.

The Manpower Services Commission (MSC), the independent labor market authority established in 1974, is the institutional core of active labor market policy. It is governed by a ten-person tripartite commission, consisting of three trade union and three employers' representatives, two representatives of local authorities, one representative from the area of vocational education, and a chairman named by the government. When it was founded, the labor market authority was given, in addition to research and planning tasks, essentially two functions: operation of the employment service and the design and implementation of adult vocational training and retraining programs. As a result of increasing unemployment and the expansion of labor market policy measures, the MSC was given additional responsibilities in the 1970s—above all, the design and execution of job creation measures and sheltered employment for the disabled. Originally the MSC consisted of two largely independent operating agencies with their own regional organizations responsible for placement services and training activities respectively. The autonomy of these divisions was subsequently limited as a result of organizational reforms, although the fragmented regional and local structures remained largely unchanged.

Tripartite Area Manpower Boards provide some limited coordination at the local level.

In addition to the central government departments and the MSC, local governments are also responsible for part of active labor market policy in Great Britain. According to the Employment and Training Act of 1973, which created the Manpower Services Commission, the local authorities are responsible for vocational counseling, training, and placement of secondary school pupils and students (Careers Service).

In Great Britain, in contrast to other countries, unemployment benefit (UB) is financed not through a separate unemployment insurance contribution but through a general social security contribution by employers and employees, which flows into the National Insurance Fund (NIF) and is also used to finance pensions, sickness, invalid and maternity benefits, and work injury insurance, in addition to unemployment benefit. The shares of the fund going for individual types of benefits (unemployment benefit accounted for about 8 percent of total expenditures in 1983) are based on the claims made for the various types of benefits; they all represent entitlements that can only be changed through changes in law (which are frequent). In order to avoid deficits, the NIF receives an annual (discretionary) grant from general government revenues which currently amounts to about 10 percent of fund expenditures. The means-tested supplementary benefit (SB) for unemployed persons without any claim to unemployment benefit (or whose benefit falls below the standard of need) is entirely financed through general government revenues. As a result of long-term and persistent mass unemployment and changes in unemployment benefit, expenditures for supplementary benefit for the unemployed now far exceed those for unemployment benefit.

Active labor market policy, which has been used on a large scale in Great Britain since the mid-1970s to alleviate unemployment for problem groups—especially youth—is almost exclusively financed through general revenues in the government budget. This is true both for expenditures of the labor market authority, MSC, which is financed almost entirely through a grant from the government budget, and for wage subsidies that are paid directly by the Department of Employment. Even the expenditures of the local authorities are predominantly financed through general and earmarked grants from central government budget.

In contrast to the situation in the Federal Republic of Germany, active labor market policy measures in Great Britain are as a rule not entitlements but cash-limited expenditures. Whereas the volume of expenditures for entitlements (in Great Britain only wage subsidies, in addition to wage-replacement benefits) is determined by uptake alone, cash-limited expenditures are limited by the amount of funds appropriated for that purpose. For these measures and programs, regulations usually define the potential participants, duration of the program, and the costs per participant. These terms and conditions, however, only exclude certain groups from participation without granting others any individual claim to a place in the program and, hence, entail only a potential upper limit on the volume of expenditures. The actual volume of expenditures is determined by the establishment of budget ceilings.

As its exclusive financing through the government budget implies, the British labor market authority only enjoys limited autonomy; the size of the government grant to the MSC is determined by the government and Parliament. Thus, not only MSC revenues but also its expenditures are decided within the government's budgetary process. Even MSC decisions with regard to the composition of expenditures—that is, their allocation among different measures and programs—can only be made with the approval of the Department of Employment, to which it is subordinate in policy questions.

Two activities (of limited significance) are carried out by the MSC on a fee-for-service basis: the placement service for managerial personnel and qualification measures for individual firms on a contract basis. A special form of financing is also utilized for the legally mandated redundancy payments, for which employers are partially reimbursed from a public redundancy fund. This fund receives revenues from a fraction of the general social security contribution earmarked for this purpose. Originally, according to the logic of a levy on firms obliged to make redundancy payments, only a fraction of the *employers'* contribution to social security was used to finance the fund; because of chronic deficits as a result of the volume of redundancy claims, a portion of *employees'* contributions to social security has also been earmarked for the redundancy fund since 1982. Figure 6 presents an overview of the financing system for labor market policy in Great Britain.

2.5 SWEDEN

In contrast to the case in other countries, labor market policy already played an important role in Sweden's full-employment policy in the 1950s and 1960s. The model of selective labor market policy,

48 *Introduction*

Figure 6
The Financing System for Labor Market Policy in Great Britain (1984)

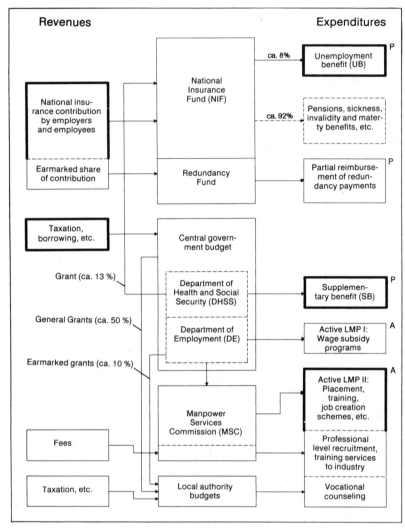

which was developed by trade union economists Rehn and Meidner, is based on three pillars: a restrictive fiscal policy, the "solidaristic" wage policy, and a selective labor market policy. Whereas the restrictive fiscal policy aims at achieving a slight underutilization of productive capacity in order to avoid inflationary bottlenecks and excess profits, the task of the solidaristic wage policy was to ensure that employees received an equal wage for equal work independent of the profitability of the employing firm. Together the two strategies give rise to an accelerated process of structural change, which is given auxiliary support by labor market policy measures. Because unproductive firms or departments of firms are more quickly driven from the market under these conditions, the adjustment costs for redundant or reassigned workers are compensated through generous support for occupational and regional mobility. This in turn enables the more productive firms or departments, whose profitability is increased as a result of the solidaristic wage policy, to quickly eliminate any shortages in qualified workers. Those persons who, for reasons of health or age, have difficulty coping with the demands of this accelerated structural change are supposed to be guaranteed work and income through public job creation programs or wage subsidies in the private sector.

The national labor market authority (AMS), which was established in 1948, is responsible for most active labor market policy measures in Sweden. The unemployment insurance system is state-subsidized but largely autonomously administered by forty-five trade union unemployment insurance funds. In contrast to other countries, Sweden originally carried out regional economic development measures primarily through the labor market authority. Since 1976, however, not the labor ministry but the ministry for industry is responsible for regional policy; since 1983, it has also been responsible for the implementation of programs in this area. Primary vocational education in Sweden takes place almost completely in the vocational education branches of the public school system.

In Sweden, the role of the labor ministry is limited to preparing legislation, developing general policy guidelines and the budget, and exercising general supervision over the labor market authority. Responsibility for the implementation of labor market policy as well as the preparation of the initial budget proposals lies largely in the hands of the labor market authority itself, which is a large nationally organized agency with regional divisions and a corporate self-governing administration in which the trade union side is in the majority. The central office of AMS formulates labor market policy on the basis of existing legislation and general policy guidelines. It is headed by a board of directors consisting of representatives of employers' associations and trade unions with the AMS director general serving as chairman.

The 24 provincial labor offices are responsible for designing and implementing labor market policy at the regional level; subordinate nate to them are 80 district employment services with 198 local placement offices. As in the Federal Republic of Germany, the public employment service enjoys a monopoly position in that private for-profit placement activities are prohibited. Its position is made even stronger by the obligation of employers to report all job openings, which was introduced stepwise beginning in 1976. In order to implement labor market training (vocational training and retraining), a system of 52 state training centers (AMU centers) was created; these centers are found in all parts of the country. In 1986, the centers were removed from the jurisdiction of the AMS and located within an independent agency that is organized more in accordance with business principles.

The labor market counseling centers (AMI centers, currently about 50), which were established within the AMS administration in 1980 and are responsible for vocational rehabilitation of the disabled and the integration of hard-to-place workers, are another innovation. In addition, 23 so-called AMI-S centers were established to specialize in the vocational rehabilitation of persons with particular types of disabilities.

Unemployment insurance is financed through employee contributions and a "state contribution," which is partly refinanced through employer contributions ("labor market fund"). The employee contributions, which are closely linked to trade union membership dues, and the state contribution flow into trade union unemployment insurance funds, which pay unemployment insurance benefits. Although employees' contributions are loosely related to the risk of unemployment in individual branches and occupations, they have over time come to be less related to the actual costs of unemployment benefits, and today more than 90 percent of expenditures are covered by the state contribution. The employers' contributions to the labor market fund are, by contrast, tied to a fixed formula: They are supposed to cover 65 percent of the costs of the state contribution to unemployment insurance.

One-third of unemployment assistance (KAS) costs is financed through the government budget and two-thirds through the employer-financed labor market fund. In 1984, approximately 55 percent of the unemployed received unemployment insurance, a further 15 percent received unemployment assistance; in case of need, the rest are dependent upon the means-tested public assistance financed by local governments. The maximum duration of unemployment insurance and unemployment assistance benefits is 300 working days (in exceptional cases 450). Unlike the situations in Austria, the Federal Republic of

Germany, and Great Britain, there is no centrally financed, unlimited means-tested benefit for the unemployed. The financing system for active labor market policy is fragmented: allowances for those in labor market training and vocational rehabilitation as well as short-time benefits (until 1984) are one-third financed through the government budget and two-thirds through employer contributions (labor market fund). The administrative costs of the state training and rehabilitation centers are borne by the government budget and to a small extent by local governments and the provincial authorities. Employment counseling and placement, job creation measures, and wage subsidies are completely financed through the government budget. The extensive system of sheltered employment in special firms for the disabled is heavily subsidized from general revenues.

In addition to the general system of financing through contributions and taxation, there is also a wage guarantee fund financed through employer levies to cover wage payments in firms that enter bankruptcy. Since 1985, "short-time benefits" have been replaced by a system of continuation of wages during "temporary layoffs." The costs of this program are borne by firms through a special fund created for this purpose (into which revenues flow from payroll levies) and by the central government budget through grants according to a prescribed formula.

This institutional arrangement and the priority given to active as opposed to passive labor market policy have resulted in a situation in which approximately 80 percent of the expenditures for labor market policy in Sweden are financed through general revenues from the government budget. However, corporate forms of labor market policy based on collective agreement are also becoming increasingly important, such as Labor Market Insurance Inc. (AFA), which is jointly controlled by the unions and employers and financed through employers' contributions. AFA provides severance pay in case of loss of employment as well as supplements to wage-replacement benefits in case of longer spells of unemployment. Another example is the Security Fund for white-collar employees in private industry, which is likewise financed through employer contributions in individual collective-bargaining districts and offers additional benefits for loss of employment and early retirement but can also be utilized for active labor market policy, that is, training or financial assistance for those entering self-employment. Figure 7 presents an overview of the Swedish financing system.

Figure 7

The Financing System for Labor Market Policy in Sweden (1983-84)

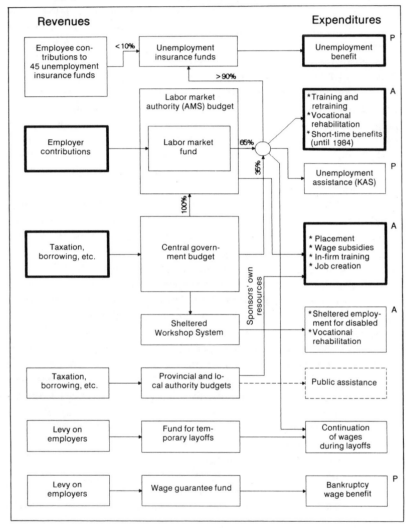

2.6 UNITED STATES

As in Great Britain, the term *labor market policy* is seldom used in the United States as an overall concept for unemployment insurance benefits and active measures to prevent or combat unemployment. Passive benefits and active measures are usually conceived in isolation and are institutionally almost completely separate. The clearest expression of this institutional separation is the fact that the most important functions of program design and financing of passive and active labor market policy are located at different levels in the federal system: unemployment insurance is largely the responsibility of the individual state governments, whereas active measures are based on federal government initiatives and funds.

The unemployment insurance system was created in 1935 through the Social Security Act under President Franklin D. Roosevelt, and it has remained essentially unchanged since that time. Because of constitutional issues pertaining to the authority of the federal and state governments, federal law does not establish a uniform federal unemployment insurance system but merely obligates the individual states to establish an unemployment insurance system and sets forth certain general requirements. It defines covered employment and provides that unemployment insurance benefits in the individual states are to be financed through employer contributions in the form of a payroll tax, for which a national lower limit is set. The law does not, however, stipulate any minimum benefit level, so that not only the contribution (payroll tax) rate but also rules for eligibility and the level and duration of benefits differ markedly from state to state. A common feature of the various state systems is the principle of experience rating. This means that the contribution rate for individual employers can also vary within a given state, with individual employers required to pay more or less depending on the extent to which, as a result of dismissals or "temporary layoffs," their employees have claimed benefits. The differentiation of the contribution rate according to the number of claims filed is intended to make the employer feel the financial consequences of redundancies and thus to provide an incentive for the stabilization of employment.

In addition to regular state benefits, there is also (since 1971) a federal program for the unemployed who have exhausted their claims to benefits under the state unemployment insurance schemes. Extended benefits are provided for up to thirteen additional weeks but only in those states in which the unemployment rate has exceeded a nationally defined threshold level ("trigger"). Half of the costs of extended benefits are financed from the individual state unemployment insurance funds and the balance through the uniform federal unemployment tax, a much lower payroll contribution levied by the federal government. Its revenues are also used to finance the placement services in the individual states and to cover the administrative costs of the unemployment insurance system. Finally, there are also a number of special unemployment benefit programs for particular groups that are financed through general federal revenues, such as a program for former employees of the federal government (who are excluded from the individual state insurance programs) as well as a special program with (limited) follow-on benefits for the long-term unemployed, which expired in 1985. In total, only 40 to 50 percent of all unemployed persons receive benefits from one of the various programs. The individual state insurance programs account for 70 to 80 percent of all benefit payments and extended benefits as well as benefits paid through special programs for about 20 to 30 percent. Unemployed persons not entitled to benefits may have recourse to the Aid to Families with Dependent Children (AFDC) program, for which only heads of households with minor children are eligible. It is financed jointly by the federal and state governments. The unemployed may also be eligible for the federally financed, means-tested food stamp program. In individual cases, limited means-tested general assistance benefits may be provided by local governments and individual states.

At the federal level two institutions are involved in the design and administration of the unemployment insurance system. The Department of Labor is the federal agency responsible for the unemployment insurance system and supervises the adherence of individual state programs to federal requirements. The Treasury administers the financial flows in the system. The revenues from contributions in the individual states flow into an unemployment insurance trust fund with accounts for each individual state and are paid out through the state unemployment benefit offices according to their respective laws and regulations pertaining to benefits. The revenues from the federal unemployment tax are also maintained in the same trust fund and utilized for the purposes described. When individual state insurance funds and the federal government are unable to finance all their expenditures for unemployment benefits or for extended benefits through revenues from contributions, they receive—as prescribed by law—loans from general federal revenue to cover the deficits in the trust fund accounts. In 1983, these outstanding loans had grown to a total of $20 billion. Federal sanctions (high interest rates, increases in the federal unemployment tax in debtor states) are used to encourage states with high unemployment and correspondingly high deficits to either raise their contribution rates or curtail benefits in order to repay their federal indebtedness. In the decentralized American unemployment insurance system, there is no permanent interregional redistributive mechanism in which the expenditures of states with high unemployment are borne in part through contributions from other states.

Active labor market policy originated in the United States at the beginning of the 1960s when sizable federally financed training and retraining programs were established for labor market problem groups. Direct job creation measures were introduced at the beginning of the 1970s—also financed through federal funds—and the legal framework for active labor market policy was consolidated in 1973 in the Comprehensive Employment and Training Act (CETA). During the 1970s, labor market policy was extended beyond its original focus on disadvantaged groups and became for a time a general instrument of employment policy. Expenditures increased dramatically until, in a shift in economic policy, the Reagan administration and Congress again cut back expenditures and reduced programs approximately to their previous scope. In 1983, CETA was replaced by new federal manpower legislation, the Job Training Partnership Act (JTPA).

The U.S. active labor market policy programs differ from those in other countries above all in the way they are planned and implemented: funds are appropriated at the federal level for certain general purposes and then allocated to individual states, localities, and service delivery areas according to a distributional formula. These operative agencies are then free to determine the precise use to which the funds will be put and develop their own policy mix based on a list of permissible uses and according to their own priorities. Active labor market policy is thus almost exclusively financed from federal budget funds but implemented and to a considerable extent shaped by decisions made by the individual states, local governments, and JTPA service delivery areas (previously CETA prime sponsors). The federal Department of Labor exercises only a support and control function over the regional and local levels through its Employment and Training Administration (ETA).

The public employment service (which does not have a monopoly on placement services) is markedly different from the other federal active labor market programs. It is run largely by the individual states and is usually administratively separate from the implementation of other active labor market programs. The employment service is the single essential component of active labor market policy which is financed not through general budget funds but—as mentioned—through the federal unemployment insurance tax. The individual states receive earmarked grants from the unemployment insurance trust fund to operate the employment service. Figure 8 presents an overview of the U.S. financing system.

Figure 8

The Financing System for Labor Market Policy in the U.S.A.

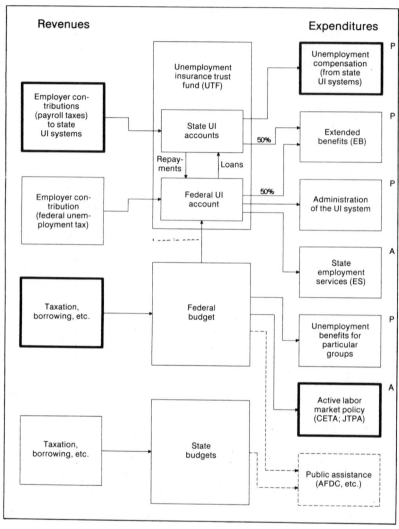

UI = Unemployment Insurance

PART TWO

The Financing and Effectiveness of Unemployment Insurance

In the following comparative analysis we will examine more closely how income security programs for the unemployed are financed and whether there is any observable relationship between different forms of financing and the type of social protection provided in the countries investigated. Because unemployment benefits represent an actual or anticipated source of income, they also affect labor market behavior, so that the interrelationship between unemployment insurance financing and the functioning of the labor market also has to be considered.

First, the questions of whether unemployment is an insurable risk and why governments have to intervene to guarantee social security in this specific case are discussed (Chapter 3).

Second, national differences in the organization of unemployment insurance are described (Chapter 4). We have examined the applicable regulations and decision-making structures on both the revenue and expenditure sides, that is, coverage of unemployment insurance, sources of financing, responsibility for deficits, the level and duration of benefits, and so on.

Third, in the core analysis of this part of the study (Chapter 5), we analyze the impact of the financing systems at several levels. We examine empirically the performance of financing systems on the revenue and expenditure sides over the course of the business cycle. Then we analyze individual aspects such as the built-in stabilizer function and redistributional effects. The "generosity" of the insurance systems is also considered, in particular the extent to which the level and duration of benefits are affected by the financing system. Another important consideration is the impact of unemployment on the totality of public budgets, that is, the direct and indirect costs of unemployment for all levels of government and for the social insurance carriers.

In a fourth and final step, we focus on the impact of unemployment insurance systems on the behavior of individual labor market actors (Chapter 6). Here we are concerned with the controversial issue of how the existence of unemployment insurance influences the labor supply and demand and in particular the thesis that generous benefits have a negative effect on work incentives and cause voluntary unemployment.

CHAPTER 3

On the Theory of Unemployment Insurance

3.1 Pure and Speculative Risks

Unemployment is one risk among many others. What kind of risk is it? In theory one distinguishes between pure and speculative risks. In the first case there is a possibility of a loss with no chance of gain; in the second situation there are opportunities for gain as well as loss (Schönbäck 1980:10). In the first case one cannot avoid the risk, whereas in the second case one deliberately takes a risk in order to make a profit. Losses as a result of fire, sickness, or accident are typical of the first case, while profits or losses as a result of playing roulette or investing in the stock market or in industry are typical of the second.

Speculative risks are called entrepreneurial risks. Strictly speaking, however, they involve not only the behavior of entrepreneurs but also that of employees in dependent employment. For example, in preferring piece-rate work to hourly work, the speculative element would be that the worker on piecework accepts the risk of premature exhaustion of his or her labor power or forsakes the advantage of a secure income in order to gain a (possibly) higher wage from piece-rate premiums (Schönbäck 1980:11).

Problems of social security result, as a rule, from a pure risk situation and not from speculative or entrepreneurial risks.[1] The latter are based on a deliberate decision to accept a risk for the sake of personal gain; any resulting losses also have to be borne by the individual.

There are in principle three possibilities for resolving the insecurity problem arising from pure risks: individual *savings* to provide resources to fall back on in case the risk materializes; *prevention* in order to minimize the risk, for example, by maintaining a healthy lifestyle and preventive measures against fire or accident; *insurance*, that is, a collective pooling of risk through contributions to a fund that reimburses individuals for any harm suffered. These three possible

59

Table 1
Methods of Coping with Pure Risks

	Savings	Prevention	Insurance
Private	1	2	3
State	4	5	6

solutions may be organized either privately, publicly through the state, or in a mixed form (see Table 1). Which strategy or strategy mix is optimal depends upon the type of risk involved. First, however, we must consider whether unemployment is a pure or speculative risk.

3.2 SPECULATIVE ELEMENTS IN THE RISK OF UNEMPLOYMENT

Involuntary unemployment seems initially, in a Keynesian perspective, to belong to the category of pure risk, because the causes of unemployment lie outside the control of the affected individual. There are, however, aspects of the situation that diminish the purity of the risk of unemployment and give rise to very controversial conceptions about how to protect against it. These aspects are considered in this section because they are basic to understanding the type of risk involved in unemployment. Although we conclude that unemployment is primarily a pure risk, speculative elements are becoming increasingly important—and have always played a role in unemployment.

The first qualification that should be noted results from the fact that the risk of unemployment only becomes a problem after an initial "speculative" decision, namely, the decision to enter dependent employment at all, which is, furthermore, always the choice of a particular employment in a given occupation and locality.

After further reflection, the first consideration does not seem to be particularly relevant. For most persons there is no alternative to earning their livelihood through employment, be it for economic or cultural reasons. The division of labor is a further reason that makes wage labor a social necessity for most individuals. As a rule, no one enters dependent employment merely for speculative reasons. However, it may be that the speculative moment has increased or is becoming more important because dependent employment has increasingly become the source of entitlements and benefits other than earnings, such as tax incentives, pension rights, and company or union fringe benefits.

The second aspect—choice of an occupation (and perhaps even of an industry), locality, and employer—appears to be more important. The choice of an occupation depends on many factors, such as traditional motives, considerations of individual talents, and altruistic motives. This choice is, however, not without a speculative motive. Many individuals work hard and make sacrifices (long course of studies, delay of marriage, etc.) with the hope of becoming—for example—a successful and well-paid pilot, engineer, physician, or computer specialist. Something may go wrong: they may fail to pass examinations, a market glut may develop because too many others chose the same career plan, or an occupation may become obsolete. Others seek a secure position in the public service instead of high income, but after completion of their education, their plans may be thwarted by a recruitment stop. The choice of an occupation is thus also the choice of a risk of unemployment, which does not vary randomly but is more or less closely associated with a particular occupation. It may be that, as a result of the increasing differentiation of occupations, we are today faced with a quite different problem of occupational risk from the case fifty or eighty years ago, when the first state or state-subsidized unemployment insurance systems were established. At that time most of those in dependent employment were unskilled, whereas today most persons in dependent employment have vocational qualifications and are employed in specialized activities with correspondingly more differentiated risks of unemployment. Surprisingly, this problem has not yet been adequately treated in the literature, and we can, therefore, offer only a preliminary assessment here.

There are a number of arguments against attaching particular significance to the speculative element in occupational choice in considering the problem of income security for the unemployed. First, the speculative motive, which is undoubtedly present, is only one of many motives or determinants and is difficult to separate from the others. Second, although the risk of unemployment at a given point in time is systematically related to the occupational spectrum, the risk associated with particular occupations may change so quickly that there is no basis for a rational speculative choice of occupation. Third, even if the relationship between occupation and risk of unemployment were stable, the individual may not be actually in a position to freely choose his or her occupation. For example, anyone today in the Federal Republic of Germany who decides to begin an apprenticeship as a baker is aware of the high risk of subsequently being unable to find employment in this occupation. Nevertheless, because of the shortage of apprenticeship openings, there is frequently no alternative for the individual, who cannot be blamed if he or she should subsequently become unemployed.

Can the choice of a location of employment be speculative? Workers in agriculture who moved to the Ruhr industrial centers in the 1950s in order to make a good income in mining could not have known then that technological developments and new sources of energy would soon make their occupation superfluous. They could have known, however, that this location and type of employer would mean a high risk in case of a crisis in the coal industry in light of the high degree of dependence of the Ruhr area on a single industry. A similar risk is incurred by a skilled worker who is hired by Volkswagen in the monostructured Wolfsburg area. The economy as a whole also profits from the acceptance of such risks, however, and the risk cannot be individualized. At most a greater willingness to accept occupational and regional mobility can be expected in return for the speculative gain (in the form of higher wages).

If one takes into account speculative predecisions (i.e., decisions that expose one to a risk in the first place), there is practically no completely pure risk except for illness. The risk of fire to real estate property is only relevant after the speculative decision to buy or build a house instead of renting; the same is true for the risk of an automobile accident. Even in the case of illness, there is the special case of occupational diseases whose risk is related to the speculative decision for a particular occupation. Speculative predecisions thus influence the type of risk but do not obviate the need for protection against risk itself.

Another way in which the risk of unemployment appears to deviate from the pure type of risk should also be mentioned. Illness, fire, and accidents cause unambiguous losses, damages, or pain for the affected person.[2] By contrast, unemployment could represent welcome free time or opportunity to engage in unpaid work (or black or unreported earnings). This possibility cannot be a priori excluded, but we do not know very much about its real significance.[3] Studies of part-time unemployment (short-time work) and temporary layoffs do show that short periods of unemployment may be welcomed by many employed persons (e.g., mothers, farmers with secondary jobs).[4] In this case, however, it is preferable to speak of windfall profit instead of speculative gain.

Summarizing our discussion, we can say that the distinction between pure and speculative risks is useful for deciding who should bear the financial risk involved. In the case of purely speculative (or entrepreneurial) risks, the possible profits and losses should be borne by the individual; insurance against this type of risk is usually uncalled for and would not even be possible on an actuarial basis. There are also private individual strategies for dealing with pure risks (saving, preventive measures); however, they are inadequate or less efficient than (private or state) collective systems of risk protection.[5] Unemployment can be characterized as being predominantly a case of pure risk, which, however, does obviously contain some speculative elements. Their significance is, on the basis of our initial assessment, not great but could be increasing for a number of reasons. These speculative elements have been the source of a great deal of controversy. How policymakers assess them—as will be shown in the course of our analysis—plays an important role in the formation of unemployment insurance systems. The following section discusses why insurance against unemployment is provided by the state or by quasi-state organizations or by a combination of state and private organizations and not solely on a private market basis.

3.3 LIMITATIONS ON THE INSURABILITY OF THE RISK OF UNEMPLOYMENT

Insurance theory provides some helpful insights into the constraints on the (private) insurance of pure risk. The most thorough analysis of this problem in the German literature is by Wilfried Schönbäck (1980), who systematized the approaches first developed by Friedman and Savage (1948) and Arrow (1971). According to his analysis, there are a number of conceivable constraints on private insurance (see also Matzner 1982:106 ff.), which are also applicable to the risk of unemployment. If one or more of these constraints are present, then private insurance either will not develop or will provide only deficient risk protection. These constraints are also indicative of the limits of insurance-type forms of risk protection for state and quasi-state unemployment insurance.

1. The damage cannot be given a monetary value. This is, at least in part, the case when one loses a job, which in addition to income also provides other highly subjective (friends at work, enjoyment of work) or social (development of social competence) values.

2. The probability of the risk is unknown. Both the amount of damages (which depends on the duration of the loss of income) and the likelihood of unemployment striking a given person are so unpredictable for a potential insurer that it would be difficult or impossible to calculate an actuarially sound insurance premium. This is because the incidence of unemployment is not a random event in the sense of probability theory. Although the group-specific probability of unemployment can be calculated post facto, this is of no use in prognostication. There is always the possibility of an unprecedented economic crisis, which makes the level and duration of a future period of mass unemployment unpredictable.

3. The insured persons engage in hazardous behavior (risk taking). Not all but certainly many persons in dependent employment tend to value the actual loss of income through payment of insurance premiums higher than the anticipated loss in case of unemployment. Assuming rational behavior, this is particularly true of those individuals with a high marginal utility of income. If there is no risk aversion, then the maximum acceptable insurance premium will be less than the minimum premium necessary for covering the risk.

4. The persons to be insured are reluctant to accept the transaction costs associated with insurance and insurance profit (risk aversion). Insurance requires administrative overhead (transaction costs), and market-organized insurance must be profitable (insurance profit). The latter increases with diminishing competition among insurance firms. This means, in turn, that the objective and subjectively perceived burden of the transaction cost increases as the anticipated magnitude and the probability of damages decline. In the case of

the risk of unemployment, that would presumably mean that employed persons with low income, on the one hand, and those with high income but an extremely low probability of unemployment (e.g., white-collar employees with middle and upper incomes and unlimited employment contracts that can hardly be dismissed), on the other, would not insure themselves.

5. The persons to be insured cannot afford the required insurance premium (relative poverty). If the magnitude of the risk relative to the income of the individual seeking insurance is so great that the insurance premium necessary to cover the potential loss of income pushes take-home pay below a subsistence level (relative poverty), and if a redistribution at the expense of those with a smaller risk is not possible because they would be unwilling to accept a pooling of such heterogeneous risks, then private insurance organized according to market principles will not be possible. This constraint is of great significance for insuring against unemployment. Relative poverty affects in particular unskilled or low-skilled persons as well as individuals at the beginning of their occupational careers, persons who as a rule are subject to high risk of unemployment. For such persons a premium appropriate to the risk might push them below a subsistence level. The constraint of relative poverty can be circumvented if groups with high income but an (extremely) low risk of unemployment would voluntarily join the private unemployment insurance scheme. Then an average premium could be established, which most of the above-mentioned groups would also be able to pay. However, this would assume that the groups with an objectively low risk were subjectively unaware of this fact. This assumption is improbable; for many (e.g., white-collar employees and civil servants), the low objective risk is manifest in quite visible job characteristics (e.g., job security provisions). For this reason it is not feasible to mix blue- and white-collar employees and civil servants in a common private unemployment insurance scheme. Permanent interpersonal redistribution in the context of private insurance (mixed risk insurance) is improbable when the individual differences in the level of risk are obvious and explicit. This leads us to the next constraint based on the inequality of risks, which is closely related to relative poverty.

6. Inequality of risks is a constraint for private insurers (a) when this inequality is not known in advance by the insurer, or (b) when—if it is known—a low-risk group is only willing to pay a premium lower than that necessary for covering the average risk. Both situations are relevant to the risk of unemployment (see constraint 2), particularly the second one. One can clearly distinguish a high- and a low-risk group in the recent history of the labor market, whereby the risk is not even distributed normally within the high-risk group itself (see inter alia Büchtemann and Brasche 1985:14 f. and Karr 1983 for the case of the Federal Republic of Germany). Regional and sectoral inequalities further exacerbate this problem. Case (a) can lead to a concentration of poor risks, which may lead to a collapse of this area of the insurance market (comparable to the failure of travel insurance against bad weather). Not knowing the actual individual risk involved, insurers would calculate a premium that is too high for individuals with a (subjectively) low risk, resulting in their withdrawal from the insurance market. The insurer would then be left with only the poor risks, for whom the premium would be too low. This constraint loses its relevance to the extent to which insurers are able to correctly calculate risk and correspondingly differentiate premiums—if need be post hoc (experience rating). Given current knowledge of differences in the risk of unemployment, this subtype of constraint cannot play a central role in explaining the failure of private unemployment insurance (CRESGE 1986:21). Case (b) would be no problem for insurers if a "solidaristic" uniform premium were established that covered the average risk of all risk groups in each situation. Private insurance based on market principles is, however, not capable of implementing such a solidaristic (i.e., redistributive) scheme. Even nonprofit associations can only do so to a limited extent. This is shown, for example, by the experience of labor union unemployment insurance funds (which still exist in Sweden), which can only survive on the basis of a large state subsidy.

7. Insurance claims (and hence benefits) can also be affected by the behavior of the insured ("moral hazard"). If this is the case, the existence of insurance can increase the likelihood of a claim by affecting that behavior. If this leads to an increase in premiums, some persons previously willing to pur-

chase insurance may cancel it or exert pressure for the exclusion of poor risks (more on this below). Moral hazard is manifest in labor market behavior, for example, by employees quitting more readily and perhaps remaining unemployed longer than absolutely necessary. Firms may also tend to discharge employees more readily because they regard themselves as being free of any social responsibility for the unemployed. Unemployment would be endogenously induced and increase as a result of such reflexive behavior. Moreover, the existence of unemployment insurance could conceivably induce persons not in the labor force to register as unemployed. Finally, the existence of insurance protection could also have a negative impact on otherwise usual individual precautionary behavior (saving or risk avoidance through occupational or regional mobility). There are a number of possible ways of controlling moral hazard that private insurers might use. One effective method is to differentiate premiums according to the number of claims made (Eisen 1976:198), which provides an incentive to avoid or reduce damages. The most important forms are deductibles—payment of part of the cost of damages by the insured person (only partial coverage of the loss of income resulting from unemployment)—and experience rating systems with rebates for insured without claims and premium surcharges for those with a high number of claims. Waiting periods, disqualification periods for persons voluntarily leaving employment, and various other control mechanisms are traditional instruments for dealing with the problem of moral hazard, which can also be used by private insurers. The resulting increased transaction costs could, however, have the effect of causing some potential insurance users to cover their risk individually. Moral hazard does not, however, represent a fundamental obstacle to the private organization of unemployment insurance.

8. Mass claims can occur when individual risks depend on one another (interdependence). Events of unemployment are not (statistically) independent of one another but can cause a chain reaction. This is because of the interrelatedness of firms; of capital, commodity, and labor markets; of market and state, and the internationalization of markets (imported or exported unemployment); the linkages among social security systems; and finally the "endogenization" of unem-

ployment, that is, increased risk of unemployment for the individual as a result of multiple spells of unemployment or the increasing duration of unemployment. Unemployment can be spread like a disease. However, unlike most other types of disease, one case of unemployment infection does not make the individual immune but usually makes him or her even more susceptible in the future. The interdependence of risks is probably the most decisive constraint on the possibility of private insurance against the risk of unemployment. There is general agreement on this point in the relevant literature; private insurance would simply not be credible. Burtless (1986:29 f.) compares the situation with that of private fire insurance in an overpopulated city without a fire department in which buildings are built of wood. Private insurance would be bankrupt after the first fire, which would probably spread to large sections if not through the whole town. Effective unemployment insurance cannot just provide protection in case of minor fires (frictional unemployment); it must also be capable of coping with situations in which kitchen fires develop into major conflagrations (structural, cyclical or demand-deficient unemployment).

In summary, not all types of constraints are relevant for explaining why insurance against unemployment is organized or financed not privately but on a mixed or state basis. The following factors are particularly important: not all damages as a result of unemployment can be expressed in monetary terms; the risk of unemployment is difficult to forecast; many persons would not be able to pay an insurance premium reflecting their actual risk of unemployment; willingness to engage in voluntary redistribution (solidarity) is limited; and, above all, unemployment can cause chain reactions and can be self-reinforcing.

A number of these constraints could be eliminated by state regulation as is usual in the case of private insurers (health or accident insurance)—that is, through a favored tax treatment or direct subsidies, state compensation for damages not covered by private insurance, or compulsory insurance with free choice of the insurer. The social and psychological costs of unemployment (which prevent it from being given a monetary value), relative poverty, and the interdependence of the risks of unemployment are, however, the decisive factors in explaining why unemployment insurance is largely organized and financed on a state or quasi-state basis. It is, above all, the increasing national and international interrelatedness of finance and commodity markets (and hence the increasing interdependence of the risks of unemployment) that explains why regional, local, and sectoral schemes of protection against unemployment developed into nationally organized systems of unemployment insurance in all developed industrial nations in the first half of the twentieth century.

The possible variations in the concrete form taken by unemployment insurance, which depend on the historical-institutional context as well as on goals that transcend the immediate aim of social security (redistribution, economic efficiency, and economic stabilizer function) are the object of the following empirical parts of our investigation.

CHAPTER **4**

The Organization and Financing of Unemployment Insurance in Comparative Perspective

4.1 THE ORIGINS OF UNEMPLOYMENT INSURANCE AS AN INSTITUTION

Unemployment insurance is organized and financed in very different ways in the countries included in this study. One reason among many others may be that the countries introduced their systems at different points in time and under quite different circumstances. Almost half a century had elapsed between the establishment of the first unemployment insurance system in Great Britain (1911) and the newest in France (1958). The different systems of unemployment insurance do, however, have one thing in common: the introduction of unemployment insurance was preceded by vehement political conflicts, which were much more difficult to resolve than in the case of health, accident, and pension insurance. Unemployment insurance was, therefore, in most countries the last component of the system of social security to be established (Leibfried 1977), and the systems finally introduced tend to reflect political compromises and previous institutional traditions more than logically coherent principles. In addition to the technical complexity of unemployment insurance, which is evident from our discussion in Chapter 3, the formation of unemployment insurance institutions was also delayed by principled opposition. This was caused especially by the fact that provision for the material needs of the unemployed also establishes minimum conditions of work on the labor market. Thus, unemployment insurance intervenes much more directly in the world of work than do other types of social insurance, and it goes far beyond Bismarck's social reform, which was primarily aimed at fostering the social integration of workers and providing security against more or less natural social risks (illness, accident, age).

70

This historical legacy has to be taken into account in considering the recent history of unemployment insurance systems because "institutional logic" is different from economic or purely actuarial principles. Jens Alber has convincingly shown in his analysis of the origins and development of unemployment insurance systems that history is one of the principal determinants of modern social security systems, including—and perhaps especially—unemployment insurance:

The original legislation retains a clear influence on current regulations. The strong persistence of traditional institutions makes it apparently easier to introduce new insurance systems with high levels of benefits than to adjust existing systems to modern standards. The extent to which their past determines the present is clearly evident in a correlation analysis of contemporary and original regulations. Contemporary benefit levels for social insurance reflect to a large extent the original ones. . . . There is also a similar persistence of original regulations with respect to the duration of benefits . . . and the length of waiting periods. . . . (Alber 1982:182).

Alber's findings are based on observations through the mid-1970s. Do they still hold true after the experience of two major economic recessions (1974–75 and 1981–82)? Have the unemployment insurance systems withstood this test in recognizable form, or have there been abrupt changes? In a period of increasing economic and political integration, one might also expect to find a process of institutional assimilation, or at least that individual countries would be guided by the strengths of other systems in undertaking necessary institutional reforms, incorporating certain elements without entirely abandoning their original structure. Before discussing the organization and financing of the various systems of unemployment insurance in detail, this section briefly describes the historical and institutional background in the individual countries.

4.1.1 Austria

In Austria a national unemployment insurance was established in 1920 during a brief period of socialist government. Introduced simultaneously with a national employment service, coverage became mandatory for about one-third of the labor force. Insurance contributions were related to wages and to the risk of unemployment, with fixed percentage rates in various wage and risk categories. Employers and employees each bore about 40 percent of the cost with the balance being borne by the federal government. As a rule, the government initially paid the entire costs for which it was subsequently reimbursed at the end of the fiscal year. Twenty weeks of covered employment sufficed to establish eligibility for benefits, which averaged 36 percent of gross wages and were paid for a period of twelve weeks after a seven-day waiting period. Workers who had left their previous jobs voluntarily or refused placement offers could be temporarily disqualified for a period from four to eight weeks. The Austrian unemployment insurance was from its beginnings closely linked both organizationally and financially to the services for placement, counseling, retraining, and work relief.

The first basic change in the system took place in the 1930s with the introduction of the temporary work relief program (PAF, "productive work promotion"), intended to alleviate seasonal winter unemployment, which is particularly high in Austria. PAF, which was financed through unemployment insurance funds, is an institutional innovation that is still important today. After passage of the Labor Market Promotion Act (AMFG) in 1968, which resembles the West German Employment Promotion Act, the expenditures were also authorized for various other and in part new instruments of labor market policy, although until 1972 expenditures were predominantly for PAF. Despite this expansion of functions, no changes were made in the basic mode of financing, that is, the financing of passive and active labor market policy through the same fund; only the regular state subsidy was abolished.[1]

4.1.2 Federal Republic of Germany

After trade union unemployment insurance funds had proven to be inadequate, and after local placement offices and a state-subsidized local assistance program had already been established, the Reichstag passed the Placement and Unemployment Insurance Act (AVAVG) in 1927. Following an extended period of discussion lasting several years, the legislation, based on a broad consensus of four-fifths of the Reichstag, was finally passed under a conservative government. It established the National Office for Placement and Unemployment Insurance, whose tasks were job placement, unemployment insurance, vocational counseling, and placement for apprenticeship positions. Reflecting the tradition of the trade union insurance funds and the local labor exchanges, the law also provided for group participation in administration (employees, employers, local and state officials) and for financing through contributions to a separate trust fund.

About 40 percent of the work force was originally covered by unemployment insurance and subject to compulsory contributions. The payments, which were borne equally by employers and employees, were wage-related with constant percentage rates in various wage categories. Twenty-six weeks of covered employment were necessary to qualify for a maximum of twenty-six weeks of benefits amounting to approximately 35 percent of previous gross wages. Benefits were only paid after a waiting period of seven days, and those who had voluntarily left their previous employment or refused placement offers were disqualified for a four-week period. In addition to the close linkage between unemployment insurance and the placement service, the National Office could also finance certain other active labor market policy measures from the insurance fund: short-time benefits, temporary public works, and placement subsidies.

The system was unable to cope with its first test, the depression of the early 1930s. It had already come under pressure by the end of the 1920s as a result of increasing deficits, which, in combination with the obligation of the Reich government to make loans to the system to cover its deficits, were an occasion for constant changes: increases in contributions, exclusion from coverage, reductions in the level and duration of benefits, and finally even a means test (incompatible with insurance principles) for the insured. These measures led to the paradoxical result that the National Office ran a surplus in 1932–33 at a time when there were 5.6 million unemployed. The funds were used to finance public assistance benefits for the jobless. At the end of the Weimar Republic only 11 percent of the unemployed were receiving benefits, which had been cut by 46 percent since the introduction of the system and were even lower than in the 1927 public assistance program for the jobless.

In 1952, the Federal Institute for Job Placement and Unemployment Insurance assumed the functions of the former National Office, but the essential features of the previous legislation remained unchanged. The legislative basis of the current organization and financing of unemployment insurance and the Federal Employment Institute is the Employment Promotion Act (AFG) of 1969, which, above all, institutionalized an expansion of the instruments of active labor market policy.[2]

4.1.3 France

A comprehensive and originally voluntary unemployment insurance was first introduced in France in 1958 as a result of an agreement between employers' associations and trade unions and transformed into compulsory insurance in 1967. Social security for the unemployed was previously limited to a welfare type, which was initially established in 1915 in the form of public and tax-financed assistance funds for the jobless administered by local governments and departments and subsidized by the central government. In addition, there were also publicly subsidized assistance funds for the jobless organized by trade unions or private welfare organizations, which, however, had largely disappeared by the beginning of the 1950s.

The public unemployment insurance system consists of forty-six regional insurance societies (*Associations pour l'Emploi dans l'Industrie et le Commerce/ASSEDIC*), which are controlled by commissions in which the employers and trade unions are equally represented. The *Union Nationale pour l'Emploi dans l'Industrie et le Commerce (UNEDIC)* serves as their national organization, which negotiates with the government and provides a national fund for the interregional sharing of the financial burden of unemployment. The determination of benefit regulations in the system takes place in the form of a "legislated partnership" between management and labor. The state passes framework legislation which the social partners elaborate in detail or supplement in negotiations. These agreements themselves then have to receive government approval and are made binding in the form of government regulations.

At the time of the transition from voluntary to compulsory insurance about 50 percent of the French work force was covered. Only twelve weeks of qualifying employment were required to establish eligibility for benefits averaging 56 percent of previous gross earnings for a maximum of fifty-two weeks. Because benefits consisted of a uniform lump-sum payment plus an earnings-related supplement, the overall structure of benefits was degressive; that is, the wage-replacement rate varied inversely with the wage level. There was no waiting period, but disqualification periods of six weeks were foreseen for the usual reasons. Contributions were deducted from wages and salaries at a fixed percentage rate, with employers being required to contribute a total of 58 percent of revenues from contributions and employees 14 percent. A regular state subsidy provided 28 percent of funding because the benefit system initially was characterized by an integration of insurance and welfare principles. As a result of subsequent reforms, these functions were, however, clearly separated both institutionally and financially.[3]

4.1.4 Great Britain

In 1911, Great Britain was the first country to introduce a public unemployment insurance system. It had been preceded by the establishment of public labor exchanges in 1909, which then assumed the task of administering unemployment benefits. Compulsory insurance was initially limited to seven branches of the industry and initially covered about 10 percent of the labor force. Coverage was quickly expanded in the 1920s and the 1930s, and by the beginning of World War II about two-thirds of the work force was covered.

Contributions as well as benefits consisted of lump-sum payments, with benefits on the average replacing about 20 percent of gross wages. The first system of compulsory insurance was thus more oriented toward the social goal of guaranteeing a minimum income than based on strictly actuarial principles. Contributions to the insurance fund were borne by employers (37.5 percent), employees (37.5 percent), and the central government (25 percent). The unemployed were eligible for benefits if they had paid contributions for twenty-six months and after a waiting period of six days; the maximum duration of benefits was initially fifteen weeks. Those who had voluntarily left their previous employment or refused placement offers were disqualified for a period of from one to six weeks.

This system consisting of uniform and relatively low contributions, short duration, and low benefits was overwhelmed by the mass unemployment of the 1930s, and in the middle of the 1930s it was supplemented by a means-tested unemployment assistance program. A reform of the entire system took place on the basis of the famous Beveridge Report (1942), the essential element of which was an integration of all types of social security without, however, changing many basic principles. Social security contributions and benefits continued to take the form of lump-sum payments and were intended only to guarantee a subsistence minimum and leave room for supplementary private insurance. Earnings-related contributions were first introduced in the early 1960s, and after 1966 the uniform unemployment benefit was supplemented by a system of income-related benefits, which, however, was then abolished in 1982. The dominant historical tradition of benefits based on need (in contrast to the principle of income security) has thus recently reasserted itself.

A slight break with the institutional tradition occurred in the 1970s when the administration of unemployment insurance was separated from the placement services. This separation was—in contrast to the tradition in Austria, the Federal Republic of Germany, and Sweden—facilitated by the fact that placement offices in Great Britain have never had any further functions for active labor market policy: neither vocational counseling, short-time benefits, subsidies for winter construction, nor job creation measures. The labor market authority MSC was created in 1974 as a special organization to perform these and similar tasks; it also was given responsibility for placement activities.[4]

4.1.5 Sweden

The Swedish unemployment insurance system has its origins in the state subsidy for local unemployment funds first introduced in 1922. This precedent led to the introduction of the so-called Ghent system. This type of unemployment insurance, which is older than compulsory state insurance, is based on the insurance activities of voluntary bodies (originally mostly trade union unemployment insurance funds), which receive public support based on the amount of benefit expenditures when certain conditions are fulfilled. Funds have to be handled separately from those of the parent organization, and there has to be a certain minimum number of members, external auditing of accounts, and official approval of fund regulations. The Ghent system, named after the Belgian city that first introduced it, was the most widespread insurance system prior to World War I and was used by many communities (also in Germany).

The advantages of the Ghent system are simplified collection of contributions (which can be included as part of union dues), simplified examination of claims (personal contact within the union), and the fact that the fund members all have similar occupational risks. The disadvantages are the (difficult to realize) requirement of a high degree of trade union organization and the limited ability to cope with economic crises that transcend a particular occupation or sector. This was probably why this system was rejected by the German trade unions in the Weimar Republic, which—after having originally favored it—advocated a compulsory insurance following their experience with the economic crisis after World War I.

Not only communal but also trade union unemployment funds were established in Sweden. Furthermore, the Swedish government was able to combat the depression at the beginning of the 1930s at an early stage and relatively successfully through state job creation programs and other expansive (Keynesian) measures, which facilitated the retention of the Ghent system. In 1934–35, the existing trade union unemployment funds became officially recognized and were subsidized at the rate of about 30 percent of their benefit expenditures.

In union-organized unemployment insurance funds it is naturally the employees who pay contributions, and membership—as in the unions themselves—is voluntary. Contribution rates and benefits were largely determined by the individual unions. Because contribution rates reflected the risk of unemployment, which differs from occupation to occupation, they also differed from fund to fund. Moreover, it was also possible to choose among insurances with different benefit levels. The benefits paid varied accordingly but were always a flat rate within each benefit level and not paid as a percentage of earnings. The essential elements of this system are still present today.

Fifty-two weeks of membership were a prerequisite to receiving benefits. There was a six-day waiting period, and claimants were subject to disqualification periods of four or more weeks. Initially only a small percentage of workers were covered, and even at the beginning of the 1960s only about one-third of all employees belonged to the voluntary insurance funds.[5]

4.1.6 United States

Up until the world economic crisis of the 1930s, only few American employees were insured against unemployment (235,000 in 1934). They were covered by trade union self-help organizations or voluntary agreements between unions and employers in individual industries and firms. In the 1920s and early 1930s, there had been attempts in individual states to establish a compulsory public employment insurance system financed through contributions, following the British or German model. However, these efforts all failed, mostly because of the increased financial burden of contributions on employers, which would have entailed a competitive disadvantage in comparison with firms in other states. A uniform federal unemployment insurance system was at first not considered because it was assumed that it would exceed the constitutional powers of the federal government and, therefore, be ruled unconstitutional by the Supreme Court.

Only under the impact of mass unemployment were there serious efforts beginning in 1933 under President Franklin D. Roosevelt to find a legal basis for establishing a general public unemployment insurance system, despite the constitutional problems and opposition of individual states. As part of the Social Security Act of 1935, a national 3 percent payroll tax applicable to employers with more than seven employees was finally introduced. The act provided that the payroll tax could be reduced by 90 percent (that is, to 0.3 percent of payroll) if employers paid wage-related contributions to state unemployment insurance programs that satisfied certain minimum requirements. This legislation thus provided individual states with a financial incentive to create their own unemployment insurance programs and removed the most important argument against individual state programs, that is, that there would be an unfair financial burden on employers in states with insurance systems, because employers in states that failed to establish an unemployment insurance program would now be subject to the higher federal tax. As a consequence, all states passed their own unemployment insurance laws between 1935 and 1937, establishing individual state unemployment benefit systems. The federal payroll tax (which subsequently was earmarked for three activities—extended insurance benefits, the employment service, and the administrative cost of unemployment insurance—and thus came to have the character of an additional contribution) was as a consequence paid everywhere only at the reduced rate.

The unemployment insurance system thus established has retained its basic features to the present day. Because the federal Social Security Act did not prescribe any minimum benefit standards, the eligibility requirements, level and duration of benefits, and contribution rate differ from state to state. Merely some basic features are similar in all states: a minimum earnings or period of employment during the preceding year is a prerequisite for eligibility; the level of benefits is related to previous earning and averages—within minimum and maximum benefit levels—about 50 percent of gross earnings. The maximum duration of benefits is as a rule twenty-six weeks. Follow-on extended benefits financed through federal and state funds have been available since 1971 under certain conditions.

The U.S. system differs from European unemployment insurance systems in that its focus is not primarily on the individual employee but on the employing firm. Only individuals employed by a firm that participates in the system (covered employment) can be eligible for unemployment insurance benefits (in 1935, only employees in firms with more than seven employees with certain exclusions; thereafter coverage was systematically expanded so that 75 percent of all employees were covered by 1965). Because of this organizational principle only employers pay contributions to the unemployment insurance system (except in three individual states). A further characteristic is that the level of contributions paid by firms is experience rated; that is, the contribution rate is higher for firms that have laid off or dismissed more workers in the past (more on this below). In 1935, the task of administering unemployment insurance in the individual states was given to the employment service offices which had been created two years previously; both activities were financed through the federal unemployment insurance payroll tax (contribution). Most states have retained this structure in which unemployment insurance and employment service are jointly administered. The implementation structure for new active labor market policy measures created since the 1960s has usually been separately organized through individual states, local governments, and special-purpose organizations.[6]

4.1.7 Summary

This historical survey confirms both the restrictions on unemployment insurance derived from insurance theory and the political sensitivity of unemployment insurance. The labor market did not give rise to any private insurance carriers able both to operate profitably and to provide adequate insurance against unemployment to a relevant group of persons. The initially voluntary forms of insurance were not commercially organized but based on group solidarity and proved inadequate at the least with the onset of mass unemployment transcending individual occupations, sectors, and regions. The oldest historical solution to this problem consisted in regular state subsidies to the voluntary unemployment insurance funds (Ghent system) and/or the expansion of the largely locally organized and later more or less state-subsidized means-tested welfare system for the jobless. The Ghent system has been retained only in Sweden; in France, the combination of this system with a comprehensive welfare system led to the relatively late establishment of a modern compulsory unemployment insurance system.

The first system to introduce compulsory contributions and legal entitlement to benefits following Bismarck's model—the British system—had no other characteristics of modern social insurance: contributions and benefits were uniform and low, corresponding more to welfare than to insurance principles. This tradition has survived in Great Britain to the present day.

Austria and Germany established compulsory insurance systems in which employers and employees played an equal role in both administration and financing and which were from the beginning closely linked with the classic functions of active labor market policy (placement service, vocational counseling, certain special employment measures). The insurance character of these systems was already relatively well developed, although the earlier means-tested welfare systems for the jobless were retained in a modified form as a supplementary type of protection. Insurance principles were, however, successively abandoned on the benefit side as mass unemployment increased, until the introduction of compulsory labor service by the fascist regime finally eliminated the last formal entitlement to benefits. With the reestablishment of the unemployment insurance system after World War II, the original legislation was revived in its essential features, and the integration of labor market services and unemployment insurance was retained and further extended.

The American system has displayed an astonishing stability to the present day—which is presumably a result of the fact that it was only established after the world economic crisis. In contrast to the European systems, the American system of unemployment insurance is predominantly financed through risk-related employer contributions, and its financing and administration are largely decentralized to the level of the individual states; despite a great deal of variation in regulations in the individual states, the system is still uniformly and strongly oriented toward insurance principles.

4.2 THE REGULATION OF CONTRIBUTIONS TO UNEMPLOYMENT INSURANCE IN 1973 AND 1985

This section describes and compares the regulations on the input side of unemployment insurance systems at two points in time: in 1973, the year before the first large postwar recession; and in 1985, a recent year in which the impact of both major postwar recessions on the structure of unemployment insurance systems should be apparent. In the next section we will consider the output side.

The input side is first described in terms of the criteria of *membership* (eligibility, compulsory coverage), which determine the *extent of coverage*, that is, the percentage of all persons in dependent employment (including the unemployed) who are insured. Then different possible ways of *structuring contributions* are examined: choice, level, and risk-relatedness of contribution schedules; the ceiling on covered earnings; and the employer and employee shares in financing. The structure of contributions to unemployment insurance reflects the historical tradition and, in particular, the philosophy of unemployment insurance that individual countries have adopted. Finally, two important characteristics of financing are considered: *fund administration* and *state subsidies*.

The regulations pertaining to contributions and benefits are closely related, and some overlap cannot be avoided in the presentation. For this reason, too, a summary assessment is first presented after benefit structures have been described. The discussion of the input side in this section follows the structure of Table 2.

4.2.1 Insurance Coverage

Except for Sweden, all the countries examined have systems with compulsory coverage, covering almost all persons in dependent employment. The earlier practice of excluding entire groups, such as construction workers or other seasonal occupations, is now rare. Only civil servants and the self-employed are as a rule not covered today. Nevertheless, until 1977 married women could be exempted from unemployment insurance coverage in Great Britain; their correspondingly reduced social security contributions did not entitle them to benefits in their own right. Most women opted to be exempted; this option no longer exists for women entering the labor force for the first time.

4.2.2 Earnings Threshold

The practice of exempting those with earnings above a certain limit from compulsory unemployment insurance coverage, which existed in a number of countries, has been abolished over the course of time (e.g., in 1968 in the Federal Republic of Germany), so that, with increasingly comprehensive coverage, the element of solidarity in the system was strengthened. Most countries, however, still have, as in the past, a lower threshold for insurance coverage, which is defined in terms of a certain minimum income and/or working hours. As a rule, however, this limit is so low that only casual laborers and some part-time employees are not covered, affecting particularly women and youth.

4.2.3 Extent of Coverage

For systems financed through contributions with compulsory insurance coverage, there is an observable trend toward universal coverage, which has peaked in the 1980s. In the United States only about 75 percent of persons in dependent employment were covered in

Table 2
The Regulation of Contributions to Unemployment Insurance (1973 and 1985)

	Criteria of Membership						Structure of Contributions						
	(1)	(2)		(3)		(4)	(5)		(6)		(7)	(8)
	Coverage	Earnings Threshold		Extent of Coverage		Types of Contributions	Level of Contributions		Ceiling on Covered Earnings		Employee Share	Employer Share
	1973-85	1973	1985	1973	1985	1973-85	1973	1985	1973	1985	1973-85	1973-85
Austria	Compulsory	Low	Low	85	84	Proportional	2.0	4.4	60	120[a]	50	50
Fed. Rep. Germany	Compulsory	20 hrs.	20 hrs.	90	92	Proportional	1.7	4.6	135	140	50	50
France	Compulsory	Low	Low	Inter-mediate	High	Proportional	0.7	5.8 (1983)	150	160[a]	20-27	73-80
Great Britain	Compulsory	Low	23 hrs.	Inter-mediate	90	Proportional, since 1985 progressive	14[a]	10[b]- 19.45	142	165[b]	39-50[a]	50-61[a]
Sweden	Voluntary	None	None	62	80	Lump-sum[a] payment vary-ing according to benefit level and risk-related	Unions:[c] 0.5-1 0.1- 0.5 Employers: 0.4 1.9 (1974)[c]		None	None	100	-
U.S.A.	Compulsory	Low	Low	High	97	Proportional and risk-related	Fed. govt.: 0.5 0.8 States: 2.7- 5.4- 4.2 10.5		46[c]	34[c]	- [b]	100 100[b]

Notes to columns:

(1) Certain groups are usually explicitly exempted from compulsory coverage, such as the self-employed and civil servants. In Great Britain married women could be exempted until 1977. The voluntary unemployment insurance contribution in Sweden is closely tied to trade union dues.

(2) As a percentage of the average wage and salary per employee. Germany: lower threshold for compulsory coverage in terms of weekly working time. Where no quantitative data given, low = up to 10 percent, intermediate = 10 to 25 percent, and high = more than 25 percent of average earnings.

(3) Where no quantitative data available, low = up to 50 percent, intermediate = 50 to 75 percent, and high = more than 75 percent of employees covered by insurance.

(4) a) In Sweden it is possible to choose among twelve different benefit levels with correspondingly different contribution rates; moreover, the contributions also vary (crudely) according to the risk of unemployment in a particular trade union; the differentiation according to benefit levels has become increasingly less important; in 1980, 88 percent of insured persons were in the highest benefit category, and by 1985, 97 percent.

(5) Data in percentage of gross wages. a) In Great Britain the unemployment insurance contribution is included in the general social insurance contribution and cannot be isolated. b) Since 1985, progressive social insurance contributions from 10 percent to 19.45 percent. c) Trade union contributions estimated; since 1974, employer contributions to the labor market fund.

(6) Data in percentage of the average wage and salary of employees. a) Approximate data. b) Since 1985, no ceiling on covered earning for employer contributions. c) The federal minimum ceiling - actual ceiling higher in individual states.

(7)/(8) a) Since 1985, the employer's share is actually higher for wages that are considerably above the ceiling on covered earnings, because the ceiling is now only applicable to employees' contributions. b) In four individual states contributions have at times been required of employees.

1965, whereas today about 95 percent are covered (Albeck and Blum 1984:238).[7] In the Federal Republic of Germany, too, "only" three-quarters of all persons in dependent employment were covered in 1965, whereas by 1973 this figure had increased to 90 percent and by 1985 to 92 percent. Similar trends can be observed in other countries.

Even Sweden shows a trend toward near universal coverage. Membership in the forty-five union-organized unemployment insurance funds in Sweden is voluntary but in practice almost obligatory as a result of the linkage between insurance contributions and trade union membership dues and the high percentage of trade union members (about 80 percent).

4.2.4 Types of Contributions

Sweden is also a special case in terms of the type of contributions. Following strict actuarial principles, the Swedes may choose among insurance at twelve different benefit and contribution levels according to their income. Within each level the employed pay a lump-sum contribution and the unemployed receive a uniform payment. This system is, however, now hardly recognizable in practice, because insurance principles have been increasingly displaced by a philosophy maintaining the insured's previous standard of living: 97 percent of the insured today are in the highest benefit category of the system. On the other hand, lump-sum contributions (premiums) have been retained; if they had been increased corresponding to increases in benefits levels, the regressive character of the lump-sum contributions (low-income persons pay relatively more as a percentage of income than do high-income persons) would have become increasingly obvious. This is probably the most important reason why contributions have not increased at the same pace as benefits and the share in financing of the Swedish state has steadily increased. A payroll tax on employers introduced in 1974 provides revenue for a labor market fund out of which the state contribution is partly refinanced.

In all other countries contributions are set as a percentage of earnings, and the same principle is also used to determine benefits,[8] which, as a rule, are income-related in the event of a claim (insurance principles).[9] In the recent past, only Great Britain has deviated from the principle of pure proportionality. Since contributions to social security were reformed in October 1985, the contribution rates (in which unemployment insurance is included)[10] are lower for lower-income wage earners in order to promote the creation of low-wage jobs.[11] Insurance principles were already greatly weakened with the abolition of the earnings-related supplement to unemployment insurance in 1982, and there was no opposition to this reform.

Strict insurance principles would require a variation in contributions according to the risk of unemployment. This is, however, only realized in two of the countries investigated: Sweden and the United States. Contributions to the different trade union unemployment insurance funds in Sweden are loosely related to the risk of unemployment in the particular industry or occupational group. University graduates, bank employees, or insurance employees, for example, pay the lowest contribution rates (8, 3.25, and 8 kronor per month, respectively), while construction workers, hotel and restaurant employees, and musicians, for example, pay the highest rates (19, 25, and 45 kronor per month, respectively; the figures are for 1983 and in each case for the highest benefit level). Because the insurance is voluntary, the trade unions themselves set contribution rates. No information is available on whether differences in contribution rates actually reflect different degrees of risk or whether they are only an outdated relic of the past.

The risk factor is integrated differently in the United States because only employers pay contributions (see below). The American principle of experience rating means essentially that the contribution rates for individual employers are based on the extent to which their employees have drawn unemployment insurance in the past. Experience rating is applied only in determining the contribution rates for the individual state unemployment insurance systems and not for the uniform federal contribution. The experience-rating system thus varies state to state, although its basic features are based on common national guidelines. In most cases, the system functions as follows. Points are assessed to each individual employer for dismissals and temporary layoffs that lead to unemployment benefit claims. The contribution rate the employer pays is based on this point system. If an employer has had few redundancies and therefore a low number of points, only a reduced contribution rate is applicable, whereas an employer with frequent layoffs and dismissals and a high number of points must pay the regular contribution rate set by law.

The goal of the experience-rating system is to shift part of the societal costs of layoffs and dismissals to the individual employer in a system with extremely low barriers to layoffs and dismissals (e.g., through employment protection legislation). The impact of the experience-rating system is, however, usually considered to be incomplete. This is, above all, caused by the fact that many firms, particularly those in the construction industry, have accumulated such a high number of points on their individual accounts that they already pay the highest contribution rate. For them, experience rating no longer provides an incentive to avoid dismissals.

The contribution systems with risk rating also function as control mechanisms to prevent unjustified claims by individuals for unemployment benefits. In Sweden, it is the local representatives of the trade unions who monitor for possible abuses (possible sanctions would be, for example, expulsion from the union or denial of benefits). In the United States, it is individual firms themselves who have an interest in reporting those unemployed who have quit or brought about dismissal through their own conduct; employers can avoid accumulating additional points on their individual accounts only by reporting such persons. Employers' reports enable the labor administration in the individual states to exclude such persons (temporarily) from benefits. Despite weaknesses in risk rating as practiced, this control aspect appears to be an essential reason for its retention.

4.2.5 Level of Contributions

The level of contributions also differs greatly from country to country. Only Austria, France, and the Federal Republic of Germany have a comparable structure. In these countries the contribution rate in 1973 was between 0.7 and 2 percent of gross wages—the low rate in France was related to the late introduction of unemployment insurance and the close linkage with the tax-financed system of means-tested unemployment assistance. Today France has the highest contribution rate as a result of the consistent development of its insurance system, numerous special benefits financed through contributions (especially early retirement), and generous benefit levels. In Austria and the Federal Republic contribution rates increased as a consequence of increasing unemployment and the rise in expenditures for active labor market policy, which are also financed through these contributions.

The case of Great Britain is absolutely unique. Contributions to unemployment insurance have been fully integrated into a general social security contribution since the Beveridge reform. This has implications for the extent to which insurance benefits are regarded as property rights—a topic to which we shall return below in analyzing the impact of different unemployment insurance systems.

The structure of contributions in Sweden and the United States is also unique to these countries. Contributions to the trade union unemployment insurance funds in Sweden vary according to the risk of unemployment but are comparatively low and provide only a relatively small share of financing. Sweden is the only country in which the contribution rates have not kept pace with increases in expenditures. However, the revenues from a payroll tax on employers introduced in 1974 flow into a labor market fund that is in part used to finance state subsidies to the insurance funds; the contribution rate is adjusted to reflect increases in fund expenditures.

In the United States federal law establishes both the national unemployment insurance contribution (0.8 percent; in 1973, 0.5 percent) and a minimum rate for individual state insurance contributions (5.4 percent; until 1984, 2.7 percent). Beyond this minimum rate individual states can set their own contribution rates.[12] In 1973, the contribution rate exceeded the minimum of 2.7 percent required by federal law only in a few states, in which it was between 2.8 and 4.2 percent. Since then, as a result of increasing unemployment and the rise in the uniform federal minimum in 1985, all states have markedly increased their contribution rates, which now lie between 5.4 and 10.5 percent. These contribution rates are only applicable to employers who do not receive any rate reductions on the basis of experience rating. The actual average contribution rates are considerably lower because of the reduced rates paid by many employers.

4.2.6 Ceiling on Covered Earnings

There is in all countries (with proportional levies) a ceiling on earnings subject to contributions. With the exception of the United States, the historical pattern has been for the ceiling on covered earnings to rise disproportionately in comparison with gross wages. In the United States, the ceiling for the federal contribution and for most individual state contributions is considerably below average earnings and has tended over the course of time to lag even farther behind. In all other countries—a ceiling on covered wages is foreign to the Swedish lump-sum contribution system—the ceiling is now considerably above average earnings. This development has ameliorated the regressive tendency associated with every type of upper limit on covered earnings. In Great Britain, the ceiling on employers' contribution was abolished in the 1985 reform.

4.2.7 Employer and Employee Shares

Contribution systems also differ according to whether contributions are paid by employers, employees, or both. The burden of payment[13] in Sweden and in the United States follows logically from the particular concepts underlying their insurance systems: in the trade union unemployment insurance funds in Sweden, only employees pay contributions, whereas in the United States—with the exception of four individual states[14]—only employers pay contributions. Reflecting their corporate structure, contributions are paid equally by employers and employees in Austria and the Federal Republic of Germany. In France, the employers' share is substantially higher (about 80 percent), reflecting its traditions of social security law. In Great Britain, the employers' share was reduced at the beginning of the 1980s from about 60 percent to just under 54 percent and subsequently, as a result of the 1985 reform, to 50 percent for below-average wages; the employers' contribution rate is now only greater than the employees' in the case of employees with high earnings. With the exception of those countries in which the burden of payments is borne exclusively by one party, these differences probably reflect different historical traditions and not actual power relationships. In Sweden and the United States, however, patterns of influence are clearly evident. The trade unions ultimately determine the basic structure of the Swedish system of contributions to unemployment insurance; in the United States, it is the employers. In Great Britain, the shift in the burden of payments had the goal of reducing employers' nonwage labor costs, particularly for low-paid positions.

4.2.8 Fund Administration and State Subsidies

The rules governing fund administration and state subsidies or shares in financing are also important features of systems based on contributions. They determine the relationship between revenues and expenditures and also, to a certain extent, political responsibility and authority in dealing with unemployment. The greater the reliance on separate special-purpose funds and the lower the share of financing borne by the state budget, the more insurance principles will be followed and the weaker is the fiscal incentive to combat unemployment with state employment programs. Conversely, if the special-purpose fund is weakly developed (or in the extreme case of the integration of unemployment insurance in the general state budget), the linkage between revenues and expenditures is loosened; the protection enjoyed by insurance benefits as property rights will also be less. With a strong financial stake in the level of unemployment, the state will either attempt to combat it through labor market and employment programs or respond to the fiscal pressure of increasing unemployment by reducing benefits.

Except in Great Britain, contributions to unemployment insurance[15] flow into a separate "self-governing" fund, which is typically administered by a more or less autonomous, usually bipartite authority. In Great Britain, unemployment insurance is an integral component of the national insurance fund out of which also (and above all) pension and sickness benefits are financed. This fund is not independent but operates within the Department of Health and Social Security and is directly administered by it. The share of unemployment benefits in social security fund expenditures is relatively small, varying between 4 and 10 percent. The fund is essentially financed through a general (indivisible) national insurance contribution. The subsidy from general government revenues, which was originally introduced to cover benefits not contingent upon contributions (e.g., family allowances) accounts for about 8 to 18 percent of fund expenditures. This state share is not fixed by law but varies according to government policy. Because unemployment benefits constitute only a small part of total fund expenditures, these expenditures have only a small impact on surpluses or deficits in the fund as a whole. The question of state responsibility for deficits in an autonomous unemployment insurance fund is thus not relevant here. Active labor market policy is financed separately through general state revenues.

In the Federal Republic of Germany and in Austria, expenditures for active and passive labor market policy are integrated in a common fund; contributions are used to finance both unemployment benefits and active labor market policy measures. Beyond this common feature the two countries also display important differences. Most importantly, Austrian law requires a rapid balancing of the unemployment insurance fund budget by adjusting revenues to reflect changes in expenditures, whereas there are no legal limits on deficits or the build-up of reserve funds by the Federal Employment Institute (FEI) in the Federal Republic. Any shortfall (in excess of expenditures for unemployment assistance) in the Austrian unemployment insurance fund may be covered only temporarily through loans from the federal budget, which have to be quickly repaid; if necessary, the unemployment insurance fund budget has to be balanced by increasing contributions. Conversely, long-term surpluses are also not permitted, because reserve funds may only be accumulated up to a maximum of one year's expenditures. The Austrian system is thus largely based on levy financing. In the Federal Republic, there is by contrast neither an obligation to repay federal funds made available to cover FEI deficits nor an obligation to balance its budget in the long run. As a result, the German federal government has greater discretion than its Austrian counterpart in deciding on the distribution of financial burdens between taxpayers (i.e., the federal budget) and contributors to unemployment insurance. It *can* either finance a long-term deficit with federal budget funds *or* increase contributions through legislation. Conversely, it may also permit large reserves to be accumulated. The FEI's budget is thus more capable of functioning as an anticyclical stabilizer than is the Austrian fund. However, the possibility exists in both countries that balanced budgets may be achieved by adjusting expenditures to reflect revenues; that is, expenditures may be reduced in the case of deficits and expanded in the case of surpluses.

It should also be noted that since 1981 unemployment assistance in the Federal Republic of Germany has (again) been completely financed through general revenues. This means that the financial burden of increasing long-term unemployment is automatically shifted from the FEI to the federal budget. In order to offset such a trend, it is possible—when the financial situation of the FEI is favorable—to extend the duration of unemployment benefits as was done in 1985, 1986 and 1987. This is an example of how improvements in benefits not only burden one budget but relieve another and—because the decision-making institution is also the primary fiscal beneficiary—are also primarily motivated by the desire to attain budgetary relief. (In the same way, local governments would, if they were the governmental level that decided, opt for an improvement in unemployment benefits and unemployment assistance in order to reduce their expenditures for public assistance).

It is a difficult task to describe fund administration and the state subsidy in France because the relevant regulations have changed frequently during the period examined. Until 1979, the system can be briefly summarized as follows. Different sources of revenue were utilized for different types of unemployment benefits. Unemployment assistance for uninsured persons or those no longer entitled to benefits was financed from central government general revenues; other types of benefits were financed through contributions. This system led to a distribution of the annual financial burden of income security for the unemployed, which varied according to the development of unemployment and the uptake of various types of benefits. The contribution rates were set by the governing board of UNEDIC, an insurance body administered jointly by employers' and trade union representatives and adjusted at least once a year to reflect cyclical conditions and development of expenditures. This system could no longer be continued primarily as a consequence of the financial strain of the heavy emphasis on early retirement financed through contributions.

The financing system in force from 1979 to 1984 provided for a regular state subsidy to the unemployment insurance fund according to a formula that foresaw financing one-third of the fund from the state budget and two-thirds from contributions. This model presupposed that contribution rates would be adjusted through a joint decision of the social partners to reflect changes in expenditures. If they were not able to agree—as happened in 1982–83—then the state was in practice required to intervene, although not legally obligated to do so. As of April 1, 1984, a sharp separation of financing according to types of benefits was again introduced: Unemployment benefits are to be financed from a fund deriving its revenues from contributions; all other benefits (different forms of unemployment assistance, early retirement, and most active labor market policy measures) are financed solely by the state budget. The state has, however, committed itself to covering one-third of all deficits arising in the unemployment insurance system during a transition period.

In Sweden, the system is characterized by a procedure for adjusting revenues to expenditures primarily through a regularized (proportional) distribution of the financial burden between employers (the labor market fund financed by employer contributions) and the state budget. If expenditures increase, then subsidies from the labor market fund—with a constant share of financing—also increase, and the employer contributions must be increased accordingly if reserve funds have been exhausted. The employer contributions are supposed to cover two-thirds of the expenditures of the labor market fund. From a long-term perspective, it is thus in fact a type of levy financing of certain parts of labor market policy. In addition to the two main elements of financing (employer contributions and the state budget), contributions to the trade union unemployment funds by the insured constitute a third component of financing, which, however, accounts only for a small and diminishing share of expenditures for unemployment benefits. The failure to increase financing from this source during the last decades, which has in fact declined even further relative to other sources of financing, is probably largely the result of the strong position of the trade unions and their influence in the government and social democratic party.

In contrast to the Federal Republic of Germany, Austria, and in part France and Sweden, but similar to the situation in Great Britain, the financing systems for active and passive labor market policy in the United States are almost completely separate. All active labor market policy programs—except for the placement service—are financed through the federal budget. The unemployment insurance benefits in the individual states have to be financed fully through employer contributions, and, in case of threatening deficits, either expenditures have to be reduced to reflect revenues or contributions have to be raised to cover expenditures. To a certain extent, and with a short time lag, experience rating provides for an automatic linkage between revenues and expenditures because only few employers qualify for reductions in contribution rates in periods of higher unemployment whereas many qualify in periods of lower unemployment. If deficits nevertheless do develop in the state insurance programs, they receive by law loans from the federal government. The federal government attempts to compel the quick repayment of these loans by various means (including high interest rates).

4.3 THE REGULATION OF UNEMPLOYMENT INSURANCE BENEFITS IN 1973 AND 1985

Whether the unemployed receive wage-replacement benefits, for how long, and in what amount depend on numerous conditions. The most important of these are summarized in Table 3, which also shows the differences in regulations between the years 1973 and 1985. Unemployment benefits in the case of unemployment depend on the following conditions:

1. How long and/or how much was paid in contributions prior to the period of unemployment (*previous employment*)?
2. Is the unemployed person available for work, and is the unemployment the result of his or her own conduct (*availability for work*)?
3. Does the unemployed person receive unemployment benefits immediately or only after a fixed number of days (*waiting period*)?
4. What is the *duration of benefits*?
5. What is the basis for the *level of unemployment benefit*?
6. Is the unemployment benefit supplemented in the case of insufficient benefits or exhaustion of benefits by a system of *unemployment assistance*?
7. Is the unemployment benefit *taxable*?
8. Does the unemployed person continue to be covered in the other branches of the social security system (particularly *pension and health insurance*)?
9. What *additional benefits* do the unemployed receive?

Table 3: The Regulation of Unemployment Insurance Benefits (1973 and 1985)
Part 1

| | Qualifying Period for Unemployment Benefit (UB) | | | |
| | Min. | Max. | Min. | Max. |
		1973		1985
Austria	20 weeks in previous year (initially: 1 year in previous 2 years)	3 years within previous 5 years	Same as in 1973	
F.R. Germany	6 months in previous 3 years	24 months in previous 3 years	12 months in previous 4 years	6 years in previous 7 years[a]
France	3 months (91 days) in previous year		Same as in 1973	(A) 24 months in previous 3 years (B) for older persons (57.5 years): 10 years qualifying employment, 12 continuous months in last 5 years
Great Britain	25 weekly minimum contributions	50 weekly minimum contributions	Same as in 1973	
Sweden	12 months of covered employment, 5 of which in previous year		Same as in 1973	
U.S.A.[b]	In most states, minimum earning and/or 14-20 weeks employment in the previous 12 months		14 weeks covered employment and/or $150 earnings in previous year	20 weeks covered employment and/or $ 2,200 earnings in previous year

a) Qualifying period and duration of benefits dependent on age; up until age of 50 (1986: 45) years max. benefit 1 year with 3-year qualifying period.
b) Because of differences in the individual state insurance systems, data reported only for median and/or extreme cases throughout Table 3.

Table 3
Part 2

Availability for Work

	1973	1985
Austria	(A) Registration and job search (B) Availability[c] (C) 4 weeks disqualification for voluntarily leaving previous employment or refusing suitable job offer	Same as in 1973
F.R. Germany	(A) Registration and job search (B) Available for at least 20 hours/week (C) 4 weeks disqualification for voluntarily leaving previous employment or refusing suitable job offer	(A) Same as in 1973 (B) Stricter definition of suitability; part-time availability only permissible in case of child-rearing or home care of an invalid[d] (C) 12 weeks disqualification up to complete loss of benefits
France	(A) Registration and job search (b) Availability (C) 5 weeks disqualification	(A) Same as in 1973 (B) Same as in 1973 (C) 6 weeks disqualification up to complete loss of benefits (decision by a bipartite commission)
Great Britain	(A) Registration and job search (B) Availability: 30 hours/week (C) Up to 6 weeks disqualification	(A) Registration only at benefit offices but no longer with placement service (B) Same as in 1973, but now difficult to control (C) Same as in 1973
Sweden	(A) Registration and job search (B) Availability (particularly for labor market programs) (C) 4 weeks disqualification period	Same as in 1973
U.S.A.	(A) Registration and job search (except for temporary layoffs) (B) Availability (except layoffs) (C) Depending on the case (and varying from state to state) 4 to 25 weeks disqualification (on the average stricter than in Europe)	(A) Same as in 1973 (B) Same as in 1973 (C) Increase in disqualification periods up to complete exclusion from benefits

c) Above all, an obligation to accept "suitable" employment; this presupposes inter alia that the unemployed person can be contacted by the labor office at any time.
d) Availability in particular for suitable labor market programs.

Table 3
Part 3

Waiting Period

	1973	1985
Austria	3 days	Same as in 1973
F.R. Germany	None	Same as in 1973
France	None	Same as in 1973
Great Britain	3 days (2 weeks for supplement according to Part 5)	Same as in 1973 (supplement eliminated)
Sweden	5 days	Same as in 1973
U.S.A.	1 week	Same as in 1973 (only 8 of 50 states do not have a waiting period)

Table 3
Part 4

	Duration of Benefits			
	Min.	Max.	Min.	Max.
		1973		1985
Austria	12 weeks	30 weeks	Same as in 1973	1 year
F.R. Germany	3 months	12 months	4 months	18 months (1986: 24 months)[f]
France	1 year	1 year (609 days for unemployed 51 and older)	3 months	45 months (60 months for those 51 and older, 90 months for those 57.5 and older)
Great Britain	50% of lump-sum benefit for 1 year (supplement 6 months)	100% of lump-sum benefit for 1 year (supplement 6 months)	Same as in 1973 (supplement eliminated)	
Sweden	150-200 days (5 per week), depending on unemp. ins. fund; 300 days for those 61 and older		300 working days (60 weeks); 450 working days for older persons 56 and older (90 weeks)	
U.S.A.	As a rule, max. 26 weeks, varies from state to state; automatic extension of 50% (max. 13 weeks) when unemployment is high nationally or in individual states[e]		Same as in 1973, but extension now hardly possible	

e) Between 1975 and 1978 and between 1982 and early 1985 temporary extension through federal supplemental benefit programs (FSB, SUA, FSC), at times up to 65 weeks.

f) Qualifying period and duration of benefits dependent on age; up until age of 50 (1986: 45) years max. benefit 1 year with 3-year qualifying period.

Table 3
Part 5

Level of Unemployment Benefit (UB)

	1973	1985
Austria	Proportional ca. 40% of gross earnings (no minimum)	Same as in 1973
F.R. Germany	Proportional 62.5% of net earnings (no minimum)	Proportional 68% (63% for unemployed without children) of net earnings[9] (no minimum)
France	Proportional 35% (40.25% for the first 3 months) plus a uniform payment of 20% of minimum wage (cumulation of unemployment assistance possible up to 90% of gross earnings), min. and max. benefits[h]	Proportional (A) 30% plus uniform benefit of 30 francs per day (B) 42% after 6 months (C) In case of extension 85% of (A) and degressive, min. and max. benefits[i]
Great Britain	Uniform benefit with family supplements and proportional supplement of 33.3% or 15% depending on income category	Since 1982 only uniform benefit (1985 = 28.45 £/week) plus family supplements
Sweden	Uniform benefit in 12 benefit levels, max.: 11/12 of gross earnings	Uniform payment in 12 benefit levels (97% insured in highest benefit category, 1985 = 310 kronor), max.: 11/12 of gross earnings
U.S.A.	Proportional; in most states max. benefit is ca. 50% of gross earnings. Minimum benefits	Same as in 1973

g) Net earnings less special payments (premiums for night, sunday, and overtime work, one-time payments, 13th month's pay, etc.).
h) Minimum for 35% wage-replacement rate = 9.74 francs/day; max. = 96.30 francs/day.
i) (C) 85% of the regular basic grant, then 85% of the reduced payment for periods of 6 months; for those 50-55 years of age: 95% and reduction only every 9 months; after age 55: 100% of the regular basic benefit. Minimum benefit for (A) 72 francs/day, for (B) 95 francs/day, maximum benefit for (A) 56.25% of gross wages, for (B) 75%.

Table 3
Part 6

Unemployment Assistance

	1973	1985
Austria	92% of UB for single individuals, 100% with dependents; means-tested; 26 weeks with possibility of unlimited extension	Same as in 1973
F.R. Germany	52.5% of net earnings and means-tested; 1 year with possibility of unlimited extension	58% (56% for unemployed without children) of net earnings and means-tested; 1 year with possibility of unlimited extension
France	Uniform payment (A) 8.90 francs/day for the first 3 months (B) after 4th month means-tested, 8.10 francs/day for unlimited time, but reduced by 10% per year	Uniform payment (A) 40 francs/day final payment (B) 80 francs/day for workers 56 and older (max.: 75% of covered wages) (C) 40 francs/day (integration and solidarity grant)[j]
Great Britain	Uniform payment = supplementary benefit	Uniform payment = supplementary benefit (1985 = 28.05 £/week for single individuals); means-tested and for unlimited period
Sweden	None	Since 1974 uniform payment (1985 = 100 kronor), **not** means-tested, limited to 150 days (can be extended for older persons)
U.S.A.	None	Same as in 1973 (however, UB period extended by temporary programs during some periods - see Part 4)

j) Integration assistance is paid for 12 months; single women with dependent children and youths who are engaged in workfare receive a larger grant (80 francs/day); the solidarity grant is paid for a period of 6 months (may be extended); 50-55 year old persons with 10 years of covered employment receive 60 francs/day and those older than 55 with 20 years of covered employment receive 80 francs/day.

Table 3
Part 7

Taxation of Unemployment Benefit

	1973	1985
Austria	No	Same as in 1973
F.R. Germany	No	Same as in 1973 (but in part indirectly by being taken into account in determining tax bracket in annual income tax return)
France	Yes	Same as in 1973
Great Britain	No	Yes (since 1982)
Sweden	No	Yes
U.S.A.	No	Yes (since 1982), but only in case of higher income from benefits or other sources

Table 3
Part 8

Pension and Health Insurance (PI, HI)

	1973	1985
Austria	(A) Covered (B) Unemployment ins. makes compensatory payment to PI and HI systems for lost income from contributions	Same as in 1973
F.R. Germany	(A) Covered (B) Unemployment ins. pays contributions **only** to HI	(A) Same as in 1973 (B) Contributions paid to HI; contributions to PI paid proportionally to unemployment benefit or unemployment assistance
France	(A) Covered	(A) Covered (B) Payment in amount of 1% of unemployment benefit to pension insurance
Great Britain	(A) Covered (B) No transfers by unemployment insurance to HI or PI; all three insurance systems closely integrated	Same as in 1973
Sweden	(A) Covered (B) No transfers from unemployment insurance to HI or PI	Same as in 1973
U.S.A.	(A) Neither health nor pension insurance (pension entitlement, however, normally not affected) (B) Corresponding to (A), no transfers from unemployment insurance to HI or PI	Same as in 1973

Table 3
Part 9

Additional Transfer Payments

	1973	1985
Austria	(A) Family supplements (B) Family grants, family public assist- ance, housing allowance for needy (C) Exemption from fees	Same as in 1973
F.R. Germany	(A) Family supplements in amount of 12 deutsche marks per week for each dependent (B) Public assistance, if unemploy- ment benefit below threshold of need (C) Housing allowance possible (D) Reduction in or exemption from fees	(A) Eliminated in 1975 (B), (C), (D) Same as in 1973
France	(A) Family supplements in amount of 3.60 francs/day and dependent for those receiving unemployment assistance (B) Diverse means-tested and above all family-related benefits	(A) ? (B) Same as in 1973
Great Britain	(A) Family supplements (B) Supplementary benefit when un- employment benefit is below threshold of need (C) Significant housing allowances	Same as in 1973
Sweden	(A) Family supplements (B) Housing allowance possible	(A) Eliminated in 1974 (B) Same as in 1973
U.S.A.	(A) Family supplements in about 10 states (B) Public assistance (AFDC) for the needy (only for households with children) (C) Food stamps, medical care for needy (Medicaid) (D) Supplements of unemployment insur- ance based on collective agreements	Same as in 1973

The following discussion concentrates on the basic patterns in the regulation of unemployment benefits and the changes that have taken place. For details, see Table 3 and the sources indicated.[16]

4.3.1 Previous Employment

In all countries, the insured must have paid a certain minimum in contributions in order to be eligible for unemployment benefits. As a rule, this requirement is defined in terms of a minimum period in insured employment. Only in Great Britain is it exclusively and in the United States partly defined in terms of a minimum level of contributions paid. If a minimum period of insured employment is the only criterion, it is primarily new entrants to the job market who are excluded from insurance benefits, particularly youth or persons who have interrupted their working careers for a longer period of time— usually women. If only a minimum amount of contributions is required, then those with low incomes also tend to be excluded. These will often be youthful new entrants into the labor market and women reentering. Employees who have worked regularly but less than full-time or employees with very low earnings may also be excluded by such a criterion—which, strictly speaking, violates insurance principles. As already noted, insurance principles are least developed in Great Britain. The fact that it is also the only country in which the payment of a minimum amount in contributions is a prerequisite for qualifying for benefits is consistent with our interpretation of the British case.

The minimum qualifying period varies between three (France, U.S.A.) and twelve months (Sweden, Austria for initial entitlement to benefits). The countries in which the duration of benefits varies according to the length of the previous period of insured employment (Austria, Germany) require the longest periods of qualifying employment and have the longest benefit periods. Major changes in the qualifying conditions were introduced only in the Federal Republic of Germany and France. The Federal Republic increased the minimum period of insured employment required from six to twelve months during the previous four years of employment, which led to the exclusion of many unemployed from benefits. Both the Federal Republic of Germany and France have further differentiated their requirements pertaining to previous insured employment and raised the maximum conditions for eligibility in connection with the extension of the benefit period for older unemployed persons.

4.3.2 Availability for Work

In all countries studied, benefits are only provided when the unemployed (at least) are registered with unemployment benefit offices and actively seek new employment. The unemployed are obligated to accept "suitable offers"; if they reject such an offer, they may be disqualified from benefits for a fixed period and, in case of repeated refusal, their benefits are terminated. Temporary disqualification also results when the insured has voluntarily left previous employment— the regulations in this case are most strict in the United States.

In the period examined, the regulations with regard to the suitability of offers and temporary disqualification were tightened in countries in which insurance principles are strongest—in the Federal Republic of Germany and the United States. Furthermore, at least in the United States, changes in administrative practice have also led to the application of stricter controls on availability for work even apart from formal changes in regulations; in the opinion of Burtless (1983), this has contributed to the decline in the percentage of unemployed receiving benefits. However, because unemployment benefits are an entitlement—this is true in all countries—even stricter criteria of availability to work and more stringent administrative controls have had little impact on expenditures for unemployment insurance benefits. The most important factors influencing expenditures have been (in addition to qualifying employment) the regulations pertaining to the duration and level of benefits.

4.3.3 Waiting Period

In order to discourage willful abuse of unemployment insurance, a number of countries have waiting periods during which no benefits are paid. These regulations largely date back to the origins of the national unemployment insurance systems, when the tendency to blame individuals for their unemployment or to suspect voluntary unemployment was even stronger than today. The longest waiting periods are found in the United States and Sweden (one week or five working days); the Federal Republic of Germany and France do not have waiting periods.

Waiting periods are based on assumptions about the behavior of the unemployed that are highly controversial. This is probably why the provisions once introduced hardly change; a new political consensus is difficult to reach. Between 1973 and 1985, there were no changes, although there were frequent demands for introducing or strengthening these provisions in countries with no or only a brief waiting period. The institutional stability may also be rooted in a conviction that individuals would tend to exploit the system in the absence of a waiting period; this is probably the most important reason in the United States.

4.3.4 Duration of Benefits

The duration of benefits can be used as an initial indicator of the "generosity" of the systems but is not by itself very informative without also taking other criteria into consideration. We will confine our discussion at this point to a description of the structure and changes in this criterion.

The simplest and most uniform regulation of the duration of unemployment benefits is found in Great Britain. Every unemployed person entitled to benefits receives unemployment benefit for a maximum of one year (the earnings-related supplement to unemployment benefit abolished in 1982 provided benefits uniformly for six months). The duration of benefits does not vary according to the qualifying conditions (instead, the *level* of benefits varies; Reissert 1985:14). In contrast to all other countries, the duration of benefits has not changed since 1973.

Sweden most closely resembles Great Britain. There is also no relationship between the previous qualifying employment and the duration of benefits (which was extended from between thirty and forty to sixty weeks). Benefit duration is, however, dependent on age with older persons receiving extended benefits. Apart from age, there is only one uniform requirement (twelve months of qualifying employment), and because of the voluntary character of insurance in Sweden, it is more like a membership criterion: if one becomes a member, one enjoys full rights without any differentiation in the duration of benefits according to the length of the previous period of insured employment.

The United States is a special case. There is no binding federal regulation with regard to the duration of benefits, which differs from state to state. In most states, the benefit period is twenty-six weeks, and there were hardly any changes during the time period examined. In ten states, the duration of benefits—as in Great Britain and Sweden —does not vary with previous insured employment, whereas in the others it varies in different ways with the duration of previous employment and the amount paid in contributions. Until 1982, the duration of benefits was automatically extended by 50 percent (a maximum of thirteen weeks) during periods of high national or regional unemployment through a nationwide system of extended benefits. Increases in the threshold level of unemployment necessary to trigger these extended benefits in individual states and the elimination of a national trigger have led to the virtual elimination of the program. Instead, during the 1982-83 recession, a special temporary program of federal supplemental benefits—as had also existed during the period from 1975 to 1978—provided additional benefits for those whose regular entitlement had been exhausted. This program can be regarded as a substitute for a system of unemployment assistance, which does not exist in the United States. In the United States, a social security net for the long-term unemployed has been provided only on such an ad hoc basis.

In Austria, France, and the Federal Republic of Germany, the duration of benefits varies with the previous period of insured employment, and the duration of benefits has been extended in all three countries during the period investigated. This was done, however, in quite different ways. In Austria, the duration of benefits was extended from thirty weeks to one year; as in Sweden, this was done without any change in the required qualifying period. In the Federal Republic and France, the duration of benefits was extended to eighteen months (to two years in 1986) and ninety months, respectively, but the required period of previous insured employment was also increased—in both countries only older unemployed persons are eligible for these extended benefits. The unemployment insurance systems in these countries have thus clearly taken over functions of early retirement. In both cases, older unemployed persons who are eligible for the maximum benefit period no longer have to be available for work and automatically receive retirement pensions after their unemployment benefits have been exhausted. These older unemployed persons (in France after the age of sixty, in the Federal Republic of Germany after the age of fifty-eight) are also no longer required to register as unemployed, which has led to a considerable cosmetic improvement in the official unemployment statistics. The linkage between longer periods of qualifying employment, longer eligibility, and age moves both of these systems in the direction of being welfare rather than insurance systems, the aim of which is, in addition to risk sharing, the most rapid possible elimination of the circumstance giving rise to a claim (i.e., reintegration in employment). The increasing linkage of the duration of benefits to the duration of the previous period of insured employment represents a weakening of insurance principles as the system becomes more like one of compulsory individual savings for social security (CRESGE 1986:24).

4.3.5 Level of Unemployment Benefits

In addition to the duration of benefits, the level of unemployment benefits is the other decisive parameter for the "generosity" of unemployment insurance. Two different principles for calculating unemployment benefits can be identified: earnings-related payments and lump-sum payments. The earnings-related payments reflect insurance principles, that is, the principle of insuring the individual standard of living, whereas lump-sum payments are based on the principle of social welfare, that is, providing basic income security in case of need.

Lump-sum payments exist today in a pure form only in Great Britain, although from 1966 to 1981 there was also an earnings-related supplement in that country. The uniform payment guarantees a minimum of income security but does not maintain the previous standard of living. As a result of the abolition of the earnings-related supplement in 1982, benefit levels declined considerably. The lump-sum payment was also reduced in real terms as annual inflation adjustments were sometimes cancelled.

In Sweden, too, the basis for calculating unemployment insurance is not previous wages but a uniform amount within twelve optional benefit levels. Originally, these categories were a reflection of occupational differences in earnings so that the system was to a certain extent earnings-related. Today, however, the overwhelming majority (97 percent) are in the highest benefit category, for which the benefit amount is set in terms of the average national wage. In practice, Sweden has implemented a system of basic income security, which is, however, set not at the subsistence level (welfare principle) but at that of an average standard of living. Such a benefit system entails considerable redistribution, because the wage-replacement rate for low- and middle-income wage earners must necessarily be higher than that for those with higher earnings. The redistributive impact is, however, limited by the rule that unemployment benefits may not exceed eleven-twelfths of gross salary. In contrast to Great Britain, where the lump-sum benefit is financed through earnings-related (and since 1985 even progressive) contributions, there is a lump-sum contribution in Sweden corresponding to the lump-sum benefit.

In all other countries studied, unemployment benefits are earnings-related; the level of benefits is set as a fixed relationship of the previous wage or salary. An exception here is France, in two respects: the proportional unemployment benefit in France is supplemented by a lump sum (uniform payment), which again leads to redistribution in favor of low-income persons on the benefit side; and moreover, the

French system differentiates according to the duration of unemployment with benefits being paid at an initially increasing proportional rate that subsequently begins to decline after twelve months of unemployment.[17]

Earnings-related benefits can be further differentiated according to whether gross or net earnings are used as a basis for calculating benefits. Only the Federal Republic of Germany uses the net principle: unemployment benefits are calculated as a percentage of net pay after taxes and social security contributions have been deducted. However, certain special payments, which in part are included in net salary, have been excluded from the wage base used to calculate unemployment benefits as a result of cutbacks at the beginning of the 1980s. The benefit rate, which in 1975 (i.e., at the beginning of the recession) was raised from 62.5 to 68 percent, was reduced in 1984 to 63 percent for unemployed persons without children—which represents a slight deviation from the insurance principle in the direction of (assumed) need. If there are no minimum benefit levels (which is the case in the Federal Republic), benefits based on previous net earnings can lead to inadequate income provision for low-income wage earners, that is, benefits below the nationally recognized minimum income level.

Austria, France, and the United States use the gross income principle. Whereas in Austria and France there are uniform national benefit rates, benefit rates vary considerably in the United States because of the decentralized structure of the American unemployment insurance system. The gross earnings principle can also result in inadequate income for low-wage earners when there is no minimum benefit level or only a very low one, as is the case in Austria and the United States, respectively. In France, the lump-sum supplements as well as the regulations providing for minimum benefit amounts guarantee a minimum of income security for the unemployed. Where the gross earnings principle is used, the actual wage-replacement rate is more dependent on the tax system than is the case using the net principle (see below).

4.3.6 Unemployment Assistance

Because insurance benefits in a strict sense (unemployment benefits) are of limited duration, but individual unemployment can last longer (especially as a consequence of severe economic recessions), almost all countries have a second system of income security, a type of means-tested unemployment assistance or supplementary benefit for the unemployed. A further reason for the existence of such a system is the fact that many unemployed persons, consistent with insurance principles, have not yet become eligible for insurance benefits. The essential difference between unemployment assistance and insurance benefits consists in the fact that unemployment assistance is lower, usually means-tested, and as a rule financed not through contributions to the social insurance but out of general revenues.

The United States is the only country without such a regular second security net for the unemployed.[18] In Great Britain, it is the national supplementary benefit program that assumes the functions of both unemployment assistance and public assistance and has now become the most important security net for the unemployed. In Sweden, such a program was first introduced in 1974, the KAS (Kontant Arbetsmarknadstöd). It provides unemployed persons not eligible for unemployment insurance with a level of support significantly lower than regular unemployment benefits (new entrants into the labor market are first eligible after a three-month waiting period). KAS is also provided after the exhaustion of regular insurance benefits, but only to older unemployed persons shortly before reaching pension age. KAS consists of a uniform benefit, which is paid for a maximum of 150 days (450 days for older unemployed persons). In contrast to similar benefit programs in all other countries, KAS is not means-tested.

Lump-sum benefits are also paid in France. The French unemployment assistance, however, varies according to individual characteristics and is limited in most cases to twelve months. Only Austria and the Federal Republic of Germany have proportional, wage-related unemployment assistance systems that are in principle of unlimited duration but means-tested.

4.3.7 Taxation of Unemployment Benefits

In 1973, unemployment benefits were taxable only in France. By 1985 the group of countries in which unemployment benefits were at least in part taxable had grown to include Great Britain, Sweden, and the United States. Austria and the Federal Republic of Germany still do not tax these insurance benefits. In the Federal Republic, such insurance benefits have, however, been taken into consideration since 1982 in determining annual income tax liability in order to avoid disproportionately high wage-replacement rates that might otherwise result for short spells of unemployment caused by the effect of tax progression.

If unemployment benefits are not (or are hardly) taxed, the use of previous gross income as a basis for determining benefits may result in regressive redistribution—an effect that is most visible in Austria (Fischer and Wagner 1985:236). The wage-replacement rate as a ratio of the (untaxed) unemployment benefit to (progressively taxed) previous earnings is actually higher for those with higher incomes. In France, Sweden, and the United States, taxation is a reflection of the fact that unemployment benefits are based on (or, as in the case of Sweden, limited by) gross earnings. Great Britain is the only country in which the introduction of taxation of benefits cannot be explained by such considerations, because the British unemployment benefit is not earnings-related but a lump-sum payment. In this case taxation had primarily the function of reducing benefits.

4.3.8 Pension and Health Insurance Coverage

Regulations with regard to continued pension and health insurance coverage in case of unemployment are relevant both for individual income security and from the point of view of the interdependence of the different social security systems. Individual income security can be considerably diminished when the unemployed individuals themselves have to pay the premiums for coverage in other social security systems, and this is even more true as the duration of unemployment increases. With the exception of the United States, pension and health insurance coverage of the unemployed is, however, maintained; that is, they continue to be insured in these other social security systems and do not have to pay premiums during the period of unemployment.

There are great differences among countries regarding which institutions ultimately bear the burden of the loss of contributions from the unemployed whose social insurance coverage is continued. In Sweden and to a large extent in France, it is the pension and health insurance carriers themselves; in Austria and the Federal Republic of Germany, these two insurance carriers receive compensating payments from the unemployment insurance system. In Austria, the pension and health insurance systems are hardly financially affected by unemployment because health insurance contributions for the insured unemployed are paid by the unemployment insurance system and the pension system also receives an offsetting payment. A significant loss of revenues can only occur as a result of the uninsured unemployed. In the Federal Republic of Germany, the unemployment insurance system pays contributions for the unemployed fully only for health insurance. Until 1978, the pension insurance system experienced a loss of revenues proportional to the increase in unemployment because no offsetting transfer payments were made. Between 1979 and 1982, the Federal Employment Institute paid the full pension insurance contributions of the unemployed, corresponding to their previous gross earnings. As a result of deficits in the unemployment insurance system and the relatively favorable financial situation in the pension insurance system, these contributions were again reduced in 1983. The benefit entitlement of the insured rather than previous earnings became the basis for calculating these contributions. The pension insurance system thus now experiences a loss of revenues from contributions not only from the uninsured unemployed but also for benefit recipients corresponding to the difference between their previous gross earnings and their entitlement to unemployment benefits or assistance. This new regulation has resulted in a yearly loss of revenues on the order of 5 billion deutsche marks for the pension system (Bruche and Reissert 1985:87 ff.; Schmähl 1986:562).

4.3.9 Additional Transfer Payments

A complete picture of income security for the unemployed also requires consideration of additional transfer payments which are available in case of loss of regular income and can supplement unemployment benefits. The list contained in Table 3 is necessarily incomplete because of the difficulty of assembling a complete picture of this gray area of social transfers. Our discussion will therefore be limited to a general observation: the better individual standards of living are protected by unemployment insurance, the less such supplementary transfer payments are necessary. The manifold number of additional transfer payments listed can therefore be said to reflect shortcomings in the respective systems of unemployment insurance.

In 1973, all countries studied still had a family supplement to unemployment benefits. This suggests that at that point in time none of these systems of unemployment insurance had achieved the goal of providing adequate protection for individual standards of living (insofar as this was a policy goal at all). However, as early as 1974 and 1975 such supplements were abolished in Sweden and the Federal Republic of Germany, which was linked in both cases to a substantial improvement in the wage-replacement rates. In all other countries, wage-replacement benefits in 1985 were still supplemented through such family grants (only in individual states in the United States).

The necessity of additional transfer payments is also related to relative poverty, that is, when caused by low income the insurance benefit falls under the subsistence minimum. A possible preventive measure is to provide minimum benefit levels for income-related unemployment benefits, which are found only in France and (at a low level) in the United States, or very high wage-replacement rates (declining with increasing income), which are found only in Sweden. In most countries, therefore, some wage-replacement benefits must be supplemented through public assistance and/or other types of supplementary benefits. In Great Britain, the supplementary benefit, which also performs the function of unemployment assistance, has even replaced unemployment benefits as the most important instrument for the income security of the unemployed; it serves on the one hand as a supplement to unemployment benefits, but mostly as a last safety net for the numerous unemployed who, because of insufficient contributions, fail to qualify for unemployment benefits or whose benefits have been exhausted.

4.3.10 Summary

The analysis of the regulation of unemployment insurance on the revenue and expenditure sides has again shown the complexity of our subject. Unemployment insurance contributions and benefits are regulated by a multiplicity of conditions in which it is difficult to see overall patterns. The differences among the six countries examined seem to be greater than the common elements. There is no evident tendency for the individual systems to become more similar. The responses to the employment crisis in the mid-1970s and early 1980s can be more accurately described as different developments within individual national systems. Most changes within the systems seem to reflect more pragmatic "muddling through" than any inherent logic of the respective systems. Only a few clear patterns can be recognized.

All unemployment insurance systems manifest a trend toward universal coverage. Whereas at the time of the introduction of the systems only a few categories of employees were covered, the degree of coverage—that is, the percentage of insured in the labor force—is today high in all countries. In countries in which the degree of coverage was relatively low in 1973 (France, Great Britain, Sweden), the employment crisis accelerated this process of convergence.

A further common feature is what can be called the reassertion of institutional principles. Systems with a sharply defined insurance character (Austria, Federal Republic of Germany, United States) reacted to the crisis by increasing contributions (Germany, Austria, United States), raising the upper limit on earnings subject to contributions (Austria, Germany), extending the required qualifying period of insured employment (Germany), raising the qualifying amount of contributions (United States), or introducing more stringent requirements of availability for work (Germany, United States). They have thus further intensified their insurance character. Systems characterized by a mix of insurance and welfare principles (France, Great Britain) have proved to be unstable and shifted either more toward insurance principles (France) or to welfare principles (Great Britain). In Great Britain, this trend has been emphasized by real cuts in unemployment benefits, the abolition of the earnings-related supplement, the increased importance of supplementary benefits, less control with respect to availability for work, and the introduction of progressive contributions. The fewest changes are found in those countries in which the increase in unemployment could be limited by labor market and employment policy measures (Austria and Sweden).

A final common feature is the instrumentalization of unemployment insurance for purposes of early retirement by extending the duration of benefits for the older unemployed and relaxing the requirement that they be available for work. There are, however, considerable differences in extent and manner in which this has occurred. The trend is strongest in France and somewhat less strong in Germany, but it is also found in Austria and Sweden. In the United States, there was also at times an extension of the usual period of eligibility for benefits, which probably was particularly beneficial to older unemployed persons. In Austria and the Federal Republic of Germany, the means-tested but in principle unlimited and income-related unemployment assistance programs certainly also facilitated the de facto exclusion of older unemployed persons. Only in Great Britain was there no age-specific extension of unemployment insurance benefits. This would also have been foreign to the British system, because the means-tested supplementary benefit is available to the unemployed who have exhausted their benefits and provides a level of support that is hardly less than the unemployment benefit. With the loosening of the registration requirement in Great Britain, a great many older unemployed persons were, however, also practically written off.

If the instrumentalization of unemployment insurance on the benefit side to exclude some persons from the labor force and hence to relieve the labor market is conspicuous, this raises the question of whether there is any similar phenomenon on the contribution side. A parallel can be found in Great Britain, where contributions have been restructured to make them progressive with income. This change is based on the assumption that low nonwage labor costs for employers and low contribution rates for employees could create more employment, particularly low-income employment. In France, there are also special programs in which employers are freed from social security contributions (including the unemployment insurance contributions) when they hire unemployed youth. In Sweden and the United States, there have always been risk-related contribution rates which, like a self-regulating system, are supposed to counter increasing unemployment by influencing the reaction of the insured themselves. These different regulatory systems are, for quite different reasons, of only limited effectiveness. The existence of the regulations has, nevertheless, not been questioned in either of these countries. Rather, the unresolved problem of mass unemployment has given rise to discussions of how the labor market could be made more flexible and unemployment eliminated by improving risk-related contribution rates and thereby increasing individual responsiveness.

We shall return to these and other questions in our concluding observations after we have examined the effects of unemployment insurance regulations and active labor market policy as an alternative to reliance on wage-replacement benefits alone.

CHAPTER 5

The Effects of Unemployment Insurance on the Income Security of the Unemployed and on Public Budgets

After having described the evolution and regulation of unemployment insurance systems in six countries, this chapter examines the effects of administrative and financing structures on the income security of the unemployed and on public budgets.

The analysis is carried out in four steps. First, we investigate the extent to which different unemployment insurance systems have been able to finance unemployment benefits through their own resources or have become dependent on government subsidies. We assume that increasing subsidies are indicative of the limits of the insurability of unemployment and of increasing political intervention in income security programs for the unemployed. This may not necessarily be a threat to the social security of the unemployed but does tend to undermine the strength of the claim to such benefits as a property right based on insurance principles.

In a second step, we investigate the effects of the different organizational and financing structures for unemployment insurance on the development of expenditures for wage-replacement benefits. We are concerned here with the question of whether and how different systems have reacted to the financial problems associated with increasing unemployment. In particular, we examine whether financing problems in different systems of unemployment insurance have tended to lead to general reductions in benefits or to the exclusion of unemployed persons from receipt of benefits.

In a third step, we examine the extent to which different systems of unemployment insurance compensate the loss of income caused by unemployment. In using the customary term *generosity* to describe this characteristic of unemployment insurance systems, we do not mean to imply any connotation of benevolence. The wage-replacement rates for various types of households and durations of unemployment are considered in assessing generosity. Based on a survey of available literature, we attempt to assess interrelationships between differences in financing systems and different degrees of generosity.

In a fourth and final step, we broaden our focus and investigate the total burden of unemployment on public budgets in different countries and how this burden is distributed among the various individual budgets (unemployment insurance system, central government, regional and local governments, and other social insurance carriers).

5.1 Financing Systems and the Development of Revenues for Unemployment Benefits

Our description of unemployment insurance regulations has shown that the financing of economic security for the unemployed does not take place exclusively through contributions but, to a greater or lesser extent, also through general tax revenues. The role of general revenues in financing results in part from the necessity of covering deficits in the unemployment insurance because of the limits of insurability in case of interdependent risks. Considerations of redistribution, the inclusion of more or less uninsurable risks, special benefits, or simply institutional traditions also play a role. A third intermediate category of financing has not yet been mentioned, namely, special-purpose levies. These could be taxes earmarked for particular uses (which, in contrast to contributions, do not give the payer any claim to benefits), such as the Swedish levy on employers for the labor market fund and the solidarity levy in France, or contributions to special funds that are intended to protect against either a risk specific to an individual sector (e.g., the German winter construction levy) or a specific risk of unemployment (e.g., short-time work, bankruptcy, or insolvency wage benefits).

Table 4 summarizes the financing sources of wage-replacement benefits at three points in time: in 1973, before the beginning of the employment crisis, the "normal" situation under which the financing structures were institutionally established; in 1975, after the onset of the crisis, the first "test"; and in 1983, in order to observe the "adjustment" of financing systems to continuing mass unemployment.

In the period before the first recession (normal situation), two groups of countries can be distinguished. Austria, the Federal Republic of Germany, and the United States financed wage-replacement

Table 4
Sources of Financing for Wage-Replacement Benefits in Percentage of Total
Expenditures

	Contributions to Un-employment Insurance[a]			Other Special-Purpose Levies			Central Government Budget		
	1973	1975	1983	1973	1975	1983	1973	1975	1983
Austria	99	99	79	-	-	18	1	1	3
F.R. Germany[b]	98	55	65	-	1	3	2	44	32
France	50	73	45	-	-	-	50	27	55
Great Britain	43[c]	41[c]	25[c]	9	11	7	48	48	68
Sweden	37[d]	33	8	2[d]	35	33	61[d]	32	59
U.S.A.	93	46	66	-	-	-	7	54	34

Notes:

Wage-replacement benefits: expenditures for unemployment benefits, bankruptcy wage benefits, early retirement (France and Austria), excluding administrative costs.

Data for Austria for the years 1973, 1975, 1984; for Sweden 1973, 1976, 1983; for the U.S.A. 1973, 1976, 1983.

a) Includes funds drawn from accumulated reserves of the unemployment insurance systems because they are derived from contributions.

b) FEI contributions and the federal subsidy are used to finance both wage-replacement benefits and active labor market policy. We assume here that both sources of financing are used proportionally (i.e., according to their respective shares in total expenditures) to finance wage-replacement benefits and active measures.

c) General social insurance contribution.

d) Estimated.

benefits almost fully through contributions to unemployment insurance. By contrast, in Sweden, France, and Great Britain, a large share of expenditures for the unemployed were financed through general revenues of the central government. In Sweden, this financial structure reflects the original decision to organize unemployment insurance according to the Ghent system; in France, it reflects the earlier characteristic mixture of welfare and insurance systems; in Great Britain, the means-tested supplementary benefit financed through the central government budget is clearly an important pillar of the system of social security for the unemployed.

During the 1975 recession, the ratio of financing unemployment insurance through contributions remained stable only in three countries: Austria, Great Britain, and Sweden. In Austria and Sweden, this stability is primarily the result of the fact that unemployment only increased slightly. Moreover, Sweden introduced the labor market levy for employers as a new source of financing in 1974. In France, the ratio of financing through contributions even increased as the originally very low contribution rates were disproportionately raised.

The largest shifts in financing are in the Federal Republic of Germany and the United States. In the United States, the revenues of the individual state unemployment insurance systems were not increased rapidly enough to cover increasing expenditures, so that the federal government was obligated to cover these deficits through loans. In Germany, too, contributions covered only about half of the costs of wage-replacement payments, so the resulting deficits had to be met by the federal government. The deficit in the Federal Republic was also caused by the fact that contributions are used to finance not only wage-replacement benefits but also active labor market policy (see note *b* to Table 4).

How one regards this instability in financing sources depends on one's analytic perspective and on whether the increased share borne by government budgets is financed through taxes or borrowing. If additional expenditures in the central government budget to cover deficits in the unemployment insurance system are financed through new borrowing, which seems to have been the case in Germany (Bruche and Reissert 1985:144), then this shift in financing from contributions to the state budget represents a textbook example of the built-in stabilizer: increased wage-replacement benefits despite declining contributions to unemployment insurance stabilize aggregate demand in a recession. From this point of view, the financing systems in the Federal Republic of Germany and the United States are to be regarded positively.

In the third period—the reaction to the extended crisis and mass unemployment—the following changes can be observed:

1. The Austrian financing structure continues to be stable; the only innovation here is the introduction of a levy on employers to finance bankruptcy wage benefits. With the exception of France and the United States, all the countries have introduced such special funds. Great Britain, Sweden, and Germany did so between the mid-1960s and the beginning of the 1970s; however, these funds became significant only in the middle and latter part of the 1970s, particularly in Austria, Great Britain, and Sweden.

2. The other two systems originally based purely on contributions—the United States and the Federal Republic of Germany—manifest similar reactions. Under the pressure of federal budget deficits, the financial burden in both countries was, despite continuing high levels of unemployment, shifted back onto contributors. This was accomplished pri-

marily through raising contribution rates and secondarily (particularly in the United States) by reducing benefits, which made it possible to finance benefits to a greater extent through contributions.[1] In any case, the shifting of the financial burden back onto contributors has reduced the economic stabilizer effect of wage-replacement benefits.

3. In the other three countries, by contrast, the share of the central government budget in unemployment insurance financing increased for reasons that were different in each case. In Great Britain, long-term unemployment (with corresponding reduced eligibility for insurance benefits) and cuts in the unemployment benefit have led to a situation in which supplementary benefit financed through general government revenues has become by far the most important income security program for the unemployed. In France, special benefits for the unemployed have been increasingly financed through general revenues, and the government subsidy to the unemployment insurance system has been raised primarily in order to finance early retirement policies.[2] In Sweden, one can speak of an erosion of the contribution-based system: the Swedish government has not been successful—in fact, it made no serious efforts to do so—in shifting the burden of increasing expenditures for unemployment onto the trade union unemployment insurance funds. By contrast, the special-purpose employer contribution (a payroll tax to finance unemployment insurance through the labor market fund) has proved to be a bountiful auxiliary source of financing benefits. Because this levy is based on a fixed financing formula—that is, it must cover two-thirds of the state contribution to unemployment insurance financing—and because the state contribution itself is in principle unlimited, there is no pressure to adjust trade union contributions to reflect actual expenditures.

5.2 FINANCING SYSTEMS AND THE DEVELOPMENT OF EXPENDITURES FOR UNEMPLOYMENT BENEFITS

Under conditions of high and persistent mass unemployment, adjusting revenues to reflect expenditures no longer suffices to cope with the increasing burden of benefits on the finances of unemployment insurance systems. Cutbacks in benefit expenditures are likely to be implemented. Because they are based on entitlements, expenditures for wage-replacement benefits can only be reduced through changes in law. In principle, there are two strategies available for limiting expenditures: tightening eligibility for benefits and limiting (or not extending) their duration or reducing benefits themselves.

Exclusion of the unemployed, resulting in a smaller percentage of the unemployed receiving benefits, can be achieved by extending the period of qualifying employment, enforcing stricter criteria or control of availability for work, and reducing the duration of benefits. The same result can be achieved without any changes in law when, as a result of persistent unemployment, an increasing percentage of the unemployed exhaust their entitlement to benefits. Cuts in unemployment insurance benefits for individual recipients can be achieved by introducing criteria similar to a means-test which, although at odds with the insurance principle, can be readily legitimized politically, for example, by differentiating benefits according to family status or the presence of dependent family members. A more far-reaching effect can be achieved by a general reduction in the wage-replacement rate, which is, however, politically more difficult. There seems to be a sort of ratchet effect: benefits are easy to raise but difficult to reduce. Another possibility is to reduce the wage base in terms of which insurance benefits are paid—this happened in the Federal Republic of Germany in 1982; because the effects are less apparent, this is presumably easier to achieve. The most radical approach would be to abolish proportional wage-replacement rates and return to the provision of a basic subsistence benefit or public assistance; this actually happened in Great Britain (more on this later). Table 5 shows that between the troughs of the economic crises in 1975 and 1982, individual countries have attempted to influence the development of expenditures for unemployment benefits in different ways by means of changes in these parameters.

Noteworthy in Table 5, first of all, is the fact that changes in expenditures for wage-replacement benefits as a percentage of gross domestic product (GDP) varied greatly among countries, although all experienced—to varying degrees—a large increase in unemployment. In the United States, the unemployment rate increased by more than one percentage point between 1975 and 1982, but the level of expenditures actually fell (see column 1). In Great Britain, the rate of unemployment increased almost threefold, whereas the level of expenditures was only somewhat more than twice as high in 1982 than in 1975. By contrast, unemployment doubled in Sweden while the level of expenditures as a percentage of GDP tripled. A similar pattern

Table 5
Expenditures for Unemployment Benefits and Factors Affecting Expenditure Trends
(1975 and 1982)

	(1) Expenditures for Unemployment Benefits as a Percentage of Gross Domestic Product (Unemployment Rates in Parentheses)		(2) Expenditures for Unemployment Benefits per Unemployed Person as a Percentage of the Average Earnings of Employees in Dependent Employment		(3) Recipients of Unemployment Benefits as a Percentage of All Unemployed (%)[a]		(4) Expenditures for Unemployment Benefits per Benefit Recipient as a Percentage of the Average Earnings of Employees in Dependent Employment	
	1975	1982	1975	1982	1975	1982	1975	1982
Austria	0.25 (1.5)	0.61 (3.1)	21	26	73	75	29	34
F.R. Germany	0.85 (4.0)	1.44 (6.7)	30	31	76	66	39	46
France	0.47 (4.2)	1.36 (8.2)	16	23	62	57	27	40
Great Britain	0.81 (3.6)	1.80 (10.4)	34	24	83	84	41	29
Sweden	0.24 (1.3)	0.70 (2.6)	22	32	63	77	34	42
U.S.A.	1.18 (8.3)	0.82 (9.7)	19	11	77	45	25	25

Note: Expenditures for unemployment benefits refer to passive labor market policy excluding bankruptcy wage benefits, early retirement, and administrative costs (insofar as data are available) but including pension and health insurance contributions which are paid for the unemployed, prorated on their wage-replacement benefits, out of the unemployment insurance system. The table shows the different expenditure trends and factors affecting them in individual countries (see text). It does not, however, permit any statements about differences in the generosity of benefit systems (i.e., differences in the level of wage-replacement benefits in similar cases of unemployment) because the structure of unemployment differs from country to country (see section 5.3 below).

a) Excluding unemployed persons whose applications for benefits have not yet been acted on.

can be observed in France and, more weakly, in Austria. Only in the Federal Republic of Germany did expenditures rise roughly parallel to the increase in the number of unemployed.

In the recession year 1975, the burden of wage-replacement benefits on public budgets was less than one percent of GDP in all countries with the exception of the United States—varying, of course, according to the level of unemployment. In 1982, the burden on public budgets varied between 0.61 percent (Austria) and 1.80 percent (Great Britain); the differences among countries were much less related to differences in unemployment.

Column 2 in Table 5 shows more precisely whether differences in the development of expenditures were caused by differential increases in unemployment or by changes in benefits. In Great Britain and the United States, average expenditures per unemployed person declined considerably, while they remained practically unchanged in the Federal Republic of Germany and increased markedly in Austria, France, and Sweden. Only in the Federal Republic did expenditures for unemployment benefits (in relation to GDP) vary in tandem with the rise in unemployment between 1975 and 1982; in Great Britain and the United States, expenditures increased much more slowly than did unemployment, and in the other countries (especially Sweden) much faster. Whereas in 1975 France still had the lowest level of expenditures per unemployed person, by 1982 the U.S. level was lowest. On the other hand, in 1975 Great Britain had the highest level of expenditures per unemployed person, whereas by 1982 Sweden and the Federal Republic had the highest.

Columns 3 and 4 in Table 5 show what types of changes have brought about these differences in the development of expenditures per unemployed person. They demonstrate that the similar restrictive trends in Great Britain and the United States were caused by quite different factors. In the United States, the percentage of unemployed receiving benefits declined drastically as a result of increasingly restrictive eligibility requirements and after the curtailment and elimination of benefit programs for the long-term unemployed; the average level of benefits for individual recipients has, however, remained unchanged. By contrast, in Great Britain, the average benefit for individual recipients has declined drastically as a result of cuts in the unemployment benefit and the displacement of recipients from unemployment benefit to supplementary benefit, whereas the percentage share of the unemployed receiving benefits has hardly changed. These different patterns of response reflect the different organizational principles of unemployment insurance in the two countries. The American system, which operates more strictly according to insurance principles and, moreover, because of its decentralization has only a limited capacity to pool risks, reacted to its financing problems almost entirely by excluding poor risks. By contrast, the British benefit system —which hardly has any insurance character because of extensive financing through general revenues and the lack of a relationship between the general social insurance contribution and the level of unemployment benefits and, therefore, fails to give benefits strong protection as property rights—reduced benefits.

In Germany and France, which strengthened insurance principles during the course of the crisis, one finds a pattern that is partly similar to that in the United States. Part of the unemployed have been excluded from benefits in both countries so that the already limited share of the unemployed receiving benefits was further reduced (see column 3). In contrast to the U.S. situation, however, average benefit expenditures per recipient increased markedly in comparison with the average income of employees, particularly in France (see column 4).

There are different reasons for this. In France, benefit levels for the insured unemployed were in fact considerably improved; in the Federal Republic of Germany, the fact that pension insurance contributions for the unemployed were taken over by the FEI in 1978 is of particular importance.

Austria and, above all, Sweden are the only countries in which increases in expenditures are in part a result of an increased percentage of the unemployed receiving benefits (see column 3). At the same time, the level of benefits per recipient also increased in these countries, as a result both of improvements in benefits and of structural changes in unemployment. Developments in both countries are primarily a consequence of the fact that unemployment increased only slightly during the period investigated and the unemployment insurance systems were, therefore, not subjected to strong fiscal stress.

The data presented so far showing benefit expenditures per recipient and in relationship to average earnings cannot be used to measure differences in the generosity of benefit systems; at best they provide rough indicators.[3] In order to make serious assertions about relative differences in income security provided by national benefit systems, one must compare the level of benefits for similar cases of unemployment. In other words, the expenditures for unemployment benefit per benefit recipient have to be controlled for structural differences in unemployment such as age, income, family status, and duration of unemployment (more on this in the following section).

5.3 THE COMPARATIVE GENEROSITY OF UNEMPLOYMENT INSURANCE

The usual measure of the generosity of unemployment insurance is the wage-replacement rate, the ratio of wage-replacement benefits (unemployment insurance or unemployment assistance) to the previous wage or salary. At a more detailed level, however, there are almost as many definitions of the wage-replacement rate—especially in international comparisons—as attempts to measure it. This is caused particularly by the interrelationship between wage-replacement benefits and the income tax system and other social security benefits. Further complications arise from the dependence of the wage-replacement rate on the duration of benefits (or unemployment), family status and income, and sometimes even age or the reasons for unemployment. Moreover, differences in regulations with regard to waiting periods and disqualification also affect the level of wage replacement.

Table 6
A Comparison of Weekly Gross Wage-Replacement Rates (1975)

	Wage-Replacement Rate (Unemployment Benefit as Percentage of Average Gross Wage)	
Austria	46.8	
F.R. Germany	50.3	
France	40.3	
Great Britain	67.3	
U.S.A.	51.2	= average rate
- Illinois	68.1	= maximum rate
- Texas	37.9	= minimum rate

Data source: Blaustein and Craig 1977: 68.

In the current state of research, we are in fact far removed from possessing any strictly comparable measure of wage-replacement rates. There will probably never be a uniform measure because the operationalization of the wage-replacement rate depends on the research question posed. If the primary concern is to investigate the generosity of the insurance system, then one would reasonably only include purely insurance benefits in the numerator, leaving aside family supplements or tax effects, and the denominator would logically be the previous gross or net income of the unemployed. If, however, one wishes to examine the actual disposable income during unemployment, then other transfers and tax effects would have to be considered. In the following discussion, we confine ourselves to a critical survey of the most important studies available comparing the generosity of wage-replacement benefits.

5.3.1 The Blaustein and Craig Study

In one of the first attempts to compare wage-replacement rates cross-nationally, Blaustein and Craig (1977) define the wage-replacement rate as the ratio of the weekly unemployment benefit to the average (gross) weekly wage in manufacturing industry. They compare nine countries and nine individual states in the United States for the year 1975; all of the countries in our study are included except Sweden. The findings are summarized in Table 6.

Great Britain is found to have the most generous and France the least generous unemployment insurance system. The Federal

Republic of Germany is positioned toward the middle of the group, and data for the United States reflect the large differences in the individual state insurance systems. This wage-replacement rate does not, however, consider the effects either of tax systems or of other social benefits. Furthermore, the study fails to differentiate wage-replacement rates according to the duration of benefits, family status, or earnings level. Using average wages in manufacturing industry as basis for comparison is also questionable. Although it does provide a uniform basis for defining the protection of earnings in case of unemployment in relationship to a specific average national wage income, it has the disadvantage of assuming an equal distribution of income among the unemployed and the employed. Given the concentration of unemployment among low-wage earners, such as youth, this is clearly not the case, and the wage-replacement rate defined in this way is thus not representative for most of the unemployed.

5.3.2 The 1979 OECD Study

The 1979 OECD study represents an advance in the effort to develop a comparable measure of generosity. This study relates wage-replacement benefits to the previous net income, including, in addition to pure wage-replacement benefits, any family supplements and subtracting any taxes due and, furthermore, distinguishes between two different types of households. This conception of the wage-replacement rate is based on a comparison of disposable income in case of unemployment with disposable income in employment. In order to avoid distortions caused by national differences in income taxation, a one-year period of unemployment corresponding to the tax year is assumed. The results are summarized in Table 7 (Austria was not included in the study).

The 1979 OECD study provides a more realistic picture of the generosity of insurance systems at the beginning of the first recession than does the Blaustein and Craig study. Moreover, the distinction between different types of households provides some indication of relationships between modes of financing and the structure of benefits. It is evident from these results that, with the exception of single-person households in Great Britain, the differences in wage-replacement rates among countries are not very large when net income is compared and family supplements are included. For single-person households, the United States is surprisingly in first place, followed by Sweden and the Federal Republic of Germany. The results for the United States are certainly misleading, because a large percentage of the unemployed in

Table 7
Annual Net Wage-Replacement Rates (1974)

	Wage-Replacement Rate for Single Individuals	Wage-Replacement Rate for Married Couples with 2 Children, Spouse Not in Labor Force
F.R. Germany[a]	63	68
France	58	64
Great Britain	39	61
Sweden[b]	67	60
U.S.A.[c]	68	60

Data source: OECD 1979: 78.

a) No family supplement to unemployment benefit since 1975.
b) Basic change in benefits in 1975 resulting in higher wage-replacement rate.
c) National average.

1974 were eligible for at most six months of unemployment compensation; subsequent studies confirm this high wage-replacement rate only for individual states (see below).

The low replacement rate in Great Britain reflects the weak development of insurance principles inherent in the financing system in that country. The orientation of the British system toward providing basic income security according to a standard of need is evident in the comparison of wage-replacement rates for married persons with dependent children. The higher wage-replacement rate for this type of household, which approximates that in other countries, results from the strong differentiation of British benefits according to family status. By contrast, benefit rates in Sweden and the United States in 1974 did not vary according to type of household, with the result that married couples with children even received lower wage-replacement rates because of the effects of taxation. In France and the Federal Republic of Germany, the wage-replacement rate for this type of household is somewhat higher than that for individuals, and these two countries have the highest wage-replacement rates for this type of household. As in Great Britain, this is because of the existence of family supplements, whereby the emphasis on need in contrast to insurance principles is less strongly developed and was subsequently abandoned in favor of greater reliance on insurance principles.

5.3.3 The Albeck and Blum Study

The 1984 Albeck and Blum study, which provides data for 1981, closely resembles the methodology of the OECD study. Albeck and Blum also consistently use net income in measuring both the numerator and the denominator in calculating the wage-replacement ratio. Unemployment benefits are recalculated to reflect taxation of benefits, where it exists, and contributions to pension and health insurance (where continued insurance is not provided, as in the United States), and taxes and social security contributions are subtracted from gross wages in calculating the denominator. On the other hand, the methodology of their study differs from the OECD approach in that family supplements are systematically excluded from consideration (in determining both numerator and denominator), in order to document the pure effect of insurance. Because of the different effects of annual income tax returns, a one-year period of unemployment corresponding to the tax year is assumed, as in the OECD study. The calculations are based on the average earnings of an industrial worker. In order to examine variations according to earnings, the authors construct two additional income categories: a lower-income group assumed to earn 25 percent less than average earnings and an upper-income group assumed to earn 80 percent above average earnings.[4] Moreover, not just two but three different types of households are distinguished: single-person households, married couples without children, and married couples with two children. In the case of households consisting of married couples, it is assumed in each case that only the "head of household" has earnings from employment, which for most of these households is (today) no longer true.

Table 8 summarizes the findings of this study. Austria was not included, but this methodology was extended to Austria on the basis of a study by Fischer and Wagner (1985), without, however, any differentiation according to household types. In interpreting the results, we limit our discussion to the net wage-replacement rate, the indicator most relevant to the generosity of insurance benefits.

The most generous systems for lower- and middle-income groups are those in Sweden and France. Unemployment insurance benefits have been increased most since 1974–75 in these two countries. In the United States, regional differences are again apparent: only a few individual states, such as Pennsylvania, have benefit levels comparable with those in Europe. If the imputed pension and health insurance premiums are deducted from unemployment benefits,[5] the benefit level for the lowest income category is on a par, at best, with the low level for single-person households in Great Britain.

In the upper-income groups, the rank order in generosity shifts: the Federal Republic of Germany ranks first, followed by France and Sweden. The Federal Republic is, in addition to Austria, the only country whose benefit system does not show any degressive tendencies.[6] The wage-replacement rate for the upper-income group is practically identical with those for the lower- and middle-income groups. All other countries, with the exception of Austria, show a degressive trend: the upper- income group receives relatively less in wage-replacement benefits than do the lower- and middle-income groups. In the case of Austria, the pattern is actually progressive, with the upper-income group enjoying the highest wage-replacement rate. There are various reasons for these different national patterns. The simplest case is the United States, where benefits are calculated strictly according to insurance principles but limited by a relatively low ceiling which is defined either by a limitation on covered earnings or by the average level of earnings in individual states. This ceiling is much higher in the Federal Republic of Germany. Austria also calculates benefits strictly according to insurance principles as a proportion of earnings. In this case, however, the proportional calculation of unemployment benefits is in terms of gross earnings, which—in combination with a progressive income tax schedule and the fact that benefits are not taxable—works to the benefit of higher income groups (Fischer and Wagner 1985:236).[7] The degressive effect in France is a result of the use of a lump-sum basic benefit, which is independent of earnings, and in Great Britain it reflects the limited importance of the earnings-related supplement to benefits, which was eliminated in 1982. Because most unemployed in Sweden select the highest benefit category, Swedish benefits are widely uniform. The high level of benefits (and taking into consideration the upper limit on benefits of eleven-twelfths of gross earnings) makes the degressive effect inherent in all lump-sum benefit systems, however, only relevant for high-level earnings.

With the exception of Great Britain, benefits vary little according to type of household. Such differences are also not to be expected in systems that are governed by insurance principles. Moreover, any family supplements for which the unemployed may be eligible have not been included in this study, so that the differences between household types observed in the 1979 OECD study are only partly reflected in these findings. Only in Great Britain do we again find a remarkable difference between single individuals and married couples because benefits vary according to household type reflecting the principle of basic income security according to need.[8]

Table 8
Comparative Wage-Replacement Rates for Unemployment Spell Lasting One Year (1981 and 1983)

		Gross Wage-Replacement Rate [a]			Net Wage-Replacement Rate [b]			Wage-Replacement Rate after Taxes and Transfers			Remarks
		(1)	(2)	(3)	(1)	(2)	(3)	(1)	(2)	(3)	
Austria[c] 1983		40	40	40	47	54	56	n.d. (significant family grants and supplements)			(1) lower-income group (lowest decile) (2) middle-income group (median) (3) upper-income group (9th decile) n.d. for types of households
Fed. Rep. Germany 1981	(A)	45	43	37	65	65	65	n.d. (no family supplements; may be eligible for means-tested housing allowance; otherwise no further significant transfers)			(A) single unemployed (B) married unemployed (C) married unemployed with 2 children (1) lower-income group (75% of average inc.) (2) middle-income group (100% of average inc.) (3) upper-income group (180% of average inc.)
	(B)	49	47	44	65	65	65				
	(C)	49	47	44	63	64	64				
France 1981	(A)	66 (81)	57 (68)	46 (57)	79 (98)	72 (85)	62 (77)	n.d. (may be eligible for means-tested housing allowance)			(A) to (C) same as above (1) to (3) same as above Wage-replacement rates not in parentheses = basic benefit; wage replacement rates in parentheses = special benefits for persons dismissed for economic reasons
	(B)	66 (85)	58 (72)	49 (62)	76 (97)	69 (85)	60 (75)				
	(C)	66 (85)	58 (73)	50 (63)	76 (97)	67 (84)	59 (75)				
Great Britain 1981	(A)	32 (23)	26 (17)	16 (10)	44 (33)	38 (25)	24 (14)	n.d. (but significant supplements, particularly for households with dependents)			(A) to (C) same as above (1) to (3) same as above Wage-replacement rates without parentheses include income-related supplemental benefit in first half-year Figure in parentheses without supplemental benefit in second half-year
	(B)	46 (37)	36 (28)	21 (16)	60 (49)	50 (39)	31 (23)				
	(C)	48 (40)	38 (30)	23 (17)	63 (52)	53 (41)	33 (24)				
Sweden 1981		76	71	54	88	84	61	88	84	61	practically no difference for different types of households (1) to (3) same as above assumes maximum benefit level
								(may be eligible for means-tested housing allowance)			
U.S.A.-Calif. 1981	(D)	37	33	19	45	43	29	45	43	29	(D) including pension and health ins. contrib. (E) excluding pension and health ins. contrib. Average of household types, which do not greatly differ
	(E)	25	21	7	30	27	11	30	27	11	
U.S.A.-Penn. 1981	(D)	49	49	30	60	62	42	63	64	43	
	(E)	37	37	18	45	47	25	48	48	26	

Sources: For Austria, Fischer and Wagner 1985 and our own calculations. For all other countries, Albeck and Blum 1984 and our own calculations.

a) Gross wage-replacement rate = adjusted unemployment benefit (less taxes and fictive contributions to pension and health insurance) divided by gross pay.

b) Net wage replacement rate = adjusted unemployment benefit (less taxes and fictive contributions to pension and health insurance) divided by net pay.

c) Except for Austria, the wage-replacement rate is calculated with reference to the average income of an industrial worker (= 100%), with corresponding downward (75%) or upward (180%) adjustments; for Austria, the wage-replacement rate is calculated on the basis of gross pay of the corresponding benefit recipient and income groups based on the actual income distribution of the unemployed.

n.d. = No data available.

France clearly represents a special case. Very generous wage-replacement benefits have at times been provided based on the reasons for unemployment. Unemployed persons who became redundant for economic reasons (displaced workers) received the so-called special benefit (*allocation speciale*), which guaranteed many unemployed almost full replacement of their lost net income (see the data in parentheses in Table 8; a similar but less generous special benefit—Trade Adjustment Assistance—has existed at times in the United States but is not taken into consideration here). Such a differentiation according to reasons for unemployment violates insurance principles, especially as the meaning of "dismissal for economic reasons" is subject to interpretation and was in fact used with considerable discretion. This special benefit was subsequently abolished in 1984 in the course of reforms that strengthened insurance principles.

5.3.4 The Kahn and Kamerman Study

The comparative methodology employed by Albeck and Blum provides quite useful indicators for the general level of generosity of unemployment insurance benefit systems. Nevertheless, as our interpretation of the results highlighted, it also has a number of weaknesses. There is no differentiation according to the duration of unemployment, and it is assumed that households consist of families with only one wage earner; therefore, the study is not fully representative. An exemplary differentiation according to family types is found in the transfer study by Kahn and Kamerman (1983), in which the impact of unemployment on family income under varying assumptions about the duration of unemployment is analyzed. The study distinguishes among seven different types of households, five of which are affected by unemployment. The principal results are summarized in Table 9.

The advantage of this study is that it calculates the income situation of families affected by unemployment taking into consideration other social benefits, taxation, and—in the case of families in which both spouses are employed—the still remaining wage income. Household size is also considered in order to assess the impact of disposable income on living standards.[9]

In the case of family types 1 through 3, which receive income only from transfer payments, unemployment insurance or unemployment assistance accounts for only part of transfer income. It is interesting to know the percentage share of total transfer income attributable to unemployment benefits in order to assess the perfor-

Table 9
Per Capita Family Income of the Unemployed as Percentage of Average Net Income
of a Male Production Worker (1979)

| | Family Type | | | | | Rank |
	1	2	3	4	5	
F.R. Germany	36	40	33	56	116	3
France	40	42	45	72	120	2
Great Britain	30	42	26	62	101	4
Sweden	49	50	47	65	127	1
U.S.A.-New York	28	31	26	52	89	6
U.S.A.-Pennsylvania	27	26	22	53	98	5

Data source: Kahn and Kamerman 1983: 43, table 14.2; Jungk 1984: 185.

Type 1: Family with two children; one wage earner, who has been unemployed for three months and remains unemployed for balance of reference year.

Type 2: As in 1; the unemployed wage earner, however, participates in a training program.

Type 3: As in 1; the period of unemployment has, however, lasted 13 months and will continue.

Type 4: Family with two children; two-wage-earner household; one spouse who previously earned 50% of average wage is unemployed.

Type 5: Childless couple; two-wage-earner household; the spouse who previously earned an average wage is unemployed.

Austria was not included in this study.

mance of the unemployment insurance system. For family type 1, unemployment insurance benefits are the largest source of transfer income in Sweden and in the Federal Republic of Germany (more than 75 percent); in both countries, family allowances and housing allowances represent additional transfers. In France and Great Britain, approximately one-third of total income is attributable to family benefits and housing allowances. The low level of U.S. unemployment insurance benefits is supplemented by the AFDC family assistance program as well as by food stamps—something unique to America. In New York, a family with an unemployed head receives more than one-third of its annual transfer income in the form of welfare grants and almost one-fifth in the form of food stamps.[10]

If the unemployment insurance systems are not adequately developed, many affected individuals must endure the stigma of receiving means-tested public assistance in addition to the stigma of unemployment. This problem is increasing even in countries with relatively well-developed unemployment insurance systems primarily as a consequence of increasing long-term unemployment. Families of the third type, with one wage earner who has been unemployed for more than a year and remains unemployed for an additional year, only receive insurance benefits (in the strict sense) in France (data for 1979).

In the other countries, 75 to 80 percent of transfer income received by households of the long-term unemployed consists of means-tested public assistance or unemployment assistance; the rest is provided by family allowances, housing allowances, or—in the United States—food stamps (Jungk 1984:184).

Table 9 provides yet another rank order of the generosity of social security systems in case of unemployment, which in this case also includes other social benefits. The results largely follow the pattern of previous studies: Sweden ranks first, followed by France and the Federal Republic of Germany, with the United States at the bottom of the scale and again much variation among individual states.

Some other findings should be noted. In all countries (with the exception of the U.S. state of Pennsylvania), there is a financial incentive to leave unemployment by participating in a training measure; this incentive is strongest in Great Britain (family type 2). If the one wage earner in the family remains unemployed for an extended period, the loss of income in some countries is considerable (family type 3); an exception here is France, where transfer income even increases slightly in case of long-term unemployment. In families in which both spouses work and the spouse with lower earnings is unemployed (type 4), the national differences are less, because transfer payments have a reduced impact on the income of households still receiving a full wage. The differences are, however, again large in the pure case of the two-income family (without children, type 5). The greatest difference in the relative income position of types 4 and 5 is found in the Federal Republic of Germany; the income replacement ratio for the two-income married couple in which one partner is unemployed is more than twice as high as that for the two-income family with children, in which the unemployed parent previously earned half the average wage. The situation is similar in Sweden. The priority given to replacing income in benefits is evident, whereas need is more or less strongly emphasized in other countries—particularly in Great Britain, which again coincides with our previous observations.

5.3.5 The CERC Study

The transfer study by Kahn and Kamerman provides a good overview of the effects of long-term unemployment on the income situation of various types of households, but two further studies should be mentioned that provide information on the impact of the duration of unemployment on the income of households differentiated according to earnings categories. The most detailed observations with respect to the duration of unemployment are found in the 1982 CERC study, although only the Federal Republic of Germany, France, Great Britain, and Sweden are included. The study distinguishes among three income categories (two-thirds of the average net earnings of an industrial worker, average net earnings, and twice average net earnings) and also takes into consideration any family supplements in calculating wage replacement as well as any "dynamization" of benefits, that is, an upward adjustment to reflect increases in average wage income. A further differentiation is made according to different household types (single, married without children, and married with two children), which is, however, only relevant for Great Britain, where, as we have seen, the type of household is decisive for the determination of wage-replacement benefits oriented toward need. The results are summarized in Table 10.

The comparison for the first twelve months essentially confirms the pattern already observed: generous wage-replacement benefits in Sweden, France, and the Federal Republic of Germany, especially in the case of the French special benefits for those becoming redundant for economic reasons (which, however, no longer exists since 1984) and for lower-income groups in Sweden. The degressive effect in Sweden is even more apparent in these data because the threshold for the upper-income group is higher than in the Albeck and Blum study; for the same reason, a slight degressive effect is now also observed for the Federal Republic of Germany, which results from the fact that the earnings-related wage-replacement benefits are limited by the ceiling on covered wages. In Great Britain, the degressive pattern of wage-replacement ratios as earnings increase is as strong as in Sweden, although at a considerably lower level. In Great Britain, wage-replacement rates are only roughly similar to those in other European states for households with two children in the low- and middle-wage income categories.

Table 10 offers new information concerning the periods after twenty-four and thirty-six months of unemployment. As a rule, no further wage-replacement benefits are paid in Sweden after two years of unemployment, in contrast to the Federal Republic of Germany, where means-tested unemployment assistance payments are in principle of unlimited duration. In Great Britain, the means-tested supplementary benefit, which performs the same function as unemployment assistance in the Federal Republic of Germany but is a uniform payment rather than being wage-related, is available to the unemployed after one year of unemployment. An unemployed person in France who was eligible for special benefits during the first year of unemploy-

Table 10
Net Wage-Replacement Rates according to Duration of Unemployment (1980)

	Type of household	3 Months (1)	(2)	(3)	3-6 Months (1)	(2)	(3)	6-9 Months (1)	(2)	(3)	9-12 Months (1)	(2)	(3)	12-24 Months (1)	(2)	(3)	24-36 Months (1)	(2)	(3)
F.R. Germany	(A) (B) (C)	57	56	43	56	55	42	55	54	41	54	53	41	46	45	35	46	45	35
France[a]	(A) (B) (C)	75	66	56	77	65	55	75	63	53	78	66	55	30	20	10	0	0	0
France[b]	(A) (B) (C)	100	91	82	97	84	75	94	76	67	97	74	65	79	68	57	30	20	10
Great Britain	(A)	49	36	19	47	34	18	36	24	12	31	19	6	30	19	6	30	19	6
	(B)	67	47	25	63	45	23	51	34	17	45	29	14	45	29	14	45	29	14
	(C)	77	62	32	73	58	30	59	41	20	52	33	16	52	33	16	52	33	16
Sweden	(A) (B) (C)	94	62	31	91	60	30	90	58	29	86	57	28	0	0	0	0	0	0

Data source: CERC 1982: 53 ff.

Notes: Wage-replacement rate = statutory unemployment compensation or unemployment assistance + any family supplements including any dynamization of the wage-replacement benefits divided by the net wage of three income categories: (1) 66%, (2) 100%, and (3) 200% of the average wage of an industrial worker (only males twenty-five years of age and older included in both numerator and denominator).

Types of households: (A) single, (B) married couple without children, (C) married couple with two children. Data are reported only for Great Britain, where - reflecting the orientation of the system toward a basic standard of need - wage-replacement benefits vary significantly according to type of household. In Germany, France, and Sweden, by contrast, there is little variation in benefits according to household type.

a) 15 months basic benefit + 9 months extended benefit.

b) 12 months special benefit + 15 months basic benefit + 9 months extended benefit.

Austria and the U.S.A. were not included in the study.

ment can expect to receive a lump-sum benefit in the third year; other categories of the unemployed are (as of 1980) not entitled to any further insurance benefits at the latest after the third year.

The CERC analysis does, however, have two basic shortcomings. First, it assumes that the maximum legally available entitlement is received and, therefore, overestimates actual benefits, which can be less if benefits are means-tested or in part discretionary. The latter factor is especially relevant in France, where decisions with regard to the continuation of benefits are made by bipartite control commissions. Jallade (1984:83) cites an empirical study according to which only 5 percent of those unemployed for more than twenty-eight months received the maximum possible legal benefit. The behavior of the eligible unemployed can also reduce actual benefits paid, particularly in the case of means-tested benefits if eligible persons are deterred from claiming benefits by bureaucratic controls or social stigma. The second shortcoming of the findings shown in Table 10 is the failure to consider tax effects, which can be particularly important in the case of shorter periods of unemployment, as is shown below.

5.3.6 The 1984 OECD Study

Paolo Roberti has updated and improved the 1979 OECD study (OECD 1984a:88–120).[11] Three earnings categories and two types of households are distinguished, and the net wage-replacement rates are calculated for both a three-month and a six-month spell of unemployment, taking into consideration differences in the tax systems; in the tradition of the OECD methodology, other transfers are included in both numerator and denominator in determining the wage-replacement rate. Roberti's analysis is summarized in Table 11.

The results are surprising. In the case of the three-month spell of unemployment the net, after-tax wage-replacement rates hardly differ among countries. The disposable annual income of unemployed benefit recipients is only slightly less than that of the employed when the effects of annualized income taxation are taken into consideration. This is particularly true for low-income wage earners and for married couples with two children (assuming a single-income family with unemployed head of household). The rank order of generosity found in the previous studies is still recognizable but of little significance because of the minimal differences. Families have higher wage-replacement rates than do single-person households, especially in Great Britain; the only exception is the Federal Republic of Germany in the case of the middle- and upper-income categories. A degressive ten-

Table 11
Comparison of Net Wage-Replacement Rates for 3 and 6 Month Spells of Unemployment

	Net Wage-Replacement Rate for 3-Month Spell of Unemployment			Net Wage-Replacement Rate for 6-Month Spell of Unemployment		
	(1)	(2)	(3)	(1)	(2)	(3)
Austria						
(A)	91	92	85	80	82	70
(B)	96	95	88	88	89	75
F.R. Germany						
(A)	93	96	93	87	89	84
(B)	94	94	92	89	88	81
France						
(A)	94	92	90	85	82	79
(B)	95	93	90	89	84	79
Great Britain						
(A)	93	89	83	85	78	66
(B)	99	95	87	96	90	75
Sweden	(97 96 98 96 93)			n.d.	n.d.	n.d.
U.S.A.						
(A)	95	90	87	92	80	72
(B)	n.d.	95	88	n.d.	87	74

Sources: OECD 1984a: 112 f., table 2; for Sweden, see Schmid 1984: 11.

Notes: Wage replacement rate = disposable annual income of the unemployed (earned income less taxes and social security contributions plus unemployment benefit plus other supplements) divided by the average net income. Reference year 1978, except for Sweden 1982.

Income groups: (1) 66%, (2) 100%, (3) 200% of average earnings of a production worker.

Types of households: (A) single individuals, (B) married couple with one (unemployed) wage earner and 2 children. In Sweden no information was available for either types of households or income groups. Numbers in parentheses represent net wage-replacement rates for youth, lower-ranking employees, unskilled workers, skilled workers, and higher-ranking employees, respectively.

n.d. = no data available

dency is observable according to earnings categories, which is again strongest in Great Britain and weakest in the Federal Republic of Germany.

Differences among countries are more marked in the case of a six-month spell of unemployment. Wage-replacement rates decline sharply particularly in Great Britain for single-person households and for the upper-earnings group. In other countries, the decline in the wage-replacement rate is also greatest for this income group. On the whole, the reduction in the wage-replacement rate is least in the Federal Republic of Germany. No comparable estimates are available for Sweden, but a marked reduction in the wage-replacement rate for the upper-earnings groups can be expected because of the highly progressive income tax rates. An odd result can be observed in Austria (as well as for single-person households in the Federal Republic of Germany): middle-income groups receive a higher wage-replacement than does the lower-income group, whereas the replacement rate declines sharply for the upper-income category. This result was, however, only partially reflected in a recent study by Fischer and Wagner (1985:240). After seven months of unemployment, the authors found that the upper-earnings group also receives a higher wage-replacement rate than does the low-earnings group because of the calculation of benefits on the basis of gross income, which still results in considerable tax savings for the upper-income group even after seven months of unemployment (see 4.3.7 above).

5.4 Financing Systems and the Fiscal Costs of Unemployment

Unemployment not only results in increased expenditures for wage-replacement benefits but is also a burden on public budgets in other ways. Revenues from direct and indirect taxes are lost because the unemployed have less (or no) taxable income and spend less on consumption than do the employed. Social insurance contributions likewise decline, being as a rule earnings-related. Finally, unemployment results in increased claims for other social benefits (e.g., housing allowances) compared to periods of full employment.

Studies were conducted in the 1970s and early 1980s in many OECD countries in order to survey and quantify the direct and measurable burdens of unemployment for public budgets[12]—the "fiscal costs of unemployment" (for an overview, see EGI 1984; Junankar 1985; Nordisk Rad 1983; OECD 1982:16 ff.). These studies had two main goals. Conceived in the tradition of budget reform and finance planning of the late 1960s and early 1970s, they were supposed to make public budgets and their reciprocal relationship to general economic trends transparent and show how the fiscal costs of unemployment are distributed among various public budgets and budget items. At the same time, they were also supposed to demonstrate that an effective active labor market and employment policy not only entails costs (gross costs) but can, by reducing unemployment, also yield significant savings so that the actual public costs (additional or net costs) of active labor market and employment policy are on the whole relatively small and only a fraction of the gross costs.

In light of the national differences in unemployment insurance, tax, and social security systems described above, it is plausible that the level, composition, and institutional distribution of the fiscal costs of unemployment differ from country to country. Table 12 presents comparative estimates of the burden of unemployment on public budgets in individual countries broken down according to types of revenues and expenditures as well as institutions (budgets). This attempt is necessarily incomplete and problematic because the cost estimates are based in part on different assumptions and methodologies. However, the underlying concepts are identical, and it seems legitimate to regard these estimates as being at least crudely comparable (Junankar 1985:47 f.; OECD 1982:158).[13]

Table 12 shows that the differences in the *total* fiscal costs of unemployment among countries are not all too great. In four countries the burden on public budgets per registered unemployed person is on the average approximately equal to gross domestic product per capita (see line 4.1); only the estimate for France is significantly lower (in part because of the methodology of the estimates).

National differences in the *composition* of the fiscal costs of unemployment are much greater. The share of expenditures for wage-replacement benefits in the total cost of unemployment ranges from 33 percent in Great Britain to around 48 percent in the Federal Republic of Germany, France, and Austria. The lower percentage in Great Britain attributable to wage-replacement benefits reflects the low level of benefits and the greater significance of means-tested benefits. The relatively high benefit levels and the contributions paid to the pension and health insurance systems for the unemployed by the labor market authority, the Federal Employment Institute (FEI), are important factors in the Federal Republic of Germany. The payment of health insurance contributions for the unemployed through unemployment insurance is also important in Austria. In France, the loss of tax revenues as a result of unemployment is very low because of low income tax rates and the taxation of wage-replacement benefits (as well as the very cautious assumptions on which the estimates are based); this makes the costs of unemployment lowest in that country and the share of unemployment benefits in these costs relatively high. The percentage share attributable to wage-replacement benefits is not as high in Sweden (38 percent) as one might expect; this is apparently because of the large number of unemployed ineligible for benefits (30 percent in 1982) and in particular to the high income tax and contribution rates, which make the revenue losses from these sources high (and the share of unemployment benefits, which in absolute terms are rather high, correspondingly lower) (Nordisk Rad 1983).

Table 12
The Fiscal Costs of Unemployment: Level, Composition, and Institutional Distribution

	Austria (1983) ÖS	%	F.R. Germany (1983) DM	%	France (1982) FF	%	Great Britain (1981-1982) £	%	Sweden (1982) SKR	%	U.S.A. $	%
(1) Expenditures for												
(1.1) Unemployment compensation	65,342	47	11,400	48	22,803	48	1,481	33	33,718	38		
(1.2) Other social benefits			600	3			128	3				
(2) Revenues lost												
(2.1) Income taxation	24,915	18	4,300	18	2,719	6	1,089	24				
(2.2) Excise and sales taxes	5,440	4	1,500	6	2,581	5	891	20				
(3) Contributions lost in												
(3.1) Pension insurance	31,496	23	3,700	15	} 19,382	41	} 907	20	} 54,092	62		
(3.2) Unemployment insurance	5,684	4	1,300	5								
(3.3) Health insurance	5,103	4	1,200	5								
(4) Total	137,984	100	24,000	100	47,485	100	4,495	100	87,809	100		
(4.1) As % of per capita GDP	86		88		73		98		116			
(5) Institutional distribution (affected budget):												
(5.1) Central government	13		23		32		64		XXXXX		XXX	
(5.2) Regional governments	5		9		-		-		X		X	
(5.3) Local governments	4		5		-		3		XX		X	
(5.4) Unemployment insurance	57		43		27		} 33		3		XXX	
(5.5) Pension insurance	17		15		} 41				} XX		} X	
(5.6) Health insurance	4		5				-					

Sources: Austria: Frühstück and Laschitz 1985 and our own calculations; Federal Republic of Germany: Bruche and Reissert 1985:83-87 (based on calculations of the Federal Employment Institute; for more recent calculations, see Bach, Kohler and Spitznagel 1986: 370 f.; France: Colin and Gaudin 1983:101-15 and our own calculations; Great Britain: Reissert 1985:121 (based on calculations of the Institute for Fiscal Studies); Sweden: Schmid 1984: 47 f. (based on calculations of the Swedish Labor Ministry); U.S.A.: comparable studies are not available; see, however, Note 13 to Chapter 5 and the explanation of lines 5.1-5.6 below.

Note: Average costs per registered unemployed and year in national currency and percentage shares of individual types of revenues/expenditures and affected budgets.

Notes to individual lines in table:
(1.1) Wage-replacement benefits include any payments by the unemployment insurance system for pension and health insurance for benefit recipients.
(1.1) (3.1) (5.4) (5.5) In Austria, the unemployment insurance system makes no pension insurance contributions for the unemployed but makes instead a lump-sum compensatory payment, which is largely independent of the level of unemployment. This offset payment is included in lines 5.4 and 5.5 but not in 1.1 and 3.1.
(5.1)-(5.6) For Sweden, there are still no quantitative data available on the institutional distribution of the budgetary burden of unemployment, despite the preliminary work on this topic carried out by Wadensjö (1985). Thus, the symbols in the table provide only a crude estimate of this distribution (each X representing roughly 10 percent). The distribution of the budgetary burden of unemployment in the United States can also only be crudely estimated.

The national differences in the *distribution* of the fiscal costs of unemployment among individual public budgets and levels of government are even greater than the differences in the composition of these costs. Because of the importance of supplementary benefit financed through the central government budget and the far-reaching centralization of the tax system, the central government budget accounts for almost two-thirds of all costs in Great Britain; if the National Insurance Fund is included, which is closely tied to the central government budget (it is, in fact, included legally and for statistical purposes in the government budget and is not perceived by the public as being distinct from it), then the entire budgetary burden of unemployment is borne by the budget passed by Parliament in Westminster.

The costs of unemployment are more widely dispersed in other countries. In the Federal Republic of Germany, the state (*Land*) and local governments bear a not insignificant share of the costs because of the tax revenue sharing system, and the independent health and pension insurance carriers are also affected (the latter especially since the cutback in FEI payments of pension insurance contributions for unemployed benefit recipients in 1983). Here about two-thirds of the fiscal costs of unemployment are concentrated in the (closely linked) budgets of the federal government and the FEI (which alone bears 43 percent of the burden). Because of the heavy loss of revenues in contributions to the pension system and the importance of the proportional income tax for provincial and local governments, a large share of the fiscal costs of unemployment in Sweden is also borne by institutions other than the central government, even though it still bears the principal burden.

In Austria, more than half of the costs are borne by the unemployment insurance system financed through contributions. The rest is distributed much as in the Federal Republic of Germany because of the similar tax and contribution systems. The percentage share borne by the federal budget is, however, less because unemployment assistance (*Notstandshilfe*) is not financed through general revenues in Austria, as is the case in the Federal Republic of Germany, but in principle by the unemployment insurance system. Moreover, the federal budget and the unemployment insurance fund are—in contrast to the case of the Federal Republic—completely separate in Austria because the federal budget assumes no long-term responsibility for the deficits of the unemployment insurance system and the unemployment insurance system must finance increased expenditures entirely through upward adjustments in contributions.

The fiscal costs of unemployment are most widely dispersed in France and in the United States. The loss of revenues to the pension and health insurance system is greatest in France, with a share of 40 percent. This is because both branches of the social insurance system receive practically no compensatory payments from the unemployment insurance system for continued coverage of the unemployed (see also OECD 1982:19); the central government budget and the unemployment insurance system bear about one-third each of the fiscal costs of unemployment. In the United States, the costs of unemployment are borne largely by the individual state unemployment insurance funds and the federal budget, which has to absorb the largest loss in tax revenues; the budgets of state and local governments as well as the pension systems are also significantly affected.

The national differences with regard to the costs of unemployment and their institutional distribution are not only important in themselves and as effects of differences in the unemployment insurance, tax, and contribution systems. By showing which institutions in individual countries have to bear the financial consequences of unemployment, our comparison also clearly indicates which institutions would profit most from a successful active labor market and employment policy. Whether these incentives for an active policy are actually reflected in different national activity levels of labor market policy is investigated below in Chapter 8.

5.5 Summary

The foregoing discussion has analyzed the effects of the organization and financing of unemployment insurance under four aspects. On the financing side, the following findings should be emphasized. Mass unemployment is not insurable. In case of rising and persistently high levels of unemployment, the state has to intervene to a greater or lesser extent in order to provide social security for the unemployed. All countries have increased—sometimes drastically—contributions to unemployment insurance or established new sources of revenue, but these efforts have usually not been sufficient to keep pace with the increasing costs of income security for the unemployed. From the point of view of economic stabilization, increasing contribution rates are also not necessarily the most appropriate response to increasing unemployment. The central government share of financing has increased in all countries since the beginning of the first recession in 1974–75 but most strongly in countries in which insurance principles are weakly institutionalized. In countries in which insurance principles are strongly institutionalized and unemployment is high (United States, Federal Republic of Germany, and recently France), continuing high levels of unemployment have been associated with a partial reshifting of the costs of social security onto those paying contributions into the system.

Aside from deficit financing for cyclical reasons, the central government share of financing for wage-replacement benefits is higher in those countries in which unemployment benefit regulations deviate most from insurance principles. In these countries, benefits either are oriented toward a basic income security that varies according to need (Great Britain and also, in part, France with its combination of uniform and earnings-related benefits), or they are oriented toward an average standard of living (Sweden) or provide special payments for certain groups for reasons of economic and social policy (France), which justify or make plausible a large share of financing by the central government.

On the expenditure side, mass unemployment has resulted in different patterns of response in the benefit systems of individual countries. Systems without any direct relationship between contributions and benefits (especially Great Britain) tend to reduce benefits for individual recipients (leveling response), whereas systems financed through contributions based on insurance principles (particularly the United States but also the Federal Republic of Germany) tend to limit coverage and to increasingly exclude poor risks or allow benefits to lapse for those who are currently eligible (segmentation response). Here, too, the insurance principle on which the contribution system is based explains the different responses: it provides the insured with a certain amount of protection of their entitlement as a quasi-property right and thus makes it more difficult to curtail benefits, but it tends to exclude poor risks. Benefit systems without an actuarial orientation are, by contrast, in principle open to all risk groups but hardly protected against benefit cuts for individuals. Sweden and Austria represent in this regard interesting test cases for the future. In both countries, mass unemployment has thus far been prevented by labor market and employment policy measures, and unemployment insurance systems have hardly suffered from financial problems. If unemployment increases in the future in these countries, we expect that Austria would respond by excluding poor risks and allowing benefit entitlements to expire as a result of the heavy reliance on financing through contributions, whereas Sweden would respond with general cuts in benefits as a result of its predominantly tax-based form of financing.

The comparative analysis of the generosity of insurance systems—that is, the extent to which the income of the insured is actually protected in case of unemployment—proved to be a difficult undertaking. The results depend strongly upon the extent to which the analysis differentiates according to earnings groups, household types, and duration of unemployment. The varied and sometimes confusing picture provided by these comparative studies does, however, reveal some patterns. In the case of short-term unemployment up to six months, there are hardly any national differences in the degree of income security provided—if the impact of taxation and other social transfers is considered. In the case of longer-term unemployment, the national differences are more evident and sometimes quite large. At the top of the generosity scale, one finds—depending upon the criteria employed—Sweden, the Federal Republic of Germany, and France, while the United States and Great Britain are at the lower end of the scale. In the United States, one finds, of course, a great deal of variation in income security from state to state; in Great Britain, income security varies markedly according to household type and earnings group. Only a few U.S. states provide income security benefits for the unemployed that approximate European levels, and in Great Britain only benefit levels for families with children in the lower- and middle-income categories are approximately as high as those found in Sweden, France, and the Federal Republic of Germany. When long-term unemployment is included, then the United States is the country with the least income security for the unemployed because, in contrast to other countries, there is no benefit at all comparable to means-tested unemployment assistance.

Typical patterns of response can again be observed for the different types of financing systems. Benefit systems characterized by a direct relationship between contributions and benefits hardly differentiate according to household type and earnings group and usually also offer the longest insurance protection (especially in the Federal Republic of Germany and, in part, also in France). In these countries, an increasing linkage of the duration of benefits to the prior period of qualifying employment during which contributions were paid can also be observed. By contrast, benefit systems not based on actuarial principles differentiate most strongly according to different types of households and earnings categories and offer rather limited insurance protection as far as the duration of benefits is concerned (Great Britain, also Sweden). The duration of benefits varies not according to the length of the previous period of covered employment but, if at all, for reasons of social policy (e.g., for older persons in Sweden). The U.S. system, which is financed exclusively through employers' contributions, does react strictly according to insurance principles in the short term, but the duration of benefits is quite limited (as a rule, only six months), and the wage-replacement rate declines for higher-income categories because of low benefit ceilings. By contrast, the ceiling on covered earnings in France, Austria, and the Federal Republic of Germany is much higher than the level of average earnings.

France and the United States are the only countries that have at times differentiated benefits according to the reasons for unemployment. Extremely generous benefits were offered in the case of redundancies for economic reasons or import competition—apparently in order to facilitate structural change. Such a differentiation in benefits is, however, incompatible with the insurance principle. In France, this form of "special benefit" was abandoned in the course of a policy of intensification of insurance principles. In the United States, such special benefits were, appropriately, financed separately through the federal budget and not through the unemployment insurance system.

Finally, we showed that the financial burden of unemployment on public budgets is in fact much greater than public expenditures for unemployment benefits. Lost tax revenues and social security contributions as well as additional claims for other social benefits also have to be included in estimating the "fiscal costs of unemployment." Despite national differences in the level of unemployment insurance benefits, the total burden on public budgets as a result of unemployment is surprisingly almost equally high in all countries included in the study. This is primarily the result of the fact that wage-replacement benefits constitute less than half of the total fiscal costs of unemployment—the sum of lost tax and social security revenues as well as the cost of other social benefits is greater. Given the national differences in the allocation of responsibility for financing wage-replacement benefits and in tax and social security systems, the fiscal costs of unemployment are differently distributed among public budgets and levels of government in each individual country. In Great Britain, they are concentrated almost completely on the central government budget; in other countries—particularly in France, the United States, and Austria—they are more widely dispersed among several independent institutions. Because institutions with a large fiscal burden caused by unemployment potentially benefit most from an effective active labor market and employment policy, the different national patterns in the distribution of the costs of unemployment in individual countries may also possibly reflect different incentive structures for active labor market policy. How effective such incentives are is investigated below in Chapter 8.

CHAPTER **6**

The Effects of Unemployment Insurance on the Labor Market

There is a widespread opinion that many unemployed persons abuse unemployment insurance by deliberately becoming unemployed, by refusing job offers, and by failing to energetically seek new employment. In this view, generous unemployment benefits increase the danger of abuse. Every taxi driver can provide anecdotal examples, and there seems to be a natural tendency of contributors to become suspicious of benefit recipients.

This public attitude is reflected in economic theory in two different versions. From an orthodox neoclassical perspective, unemployment insurance impedes the "clearing" of labor markets, that is, the elimination of imbalances between supply and demand through wage adjustments. Generous unemployment benefits are supposed to increase the "reservation wage," the wage at which individuals are ready to accept employment, impeding the downward wage adjustments that are necessary in case of unemployment.[1] In the search theory version,[2] generous benefits are supposed to increase the number of voluntary quits and above all the duration of unemployment because they reduce the individual cost of searching for a new job and thus increase search time. Both theoretical effects of unemployment insurance (increase in wage expectations, longer search times) induce increased unemployment; that is, unemployment insurance itself is partly responsible for the situation that it is supposed to insure against.

In the neoclassical tradition and in one of its modern variants —search theory—one finds numerous studies (first generation), particularly in the Anglo-Saxon literature, on the relationship between the generosity of benefits and the probability of voluntary quits and especially the influence of generosity on the duration of unemployment. More recent studies (second generation) expand the spectrum of possible effects to include, for example, the impact on labor force participation or on the composition of unemployment and also emphasize the differential incentive effects on various categories of supply and demand as well as the possible positive functions of longer search times for increased mobility. The most important findings of these studies as well as their underlying assumptions are the focus of the following critical survey. We first discuss the incentive effects that are to be expected and then present and assess the most important empirical studies available.

The incentives resulting from the usual form of employers' contributions as a percentage of payroll (payroll tax) should also be mentioned here. According to existing theories, this practice is not neutral. It results in a considerable (cost) burden on the factor labor but not, however, on the increased use of capital, which by increasing the tempo of labor shedding is partly responsible for the financial problems of unemployment insurance systems. As a consequence, the use of the factor labor, it is argued, becomes relatively more expensive (as a result of increasing nonwage labor costs), thus increasing unemployment. Capital-intensive industries and firms are thus said to be given (unjustified) preferential treatment and labor-intensive ones are disadvantaged. In the Federal Republic of Germany, such considerations have led to a discussion of possible changes in the determination of employers' contributions (e.g., machine tax). Although contributions to the pension insurance system have been the focus of this discussion, it is equally relevant to unemployment insurance. Nevertheless, because this effect is only an indirect incentive and the topic has already been sufficiently treated by others,[3] we do not consider it in detail here. We will return briefly to this issue when we examine intersectoral redistributive effects (see Chapter 9). Otherwise, we endorse the view of Euzeby and Euzeby that the payment of contributions as a percentage of wages and salaries is to be preferred for systemic reasons because the principal function of unemployment insurance is to provide income security during periods without earnings. Contributions thus represent a delayed (saved) component of wages, regardless of how large employer and employee shares are. The possible (small) negative employment effects can be compensated in another way, such as by financing part of the costs of unemployment benefits or pension benefits through general taxation to an extent sufficient to achieve a general reduction in the burden of wage-related contributions (Euzeby and Euzeby 1984:76 ff.; Schmähl 1986:560 f.; Schmid 1986:271 ff.).

Table 13
Anticipated Effects of Unemployment Insurance on Labor Market Transition
Probabilities according to Clark and Summers

Initial Labor Market State	Final Labor Market State		
	Employment	Unemployment	Nonparticipation
Employment	- (1)	+ + (2)	- (3)
Unemployment	- (4)	+ + (5)	-- (6)
Nonparticipation	? (7)	+ + (8)	- (9)

Source: Clark and Summers 1982: 291.

6.1 POSSIBLE EFFECTS ON LABOR MARKET SUPPLY AND DEMAND

The most comprehensive and systematic theoretical and empirical study is that by Clark and Summers (1982); Burtless (1986) has provided a helpful summary of the literature. Both studies are a useful starting point for our overview. Clark and Summers analyze the incentive effects of unemployment insurance from a microanalytic perspective in terms of the transition probabilities among nine possible labor market states:

1. From employment into (other or continued) employment, unemployment, or withdrawal from the labor force
2. From unemployment into employment, (continued) unemployment, out of the labor force
3. From nonparticipation in the labor force to employment, unemployment, or (continued) nonparticipation

Their conceptualization of the possible incentive effects on labor market supply and demand is summarized in Table 13. Although greatly influenced by the American discussion, their basic concepts are sufficiently general to be applied—with slight modification—to the European situation.

According to the table, unemployment insurance provides a strong positive incentive to enter or continue in unemployment from any possible starting point and, by contrast, a negative incentive to enter or remain in employment but also a negative incentive to leave the labor force or remain outside it. Unemployment insurance is thus said to increase the probability both of unemployment and of being in the labor force. We examine this reasoning in detail in the following critical survey of the transition probabilities from one labor market state to another and consider whether the relationships postulated by Clark and Summers are plausible (cf. the numbering of cells in Table 13). The resulting amendments to their analysis are summarized in Table 14 below.

1. *The Incentive to Remain in Employment.* Because unemployment insurance subsidizes the search costs for other and possibly better-paid employment, it reduces the costs of leaving employment and thus facilitates voluntary quits. This incentive is reduced, however, by contribution periods that are a prerequisite for eligibility for unemployment benefits. An opposite effect arises for new entrants into the labor market and casual workers, who need to remain in employment until they have become entitled to unemployment benefits. Dismissals by employers also become more likely; the affected employees will demand less compensation for their loss of employment because of the existence of insurance, and paternalistic feelings of responsibility are diminished. Employers will, therefore, be inclined to use methods of production that entail a higher risk of redundancies. This incentive is reduced when employers' contributions to unemployment insurance are partially or completely risk-related, that is, if contributions increase with the number of layoffs or dismissals.

2. *The Incentive to Become Unemployed.* Analogous to the above reasoning, the transition probability from employment into unemployment also increases. If there is an entitlement to benefits, unemployment insurance subsidizes the search for a new and possibly better-paid job. Taking into consideration the opposite effect of disqualification periods and the large number of employees not yet entitled to benefits, this relationship is not as strong as Clark and Summers suppose. The effect can be reinforced, however, by special programs for older workers that are intended to facilitate their subsequent withdrawal from the labor force after an intervening period on unemployment benefit.

3. *The Incentive to Leave the Labor Force.* Unemployment insurance reduces the transition probability from employment out of the labor force because it constitutes an incentive for certain types of employees (e.g., women, youth, or casual workers) to remain in the labor force in order to become entitled to benefits or to participate in a labor market program. This "entitlement effect" was first analyzed by Hamermesh

(1979). Special programs that subsidize early retirement through the unemployment insurance system have, however, an opposite effect. They usually provide for long-term receipt of unemployment benefit up until the regular retirement age without the normal requirement of being available for work. Where persons are no longer required to register as unemployed, they are also no longer included in the unemployment count (in countries in which unemployment statistics are based on registered unemployment instead of surveys). The overall effect—contrary to Clark and Summers's interpretation—is unclear.

4. *The Incentive for the Unemployed to Find Employment.* Generous wage-replacement benefits reduce the transition probability from unemployment into employment. This effect is reinforced by long benefit periods because the unemployed can take more time to find new employment that satisfies their expectations. This incentive effect, which undoubtedly exists, weakens as the end of the benefit period approaches and if the benefit level declines over the benefit period; wage expectations (the reservation wage) also decline. For the uninsured unemployed, an opposite effect is likely: the existence of insurance increases the incentive for them to quickly enter employment in order to become eligible for benefits. The insured and the uninsured may actually compete for jobs, and such competition would increase as vacancies become more scarce (e.g., during periods of mass unemployment). This would partially offset the negative incentive effects for the insured. The overall effect is thus quite unclear, particularly in a situation of persistent mass unemployment in which a large number of the unemployed are not (or are no longer) eligible for benefits.

5. *The Incentive to Remain Unemployed.* The incentives to remain unemployed are the same as the incentives to become unemployed. The probability of remaining unemployed undoubtedly increases, with the duration of benefits being more important than their level. Nevertheless, taking into consideration the opposite effect for the uninsured and for the insured unemployed whose entitlement to benefits will soon be exhausted, the relationship must be weaker than Clark and Summers assume. This is particularly true in the case of persistent mass unemployment, when the number of unemployed eligible for benefits declines rapidly and the number of uninsured unemployed increases.

6. *The Incentive for the Unemployed to Leave the Labor Force.*
Unemployment insurance reduces the probability of with-
drawing from the labor force for those unemployed persons
who merely wish to exhaust their benefits but de facto are no
longer available for work. This effect is mitigated by programs that explicitly foster withdrawal from the labor force
through an intermediate stage of unemployment. If in earlier periods older unemployed persons reentered employment—if only to a limited extent—today leaving the labor
force is a foregone conclusion for a large proportion of older
unemployed persons. For European conditions, in which
such programs are frequent (particularly in France and the
Federal Republic of Germany, but also in Austria and Sweden), the strongly negative relationship predicted by Clark
and Summers has to be at least qualified, if not rejected.

7. *The Incentive to Enter the Labor Force.* The entitlement
effect increases the probability of those outside the labor
force entering it. Moreover, when one household member
becomes unemployed and is not insured or is underinsured,
other members of the household not in the labor force may
be impelled to enter it. On the other hand, unemployment
insurance results in increased contributions or nonwage labor costs which, if they are effectively passed on to employees, reduce net wages, thus reducing the incentive to
enter employment. Insofar as employers' contributions cannot be passed on, they may result in a negative incentive for
employers to hire workers.[4] Whether these contrary effects
cancel each other out or whether one of them predominates
is, as Clark and Summers also see it, an open question.

8. *The Incentive for Those Not in the Labor Force to Become
Unemployed.* The relationships discussed in the previous
paragraph apply analogously here, except that the negative
incentives resulting from contributions or nonwage labor
costs are not (fully) present. Unemployment insurance increases—as a result of the entitlement effect—the probability of those not in the labor force entering unemployment.
Because those entering the labor force do not as a rule receive any wage-replacement benefits, the incentive is only
an indirect one: through registration as unemployed to find
employment as soon as possible in order to become eligible
for benefits. Because there are also contrary negative incentive effects (lower real wages and reduced hiring because of

Table 14
Anticipated Effects of Unemployment Insurance on Labor Market Transition
Probabilities: Comparison of Clark and Summers's Assumptions with Our
Expectations

Initial Labor Market State	Final Labor Market State					
	Employment		Unemployment		Nonparticipation	
	(a)	(b)	(a)	(b)	(a)	(b)
Employment	-	-	+ +	+	-	?
Unemployment	-	?	+ +	+	--	-
Nonparticipation	?	?	+ +	+	-	-

Note: (a) columns contain Clark and Summers's assumptions; (b) columns reflect our own analysis.

higher nonwage labor costs), the double plus sign assigned
by Clark and Summers to characterize this relationship (see
Table 13) seems unjustified. A more direct incentive effect
results when other entitlements in addition to wage-replacement benefits can also be acquired by registration as unemployed, such as participation in special employment
measures, use of placement and counseling services, credits
for periods of unemployment in the determination of other
social benefits. It is, of course, questionable whether these
effects should be attributed to unemployment insurance.

   9. *The Incentive Not to Enter the Labor Force.* To the extent to
which unemployment insurance promotes movement of
those not in the labor force into employment or unemployment, it also reduces the probability of individuals remaining outside the labor force. Unemployment insurance
subsidizes labor force participation. One would, therefore,
expect the incentive effect in this case to be on the whole
negative.

   Summarizing our analysis of the effects of unemployment insurance on supply and demand, we can say that we generally concur
with the findings of Clark and Summers—see the (a) columns in Table
14; there are, however, important differences in our analysis—the (b)
columns—on individual points. On the whole, unemployment insurance increases the probability of unemployment but also the probability of participation in the labor force so that the negative effects of
wage-replacement benefits on labor supply may be offset by the increase in labor supply as a result of the entitlement effect. Our analysis
has also clearly shown that the incentive effects differ according to individual circumstances and are partly contradictory. When referring

to incentives, the group of persons affected must always be clearly specified. Moreover, the transition probabilities between labor market states are in part highly interrelated, and the impact of these incentives on the functioning and efficiency of labor markets has not yet been discussed.

The existence of unemployment insurance may increase the allocative efficiency of the labor market (e.g., labor mobility) and thus the flexibility of the labor market in adapting to new technologies or new constellations of demand. From this point of view, generous unemployment insurance can then be regarded as a productive subsidy for such mobility processes. The willingness to accept temporary job offers or jobs with a high risk of unemployment, such as seasonal jobs, can be expected to be greater if generous unemployment insurance benefits are available; such jobs also have to be performed, and supporting them if not outright subsidizing them contributes to labor market flexibility.

A simple example can be used to illustrate the productive function of unemployment insurance, its contribution to the allocative efficiency of the labor market. Assuming that there are two vacancies and two unemployed job seekers, it may be economically rational to subsidize the unemployed in order to let them find the job vacancy in which they would create the greatest economic value. An extended search is probably necessary for specialized occupations so that the resulting longer duration of unemployment is desirable and not an unintended side effect of unemployment insurance (Burtless 1986:18). In addition to enhancing economic productivity, better matching can also minimize future spells of unemployment, thus reducing the likelihood of moving from employment into unemployment in the long term.

Furthermore, our theoretical analysis has shown that the causal relationship between the generosity of wage-replacement benefits and unemployment can also be reversed: a high risk of unemployment and long-term unemployment can lead to generous insurance benefits for political reasons and out of considerations of social policy. This possibility, which is a familiar constellation in Europe, is severely neglected in the Anglo-Saxon literature, but it has also been shown to exist in the United States (Leigh 1986).

Finally, it is now clear that the incentive effects depend on the labor market situation. The incentive for prolonging employment searches because of the level of wage-replacement benefits is probably especially a problem during periods in which unemployment is largely frictional, whereas generosity in the duration of benefits will be less relevant in this situation. In a tight labor market the assumptions of search theory may be realistic, that is, that the unemployed continually receive job offers and rationally compare the conditions of employment offered (especially wages) with the opportunity costs (wage-replacement benefits) and that higher benefit levels increase the probability that the job offers will be declined and spells of unemployment will be longer. These assumptions will, however, no longer be valid during periods of high unemployment because the unemployed will hardly receive any job offers. In this situation, high wage-replacement benefits will not lead to voluntary unemployment or to any significant self-induced extension of search time, whereas a long benefit period increases both the probability of becoming and remaining unemployed and the probability of subsequent withdrawal from the labor force.

6.2 EMPIRICAL EVIDENCE OF INCENTIVE EFFECTS ON LABOR MARKET SUPPLY AND DEMAND

Because the incentive effects of unemployment insurance depend on the nature of the insurance system itself, the labor market situation, and characteristics of labor supply and demand, it is advisable to examine the empirical evidence separately for each country. It is noteworthy that these relationships have hardly been studied in Europe—with the exception of Great Britain. This is clearly at odds with our findings above that the American and British insurance systems clearly rank lowest on the scale of generosity.

Why is there so little interest in this question in countries with generous insurance systems? There seem to be two plausible reasons for this pattern. First, the insurance systems in continental Europe are embedded in a corporatist system of industrial relations in which the regulation of unemployment insurance is more or less strongly influenced by employers' associations and trade unions—in some cases even largely by the unions. There is, therefore, little inclination to regard the unemployment insurance as a source of disturbance in the functioning of the labor market.[5] On the contrary, unemployment insurance is considered to be an essential component in the functioning of a system of industrial relations based upon collective agreements. Second, debate about the effects of unemployment insurance, which is also found in continental Europe, is less about rational behavioral incentives and more about abuse of unemployment insurance. Consequently, the solution is thought to lie in an improvement of administrative controls and not in regulative changes in the wage-replacement rate.[6] In countries with a well-developed labor administration organized on corporatist lines, an effective and even a restrictive control of abuse is readily possible, especially when unemployment insurance is closely linked to active labor market policy and availability for work can be easily tested by a suitable offer of employment or a place in a labor market program; neither of these conditions is fulfilled in the United States and Great Britain.[7]

In Austria, only two studies on the incentive effects of unemployment insurance are available. Fischer and Wagner (1986) examined whether higher wage-replacement rates prolonged the duration of unemployment. On the basis of a simple exploratory regression analysis of a sample of 10 percent of all unemployed persons in 1983, they concluded that there is no strong relationship between the wage-replacement rate and the duration of unemployment. Although a significant positive relationship in the expected direction was found, it accounted for only a quite small proportion of the variation in the duration of unemployment. Group differences are only weakly developed: ceteris paribus, women reacted more strongly than did men to changes in the wage-replacement rate, older unemployed persons more strongly than younger ones, and those with lower earnings more strongly than those with higher earnings.[8]

Steiner (1986) is primarily interested in the influence of personal characteristics of the unemployed on the duration of unemployment. His data on all unemployed persons between 1983 and 1986 in a local labor market in Austria did, however, allow him also to consider the wage-replacement rate as a possible explanatory variable. His estimates are based on exit probabilities according to the so-called Cox regression model. The findings of Fischer and Wagner are essentially confirmed. The probability of individuals leaving unemployment is determined primarily by individual characteristics such as previous spells of long-term unemployment, age, nationality, and training. Higher wage-replacement rates significantly reduce the likelihood of leaving unemployment, but this effect is relatively weak. For example, if the wage-replacement rate increases by 20 percent from 50 percent to 60 percent of previous earnings, the duration of unemployment increases by 5 days when the median duration of unemployment is 100 days. The elasticity of the duration of unemployment in relation to the wage-replacement rate would thus be 0.25.

In the Federal Republic of Germany, very few researchers have concerned themselves with the incentive effects of unemployment insurance, either theoretically or empirically. A study by Franz (1982) analyzes the impact of entitlement to unemployment benefits on the so-called reservation wage. If the reservation wage increases, the probable duration of unemployment also increases. The data base was all unemployed persons who left unemployment during the last week of September 1976 and included various characteristics of these unemployed (including their benefit entitlement) and their own statements about the wage at which they were ready to accept a job offer. The results showed that the reservation wage is primarily explained by the individual characteristics of the unemployed and the distribution of wage offers. Although entitlement to unemployment insurance benefits showed the expected positive association, it played only a subordinate role in explaining future wage expectations.

In another study, König investigated whether there is a significant difference between insured and uninsured unemployed with regard to the duration of unemployment. Using a Markov model, he found that the duration of unemployment for recipients of unemployment benefits is on the average greater than that for all unemployed and that "at least 10 percent of total unemployment can be attributed to this prolongation of the duration of unemployment" (König 1978:51). His results are, however, questionable because of shortcomings in the data and, above all, because of his failure to control for differences in the characteristics of benefit recipients and nonrecipients.

A more recent study by Hujer and Schneider (1986) uses panel data to estimate the determinants of the duration of unemployment. Their approach is similar to Steiner's, with numerous other individual characteristics in addition to entitlement to unemployment benefits being included as possible explanatory variables. The findings also fail to support the argument that restrictive regulation of unemployment benefits is a suitable means of combating unemployment. Individuals eligible for unemployment benefits even have a (not significantly) higher probability of leaving unemployment than do those without a benefit entitlement. The authors also tested for the existence of a special effect at the end of the benefit period (in the last two months before unemployment benefits are exhausted and wage-replacement benefits are reduced or cease entirely). In a completely flexible labor market one would expect, according to search theory, that the unemployed themselves can affect the point at which they leave unemployment. Any rational exploitation or misuse of unemployment insurance benefits would be manifest inter alia in an increase in the rate at which individuals leave unemployment shortly before benefits are reduced or cease altogether. The empirical results show, however, that the opposite is the case.

We are not aware of any empirical studies from France. By contrast, in Great Britain econometric estimates of the incentive effects of wage-replacement benefits have a long tradition. The results are, however, not unambiguous and in part contradictory. Lancaster (1979), Nickell (1979a, 1979b), and Atkinson et al. (1984) find that a 1 percent increase in the wage-replacement rate (e.g., from 50 to 50.5 percent) leads to an average increase of 0.6 to 1 percent (e.g., from 15 weeks to 15.09 or 15.15) in the duration of insured unemployment. Nearly identical coefficients of elasticity are found in U.S. studies (Burtless 1986:35 f.). However, Atkinson et al. note that these results are not statistically very robust. Moreover, they point out that this positive effect on the duration of unemployment of insured persons can be offset by the negative effect on the duration of unemployment of uninsured persons, a possibility also stressed by other authors (Burtless 1986:23). A study based on time-series data (most other studies are based on cross-sectional data) estimated an elasticity coefficient of 0.28 to 0.36 for unemployed males (Narendranathan, Nickell, and Stern 1985). In this case, the reaction of young men was found to be stronger (0.8) than that of prime- or middle-aged males (0.4), whereas —in contrast to Fischer and Wagner's results—the older men did not respond at all to variations in wage replacement by either prolonging or shortening spells of unemployment. In addition, the study found that the reservation wage declines when the duration of unemployment has reached a certain threshold; willingness to accept a job even below the original level of expectations increases as the end of the benefit period approaches.

In Sweden, there are only a few studies available on the effects of unemployment insurance on the incidence and duration of unemployment. Björklund and Holmlund (1986) present an overview of these studies. Stahl (1978) investigated whether variations in average wage-replacement rates influenced the level of unemployment between 1963 and 1973 and found no relationship. Björklund (1981) found that unemployed persons eligible for benefits could not be shown either to have been unemployed longer or to have received higher wages after leaving unemployment than was the case for unemployed persons not entitled to benefits. Heikensten (1984), using the approach of Clark and Summers, found that the insured unemployed remain unemployed longer than the uninsured. This effect is, however, mainly a result of the fact that the insured unemployed are less likely to leave the labor force; the insured unemployed as a whole are just as likely as the uninsured to move from unemployment into employment. In a similar study of youth, Holmlund (1986) found that the duration of unemployment is significantly longer (seven weeks) for the insured unemployed than for uninsured youth.

The Danish unemployment insurance system offers generous wage-replacement rates comparable to those in Sweden (Nordisk Rad 1983), and a Danish study of this issue is also of interest. Pedersen and Westergard-Nielsen (1984) found a significant positive relationship between generosity and the frequency of unemployment; that is, the unemployment insurance system increased the probability of a transition from employment or from being outside the labor force to unemployment. The effect on the duration of unemployment is also positive but statistically not very robust. If the frequency and duration of unemployment are combined (with the dependent variable being extent of annual unemployment, i.e., the unemployment experienced by individuals in one year as a percentage of potential working time), there is even an unexpected negative coefficient, which is, however, not statistically significant.

The most comprehensive and most controversial estimates are found in the United States.[9] Most studies concentrate—an American peculiarity—on the effects of unemployment insurance on temporary layoffs; more or less strong positive effects are found with the increased temporary layoffs being primarily attributed to the incomplete risk-relatedness of employers' contributions. Other studies provide econometric estimates of the duration of unemployment. Here, too, there are statistically significant positive incentive effects. However, the elasticity coefficients, which vary from approach to approach, are as a rule not very large. The most comprehensive and probably most reliable analysis is that from Clark and Summers, described above. The most important results of this study are summarized in Table 15.

The table shows that the overall effect of unemployment insurance on the three different labor market states can be ignored in the case of a 10 percent reduction in the wage-replacement rate (e.g., from 50 to 45 percent). Even the total impact of a complete elimination of unemployment insurance, while showing the expected direction, is still very modest: the unemployment rate would have been 11 percent lower in 1978 and the employment rate 1 percent lower, while the percentage of those not in the labor force would have been about 3 percent higher. In other words, although the U.S. studies confirm that unemployment insurance constitutes an incentive for more unemployment and more employment as well as for higher labor force participation, which is presumably even greater where benefits are

Table 15
The Impact of Changes in Unemployment Insurance on Employment,
Unemployment, and Labor Force Participation

UI Situation	Labor Force State (%)		
	Employment Ratio	Unemployment Rate	Nonparticipation Ratio
Actual rates in 1978	59.4	6.0	36.8
10% Reduction in Replacement Rate	0.00	- 0.08	- 0.06
No Unemployment Insurance	- 0.59	- 0.65	1.09

Source: Clark and Summers 1982: 315.

more generous, the total impact is, under all realistic assumptions (i.e., excluding the complete elimination of unemployment insurance), negligible.[10]

6.3 Summary

Unemployment insurance can affect the labor market in various ways. In this chapter we have considered in particular the individual incentive effects. Insurance guarantees unemployed persons a continuation of part of their income in case of unemployment. This fact alone, as well as the level and duration of wage-replacement benefits, influences the behavior of labor market actors. The fear is frequently expressed that high and prolonged wage-replacement benefits could interfere with the functioning of the labor market adjustment process. Exaggerated wage expectations and abuse or extensive use of benefit entitlements are supposed to reduce necessary wage flexibility, prolong the duration of unemployment, stimulate persons to register as unemployed when they are really not available for work, or even induce voluntary quits. On the demand side, too, unemployment insurance is said to encourage production methods with a high risk of dismissal and to discourage hiring because of increased nonwage labor costs.

Our theoretical analysis has shown that these plausible concerns have to be qualified by the prospect that unemployment insurance promotes greater mobility and greater allocative efficiency as a consequence of longer search periods. Thus, even if it could be demonstrated that generous unemployment benefits result in a markedly higher level of unemployment, the impact on labor market efficiency is not necessarily negative—so long as this effect remains limited. Our analysis has also shown that in the present state of research, there is no conclusive evidence for choosing between these two perspectives. It is theoretically extremely difficult to specify the incentive effects of unemployment insurance unambiguously because manifold distinctions have to be made on the basis of labor market state and labor market situation and because of the influence of political considerations. The individual effects are in part mutually reinforcing and in part contradictory.

None of the extant empirical studies possesses the methodological sophistication that the theoretical complexity of the subject matter requires. Even the authors of the hitherto most ambitious study, Clark and Summers, emphasize the shortcomings and uncertainties in their analysis. All the surveys of the extensive literature on the topic conclude that it is not yet possible to make any firm statements about the incentive effects of unemployment insurance. Most studies do agree that unemployment insurance tends to induce both higher unemployment and higher participation in the labor force. The overall effect is, however, so slight even in generous systems that there is no empirical evidence that unemployment insurance significantly impedes labor market efficiency.

These modest negative incentive effects of unemployment insurance are offset at least in part by positive effects that are even more difficult to quantify but probably no less significant. From a macroeconomic perspective, an effective system of income security in case of involuntary unemployment stabilizes purchasing power and, from a macrosociological perspective, promotes loyalty to major social institutions. From an intermediate systems or meso perspective, a functioning unemployment insurance system is of central importance to maintaining good industrial relations between capital and labor. If trade unions know that their members are adequately insured against unemployment, they will be more cooperative in adjusting the employment structure as a result of new technology or changed world market conditions. At the micro level, a reliable and generous social protection against unemployment (apart from the undoubtedly existing temptation to abuse the system) also increases employees' readiness to accept mobility in the labor market. This is especially true when mobility is further enhanced by effective measures to promote employment (active labor market policy). Linking a well-developed social security system with attractive manpower programs also considerably reduces the danger of abuse of wage-replacement benefits. Now we turn to a consideration of the interrelationship between financing systems and active labor market policy.

PART THREE

The Financing and Effectiveness of Active Labor Market Policy

In this part of our study, we first describe the administration and financing of active labor market policy in the countries studied, including the development of individual policy instruments and their financing sources. The different national systems of budget making and implementation—that is, the institutional determinants of expenditures for active labor market policy—are also compared (Chapter 7).

We then focus on the impact of national differences in financing systems on the level and structure of active labor market policy. We analyze the development of revenue sources under different labor market and financing conditions. Then we compare the development of expenditures and consider whether the national differences observed can be explained by the differences in their financing systems. We believe that active measures (training, temporary job creation, and programs to preserve employment) should as far as possible replace the "mere" passive provision of income support for the unemployed; therefore, we are particularly interested in the extent to which individual countries with different financing systems have been successful in replacing the passive acceptance of unemployment by active labor market policy. We compare the degree of activity of labor market policy in individual countries—that is, the ratio of expenditures for active measures as a percentage of total labor market policy expenditures—and look for factors and incentive effects in national financing systems that can partly explain the differences observed (Chapter 8).

161

Chapter 9 deals with the economic and social effects of active labor market policy that manifest themselves under different financing conditions: built-in stabilizer effects and regional, sectoral, and individual redistributive effects.

CHAPTER 7

The Organization and Financing of Active Labor Market Policy in Comparative Perspective

7.1 THE DEVELOPMENT OF THE INSTRUMENTS OF ACTIVE LABOR MARKET POLICY AND FINANCING SOURCES

Up until the beginning of the 1970s, labor market policy in most countries considered here consisted (in addition to the financing of wage-replacement benefits) largely of placement services and vocational counseling. This was supplemented by mobility assistance (especially in Sweden), seasonal programs such as bad weather benefits and winter allowances (especially in Germany and Austria), and, to a limited extent, vocational training and retraining measures. This set of labor market policy instruments was primarily oriented toward reducing frictional and seasonal unemployment. In most countries the classical functions of labor market policy (placement service, vocational counseling) were financed through contributions to unemployment insurance (the Federal Republic of Germany, Austria, the United States, and also predominantly in France); in Sweden and Great Britain financing was largely through funds from the central government budget.

At the beginning of the 1970s, vocational training and retraining and rehabilitation measures were expanded in almost all countries, and in some countries (especially in Sweden) public job creation measures were also initiated for reasons of structural and social policy. This active labor market policy—as it was first called by the OECD (1964)—was intended to accelerate and ease the process of structural change. Labor shortages of a quantitative and qualitative nature were supposed to be eliminated and new groups of persons mobilized to participate in paid employment. With the exception of the Federal Republic of Germany and Austria (where financing continued to be based on contributions to unemployment insurance), the expanded scope of labor market policy activities was financed through the central government budget, supplemented in France by employers' contributions to special-purpose funds for vocational training.

The 1974-75 recession initiated a third phase. In most countries, labor market policy was now confronted not only with increasing unemployment but also with a considerable structural shift in the composition of unemployment. Two trends should be emphasized. Youth unemployment became a central problem; the unemployment rates for youth were two to six times as high as those for the prime age group of twenty-five- to fifty-four-year-olds in all countries investigated here with the exception of the Federal Republic of Germany and Austria. Moreover, the persistence of high levels of unemployment led to an increasing percentage of long-term unemployed and difficult-to-place workers. By 1982, levels of long-term unemployment[1] were especially high in France and Great Britain (42 percent and 34 percent, respectively), the Federal Republic of Germany occupied an intermediate position (21 percent); the percentage of long-term unemployed in Sweden and the United States was only 8 percent and only 6 percent in Austria but also increasing in the latter countries (OECD 1985:126).

The increasing levels of unemployment and the structural changes in its composition not only increased the need for labor market policy but also led to a growing national divergence in the relative importance of different labor market policy instruments. In addition to demographic and structural economic factors, this was above all a consequence of differences in the institutional conditions of labor market and employment policy and of differences in employment policy strategies (Scharpf 1987b). The following four types of instruments can be distinguished:

1. Measures primarily designed to achieve a short-term countercyclical amelioration of a recession
2. Traditional instruments of active labor market policy, especially training, retraining, and job creation programs
3. Measures predominantly directed at youth as a target group, which are qualitatively different from the traditional labor market policy and have to be described separately
4. Measures to reduce the labor supply, especially through early retirement and restrictive policies toward foreigners[2]

Countercyclical measures have played a role primarily in the Federal Republic of Germany, Great Britain, Austria, and Sweden.[3] In the Federal Republic, short-time work has been extensively used (Schmid and Semlinger 1980; Flechsenhar 1980). In Great Britain, temporary production assistance in the form of wage subsidies was initially used and later replaced by a conventional short-time work program from 1979 to 1984. In-firm training measures have been used for countercyclical purposes ("buffer training") in Austria, supplemented by financial assistance to firms to maintain employment (interest subsidies, other subsidies, loan guarantees). In-firm training—together with stockpiling subsidies—has also been used as a countercyclical measure in Sweden. Extensive "temporary layoffs," a functional equivalent for short-time work, were utilized to cope with the crisis in the short term in the United States. Temporary layoffs as well as short-time work—which can be regarded as a form of part-time unemployment—are usually financed through contributions to unemployment insurance. Great Britain, where practically all expenditures for active labor market policy are financed through the central government budget, is an exception. In Sweden, in-firm training as well as other measures to maintain employment are financed through general tax revenues; countercyclical measures are largely financed through contributions in Austria.

Among the *traditional instruments of active labor market policy*, vocational training and public job creation programs have generally been expanded. In a number of countries, this trend has been so strong that one could say that active labor market policy developed from a necessary complement to a substitute for full employment policy. Training programs outside firms and job creation measures were used massively in the Federal Republic of Germany and especially Sweden (also for countercyclical purposes in the latter country) as well as in the United States, where a considerable percentage of the unemployed participated in job creation programs in the latter part of the 1970s. They have likewise been expanded in Great Britain in the 1980s. Out-of-firm training measures were also at times significant in Austria, although never to the same extent as in Sweden. Wage subsidy programs for the integration of the hard-to-place unemployed initially increased rapidly in importance and then declined again in the 1980s, particularly in the Federal Republic of Germany and the United States. In Austria as well as in the Federal Republic, increasing expenditures for traditional measures of active labor market policy have been predominantly financed through contributions, while the rise in expenditures in Sweden, Great Britain, and the United States has been largely financed through general tax revenues. In Sweden, a significant proportion has been supplemented through the newly created labor market fund (to which employers pay contributions).

Programs for the integration of youth are especially prominent in Great Britain and France but also play an increasingly important role in Sweden and a significant role in the United States. By contrast, youth have not been a principal target group of labor market policy in Austria or the Federal Republic of Germany because youth unemployment remained relatively low as a result of the well-developed system of apprenticeship training. In the other countries studied, labor market policy for youth has become a substitute for a poorly developed system of primary vocational training. In France, a variety of work-experience measures were established in public training centers and within firms. Programs to provide work experience for youth also expanded quickly in Great Britain and were replaced in 1983 by a new "Youth Training Scheme" with an enhanced training component. In Sweden, job creation schemes were increasingly utilized for youth in the 1970s, with the percentage of participants under the age of twenty-six reaching at times 60 percent. Since 1980, however, there are no longer any job creation measures for youth under the age of eighteen. Instead, special youth jobs (*Ungdomsplatser*) with a vocational orientation component were created, in which all unemployed youth are entitled to participate. Job creation programs with a training component were created for youths eighteen to nineteen years of age, participation in which is likewise an entitlement. There has also been an increasing use of wage-cost subsidies for the integration of youth in regular employment.[4] In the cases mentioned here, the financing of measures is predominantly, and in Great Britain exclusively, through the central government budget.

Instruments for reducing the labor supply and thus to relieve pressure on the labor market have become important primarily in the Federal Republic of Germany, France, and Austria. In the Federal Republic, the employment of foreigners was considerably reduced through a recruitment stop and restrictive controls on the issuance of work permits in the middle of the 1970s; this policy was complemented in the 1980s by financial incentives for repatriation to countries of origin. The instruments of early retirement (flexible retirement age, fifty-nine-year-old regulation,[5] expansion of disability pensions) have led to a strong decline in the labor force participation rates of men sixty to sixty-four years of age. In 1970, 75 percent of men in this age group were still in the labor force, but only 33 percent were still active in 1984. France has used similar means, if with less effect, to reduce the number of foreign workers: a recruitment stop, restrictions on work permits, and grants to promote repatriation have reduced the number of foreigners in the labor force. By far the most comprehensive early retirement initiative for labor market reasons has taken place in France, but Austrian early retirement policy also has had a considerable impact in reducing the labor supply (inter alia by means of a fifty-nine-year-old regulation for unemployed persons in industries in economic difficulty, which was extended to all industries in 1979). In both countries, the labor force participation rate for men sixty to sixty-four years of age is already less than one-third: in Austria it declined from 47 percent (1970) to 19 percent (1984), in France from 68 percent (1970) to 31 percent (1984) (OECD 1986b:461 ff.). An immigration stop and restrictive granting of work permits have also considerably reduced the foreign labor force potential in Austria. In all countries studied, the policies toward foreigners resulted not in increased expenditures but in net financial relief for labor market budgets, even in the case of repatriation grants. Early retirement measures are in part financed, especially in France and Austria, through contributions to unemployment insurance, with the main financial burden being borne by the pension insurance carriers. Only in France are the costs of early retirement pensions financed to a small extent through government subsidies (through the central government subsidy to unemployment insurance). In Great Britain, Sweden, and the United States, early retirement has also provided some relief for the labor market, but to a much lesser extent than in the above countries.[6]

Table 16 summarizes the financing sources for the most important instruments of active labor market policy in the countries compared. It shows that contributions to unemployment insurance are heavily used to finance active labor market policy only in Austria and the Federal Republic of Germany. Special-purpose levies play no role in Great Britain and the United States but sometimes do in other countries. In Great Britain and the United States (except for the employment service), active labor market policy is financed completely and in Sweden largely through the central government budget. The central government budget, on the other hand, provides only limited funding for active measures in Austria and only in exceptional cases (special programs) in Germany.

7.2 THE INSTITUTIONAL CONDITIONS FOR THE DEVELOPMENT OF ACTIVE LABOR MARKET POLICY EXPENDITURES

In this section we compare five institutional conditions that affect the level and structure of expenditures for active labor market policy: (1) the macro structure of the labor market budget, that is,

Table 16
Sources of Financing for Active Labor Market Policy

	Placement and Counseling			Training and Rehabilitation			Job Creation Measures			Seasonal and Countercyclical Measures			Integration and Training Programs for Youth			Early Retirement Programs		
	C	E	T	C	E	T	C	E	T	C	E	T	C	E	T	C	E	T
Austria	XX		X	XX		X	-	-	-	X	X	X	-	-	-	XX		X
F.R. Germany	XXX			XXX			XX		X	XX	X		-	-	-	X		
France		XXX		X	XX	X	-		-	XXX						XX	X	X
Great Britain		XXX				XXX			XXX			XXX			XXX			XXX
Sweden	X	XX			X	XX			XXX		X	XX			XXX	X	X	-
U.S.A.	XXX					XXX			XXX	-	-	-			XXX	-	-	-

C = Contributions to unemployment insurance.
E = Earmarked levies.
T = Taxation, central government budget.

XXX = Financing exclusively from this source.
XX = Predominant source of financing.
X = Partial financing.
- = Instrument not used or of only slight importance during most of the period investigated.

whether expenditures for passive and active labor market policy are financed through a common budget or more or less separately; (2) the degree to which expenditures are based on entitlements; (3) the rules for balancing revenues and expenditures; (4) the implementation structure for active labor market policy; (5) budgeting procedures, particularly the extent to which local and regional interests are included.

7.2.1 The Macro Structure of the Labor Market Budget

Three types of budgeting for labor market policy are found in the countries investigated:

1. Integrated budgeting of all (or most) passive and active expenditures
2. Integrated budgeting of part of expenditures
3. Separate budgeting of active and passive labor market policy expenditures

Largely integrated budgeting of passive and active measures occurs in three countries: the Federal Republic of Germany, Austria, and Sweden. Even though there are considerable differences among them, this type of budget structure entails some important common features. Integrated budgeting promotes a perception of labor market policy as a comprehensive policy area. At the same time, it makes the dynamics of expenditures for active and passive measures interdependent. In Germany and Austria, integrated budgeting is supplemented by a common administration of active and passive measures; the administration of Swedish labor market policy is also largely integrated, with the exception of the trade union unemployment insurance funds and the implementation of bankruptcy wage benefits.

Partially integrated budgeting is found in France and Great Britain. In France, about half of the measures included in active labor market policy together with a part of passive expenditures (the government subsidy to UNEDIC/ASSEDIC and a number of less significant passive benefits) are financed through the central government budget. Although they consist of different budget items and some even occur in the budgets of different ministries, a comprehensive overview of this government-financed labor market budget is presented in the regular program budget for this policy area ("Labor and Employment"). Nevertheless, essential parts of expenditures for labor market policy are not included in the central government budget but occur in the budget of the self-governing unemployment insurance system or in separate funds, particularly in the area of training. Labor market policy in France is, therefore, in comparison with the above three countries, less clearly identifiable and not usually regarded as a single policy area. In Great Britain, all expenditures for active labor market policy and most expenditures for passive measures (supplementary benefit) are financed through the central government budget; expenditures for unemployment benefit—which has declined in relative importance—are financed and budgeted together with other social security benefits within the National Insurance Fund.

There is completely separate budgeting of active policy measures and unemployment insurance in the United States. Active measures are financed through the federal budget and not regarded as related to the individual state unemployment insurance systems. The budgeting of active measures is sometimes related to certain public assistance programs that are financed in whole or in part by federal funds (AFDC, food stamps, etc.), expenditures for which may be reduced by active labor market policy, if it is concentrated on disadvantaged groups, potential recipients of public assistance. The problem group orientation of American manpower programs can thus be interpreted as partly reflecting considerations of federal fiscal policy. Because of their completely separate budgeting, the financing and development of the individual state unemployment insurance programs are unrelated to the dynamics of expenditures for active labor market policy.

7.2.2 The Degree to Which Active Labor Market Policy Is Based on Entitlements

In contrast to passive labor market policy, in which benefits represent legal entitlements, participation in active labor market policy programs is not usually based on individual entitlements. Expenditures for such measures can therefore be controlled not only by regulating (as in the case of wage-replacement benefits) eligibility and expenditures per participant (e.g., the amount paid in stipends to participants in training measures) but also simply through legislated budget ceilings on expenditures. In the case of entitlements (based on individual legal claims), the chain of control can be described in ideal typical terms as follows: entitlements determine uptake, uptake determines expenditures, and expenditures determine funding. In the case of discretionary programs (i.e., not based on an entitlement), the program goals typically determine appropriations (funding), appropriations determine expenditures, and expenditures determine program uptake.

Two groups of countries can be distinguished with regard to the importance of individual entitlements in active labor market policy. In France, Sweden, and the Federal Republic of Germany, a relatively large segment of active programs is provided on the basis of individual legal claims (entitlements). As a rule, only job creation measures as well as some wage subsidies and mobility grants are purely discretionary; that is, participation is at the discretion of the particular agency. By contrast, training measures represent an intermediate form between entitlements and discretionary programs because the provision of stipends is as a rule based on entitlements, although the establishment of training courses themselves is at the discretion of the responsible agency. In the other three countries—Austria, Great Britain, and the United States—there are few or no entitlements in the area of active labor market policy (in Austria only in the case of bad weather benefits, and in Great Britain in the case of wage subsidies). In the former group of countries, the level of expenditures for active measures can only be controlled to a limited extent simply through budgetary changes; in order to influence expenditure levels, statutory changes are necessary. In the latter group of countries, the level of expenditures can be controlled through changes in budget ceilings. Statutory provisions in these countries (which in the United States have usually been temporary) may, however, exclude certain categories of persons from participation in programs (without thereby granting others an individual right to participate) and in this way indirectly affect the level of expenditures and directly affect the structure of participants.

7.2.3 Decision-Making Procedures for Balancing Budgets

Two basically different situations have to be distinguished with regard to procedures for balancing budget revenues and expenditures: What happens when expenditures exceed revenues—for example, because of rapidly increasing unemployment—and what happens when revenues exceed expenditures? The decision-making procedure in the case of deficits was already described above for countries with integrated budgeting and financing through contributions (Austria and the Federal Republic of Germany; see 4.2.8). In both countries, the government initially assumes responsibility for deficits, with the rules of levy financing in Austria requiring a stricter and more rapid upward adjustment of contributions to increase revenues than is the case in the Federal Republic of Germany. In the Federal Republic, there are three possible responses to deficits, and the choice is essentially a matter of policy discretion. Either the central government subsidy to cover deficits can be reduced through an increase in contributions or cuts in programs, or it can be continued for an indefinite period of time. In fact, however, only the first two options have been utilized; in case of deficits, it is primarily active labor market policy programs that have been cut, because they enjoy less legal and political protection as property rights than do wage-replacement benefits (see 8.3 below).

When revenues exceed expenditures, the rule in the Federal Republic is that the surplus is to be used to build up reserves in order to improve the capacity of the financing system to respond countercyclically to employment crises, whereas the building up of reserves is only permitted to a limited extent in Austria. In this situation, integrated systems of financing based on contributions also tend to expand programs (for passive as well as—above all—for active labor market policy) for two reasons. First, labor market budgets financed through contributions are separate from the central government budget and thus do not have to compete with other functional budget areas (or only to a lesser extent than is the case where labor market budgets are tax financed) (Bruche and Reissert 1985:129). Furthermore, the unwritten law of incremental budgeting—that expenditures rise almost automatically because of routinized, decentralized, interest-oriented, and particularistic but in principle consensual decision-making processes[7]—is also applied to the labor market budget (and in particular to the discretionary measures of active labor market policy). Incrementalism is, however, not applicable when a budget cut becomes necessary (which would have to be termed *decrementalism*), because in this situation decision-making processes are de facto highly centralized but chaotic or at least unpredictable, politically and ideologically motivated, and conflict-laden.[8]

Insofar as the active labor market policy is financed out of contributions to unemployment insurance, French decision-making procedures for bringing revenues and expenditures into balance are analogous to those in the Federal Republic of Germany and Austria (see 4.2.8); however, no build-up of reserve funds is foreseen in France. About half of measures for active labor market policy are financed through the central government budget and general revenues; there is, therefore, no specific relationship between the financing side and the dynamic of expenditures because the normal principle in public finance is that general tax revenues are not earmarked for particular purposes (the principle of nonaffectation). De facto the above remarks on incrementalism are also applicable here when total budgets are increasing; largely unregulated and unpredictable decision-making processes also occur here when budget cutbacks (especially larger ones) are necessary.

A distinctive French institution is the training levy on firms through which a major share of French labor market policy is financed. Such a special-purpose fund financed through a levy operates according to either the levy principle (revenues are adjusted to reflect expenditures) or the budget authority principle (expenditures reflect available revenues). In France, it is revenues that largely control the level of expenditures, because there is, on the one hand, an incentive for firms to exempt themselves from the levy as far as possible through their own training efforts and/or to actually utilize available funding, and, on the other hand, there is a considerable political barrier to increasing the levy. The advantage of such a system lies in the high degree of stability on both the revenue and expenditure sides. The disadvantage is the lower level of control over the purposes for which funds are spent, such as inability to steer in-firm training to promote larger labor market policy goals.

Expenditures for active labor market policy in Sweden are mainly financed through the central government budget; additional expenditures are financed through the employers' levy that is paid into the so-called labor market fund. The employers' levy has to cover 65 percent of expenditures for certain labor market functions, including training, retraining, and rehabilitation as well as the government subsidy to the unemployment insurance funds. This represents an example of proportional division of the financial burden between employers and government budget according to a fixed formula. If expenditures increase, the size of the grant from the labor market fund increases proportionately. If the fund's reserves are exhausted, the employers' contributions are increased. There is, however, no rule requiring the accumulation of reserves in the opposite case, which means that the levy on employers would have to be reduced in case of a surplus—a situation that has not yet occurred in practice. In this system of levy financing part of labor market policy expenditures control revenues, and expenditures are heavily determined by political-institutional factors.

In Great Britain, active labor market policy is almost completely financed through general government revenues.[9] There are no special rules for balancing revenues and expenditures. Because all active labor market policy programs (with the exception of wage subsidies) are discretionary programs, the budget ceilings set in the government budget process determine expenditures. In the United

States, too, expenditures for active labor market policy, which is financed through the federal budget, are for discretionary programs and, as such, are determined entirely by authorizations in the budget process. In contrast to other countries, the U.S. Congress can also authorize expenditures in excess of the president's budget proposals and against the will of the administration. This prerogative of the Congress is of considerable significance in the area of active labor market policy; during the period investigated funding approved by Congress in this area usually exceeded the administration's original proposals.

7.2.4 The Administrative Infrastructure of Active Labor Market Policy

In contrast to wage-replacement benefits, active labor market policy requires an extensive infrastructure of program sponsors and actors with planning, administrative, oversight, and control functions without which most measures could not be implemented. Without changes in this infrastructure, expenditures for active labor market policy cannot be increased indefinitely, nor can they be arbitrarily reduced without disrupting administrative routines, frustrating program sponsors, and inducing a loss of efficiency in labor market policy. Each such institutional actor in the implementation of labor market policy develops its own momentum and vested interests, being as a rule interested in a slow expansion or at least a stabilization of expenditures in its area of activity (see, inter alia, Niskanen 1971; Schmid and Treiber 1975; Scharpf, Reissert, and Schnabel 1976).

One finds marked differences among countries with regard to administrative infrastructure. Sweden, the Federal Republic of Germany, Austria, and Great Britain have separate labor administrations for the implementation of active labor market policy that have a long tradition, their own corporate administration, organizational and personnel sovereignty, as well as an established network of cooperative relations to program sponsors. The independence of the labor administration is relatively greatest in Sweden and less in the other three countries because of limited personnel autonomy or close ties to the state administration. In France, responsibility for the implementation of labor market policy is dispersed among various government agencies; in the United States, it is delegated to individual state governments, local governments, and local special-purpose organizations. The first four countries have an established infrastructure for the implementation of active policy, which—because of its prominence and institutional self-interest and organizational rigidities—is conducive to the stability and (gradual)[10] expansion of the level of expenditures.[11] The highly fragmented and less independent implementation structures in France and especially the United States, on the other hand, facilitate rapid change in the level of expenditures (in both an upward and a downward direction) and in the orientation of labor market policies.

7.2.5 The Budgeting Process for Active Labor Market Policy

The extent to which local and regional authorities participate in the planning and preparation of the active labor market policy budget varies considerably among countries. In Great Britain, Austria, and the Federal Republic of Germany, the budgetary process is highly centralized, and participation by lower levels is as a rule limited to suggestions without binding character. In France, this is true to an even greater extent for that segment of active labor market policy that is financed through the central government budget. (Decisions with regard to the allocation of revenues raised through the training levy are, by contrast, almost completely decentralized and not subject to direct government influence.) The local and regional levels play a much more important role in the budgeting process in Sweden and the United States, although the way in which they participate is quite different. In Sweden, the preparation of the budget closely resembles a "two-stream" model: the views and requests of the regional labor offices are given considerable weight, among other reasons because they are based on intensive consultations within and decisions by the tripartite regional governing boards. In the United States, funds for various—quite broadly defined—federal programs are apportioned according to a distributional formula to local and regional organizations, which have a great deal of discretion in the allocation of these funds to individual types of measures and client groups.

The inclusion of nongovernmental actors in the budgeting process (through corporate governing boards, advisory councils, etc.) is undoubtedly most strongly developed in Sweden. There is also considerable involvement in the Federal Republic of Germany and the United States, with the difference that participation is largely at the central level in the Federal Republic and largely at the local level (private industry councils) in the United States. In France, Great Britain, and Austria, such corporate administrative entities play practically no role in the budgetary process for active labor market policy.[12]

7.3 THE INSTITUTIONAL CONDITIONS OF BUDGET IMPLEMENTATION

How funds are actually spent and whether they fulfill their intended purpose also depend on the way the budget is implemented, particularly, the degree of flexibility that the responsible agencies enjoy in implementing the budget and whether control of budget implementation is centralized or decentralized.

7.3.1 Flexibility in Budget Implementation

Flexibility in budget implementation has both a temporal dimension and a substantive one. Flexibility in timing refers to the extent to which the implementing authorities are required to spend budgeted funds for active labor market policy in the current fiscal year and whether they have the authority to exceed budgeted spending levels for a given fiscal year. From this point of view, there is a great deal of flexibility in both Austria and Sweden. The Swedish labor ministry has reserve funds at its disposal that are not allocated to individual programs, and there are also three points in time during the year at which supplementary budget requests can be made. In Austria, the responsible minister can (with the approval of the finance minister) exceed the budgeted volume of funding for active labor market policy by 10 percent (and that for entitlements by 25 percent) without having to submit a supplementary budget request to Parliament. In the United States, flexibility is in principle limited (there are no discretionary reserve funds or similar options). However, authorized expenditures can be spent either in the current or in the following fiscal year, thus increasing the flexibility of budget execution. Flexibility in this sense is particularly limited in the Federal Republic of Germany. Not only a supplementary budget request but also a complicated process of consultation among the independent labor market authority, the government, and Parliament are necessary to provide additional funds for discretionary expenditures.

"Substantive flexibility" in the implementation of the budget for active labor market policy refers to the extent to which budget resources can be shifted between individual programs and measures. A high degree of flexibility in this sense can be achieved either through providing resources for active labor market policy in the form of a block grant without detailed allocation to individual programs or by declaring appropriations for various subprograms to be mutually transferable. American labor market policy is an example of the former type of flexibility, particularly in the years between 1974 and 1978 and after 1983. Most resources made available for active labor market policy were (and still are) included in one general program in which the local and regional sponsors can themselves determine the individual program mix on the basis of a long list of authorized measures. The Austrian labor market authority followed the latter strategy at the beginning of the 1980s. All budget categories for active labor market policy were declared to be mutually transferable at the level of the regional labor offices (the regional labor offices have their own budgets).

A high degree of flexibility in the timing of expenditures (without resort to Parliament) and a high substantive flexibility in budget implementation do, of course, impinge upon the authority of Parliament in budget matters, which requires above all that appropriated funds only be spent for specific declared purposes.

7.3.2 Central Control of Budget Implementation

The problems that are supposed to be addressed by active labor market policy and the institutional, personnel, and material resources that are available vary from region to region and from one local labor market to another. Moreover, these situations can change quickly. A uniform, routinized, and centrally directed policy cannot, therefore, adequately cope with the varied and fluid problem situations with which labor market policy has to deal. Three procedural characteristics of labor market authorities that affect the problem adequacy of the use of available funds can be identified: direct influence on the regional distribution of labor market policy resources, the degree to which conditional regulations (i.e., entitlements) determine access to individual programs, and local discretion in the choice of labor market policy instruments.

The considerable regional variation in the extent and structure of employment problems in all countries has led to demands that the allocation of the scarce resources available for active labor market policy be concentrated on problem regions. Four procedures can be identified for directly influencing the allocation of resources (in addition, of course, to the differential regional impact that may be entailed, for example, by general conditions of eligibility for programs): distributional formulas, regionalized instruments, bargaining on the basis of expenditures in the previous year, and central intervention. A more or less automatic targeting of the allocation of funds to problem regions is attained through two procedures: regional distributional formulas and/or regional limitations on the availability of certain instruments. The United States provides an example of regional targeting of resources for active labor market policy on the basis of distributional formulas. The authorizing legislation for active labor market policy includes a specific formula for individual programs according to which available funds are to be distributed to individual states and implementing organizations. Since 1982, the Austrian labor market authority has also experimented with regional distributional formulas whose significance was, however, reduced by earmarking part of available program resources as a "central ready reserve." The distribution of funds available for job creation measures in the Federal Republic of Germany is now also according to a regional formula specified by the corporate administration of the Federal Employment Institute (and hence with the participation of the *Länder*; Bruche and Reissert 1985:79 f.).

The regional allocation of funds can also be controlled by limiting the availability of individual labor market programs to specific geographical areas or by making program conditions more favorable in certain regions. Swedish labor market policy uses such an approach, and—at a somewhat less formalized level—it is also found in Austria, where the so-called long-term employment grants are only available in problem regions. In Germany, such regional selectivity is only found in special programs financed directly through the federal budget, particularly the 1974-75 wage-cost subsidy program (Schmid 1979) and the 1979 program for regions with special employment problems (Scharpf et al. 1982).

The problem adequacy of the allocation of financial resources depends—as mentioned—not only on the geographic distribution of resources but also on the problem adequate composition of the local instrument mix. In most countries, there is not only central control of the geographic distribution of resources but also central budgeting of resources for individual instruments of active labor market policy. In this type of centralized programming, the budgeting of entitlements is based on projections of expected program uptake, and authorized spending levels can, if necessary, be exceeded, whereas discretionary programs are limited by a budget ceiling that may not be exceeded. While regional allocations make no sense in the case of entitlements, different procedures are possible in the case of discretionary programs. Either local agencies are allocated specific shares in the financial planning for individual instruments, or resources are allocated by the central authority as needed on the basis of local applications—possibly even in a first-come-first-served manner.[13] If expenditures approach the upper limit of planned expenditures for the fiscal year, either regional caps, a general expenditure stop, or restrictive criteria for approval of further expenditures are ordered. The United States represents a special case here. As described above, the local and regional implementing authorities can select the mix that they regard as appropriate from among broadly defined types of programs. Through bargaining and because the resources available for individual instruments are relatively large, the provincial labor office directors in Sweden also have considerable leeway in structuring their programs.

Another factor influencing the capacity to adjust active labor market programs to local problems is the degree of central fine-tuning of instruments in the sense of setting detailed parameters for decisions by lower-level authorities, possibly even with guidelines for deciding all conceivable cases. Such a strongly centralized regulation can be expected to increase the degree of uniformity in administrative practice while reducing the efficiency of instruments. The efforts of the administrative staff are likely to be diverted from the real goals of the programs by the burden of formal examination of whether certain prerequisites are fulfilled, and the adaptation of policy instruments to local conditions is made more difficult. However, a very broad and open definition of the instruments also increases the danger of misapplication of program resources and entails the danger of fiscal substitution (e.g., the performance of regular public tasks by job creation programs) or windfall effects. Among the countries included in our study, the greatest freedom for local variation in the instruments of active labor market policy is found in Sweden and the United States. For the United States, this is particularly true for the period up until 1978; participation in programs was subsequently largely limited to economically disadvantaged persons after fiscal substitution and windfall effects had greatly increased while operating under very broad definitions of the conditions for eligibility. However, this more centralized regulation had a very negative impact on the level of expenditures. State and local governments largely lost interest in the programs because of the new restriction on eligibility, so that there were no longer any strong vested interests to resist radical budget cuts during the Reagan administration. Program conditions in the other countries, especially in the Federal Republic of Germany, are generally more restrictively defined by central regulations or administrative procedures than is the case in Sweden and the United States.

7.4 SUMMARY

Three groups of countries can be distinguished with regard to the institutional conditions for the development of labor market policy expenditures. In Sweden and the Federal Republic of Germany, individual legal entitlements account for a relatively high percentage of expenditures for active labor market policy, and there is a well-established and independent administrative structure for its implementation. Both factors are favorable to stable and gradually increasing expenditures (because of legal commitments and institutional self-interest and rigidities). In Sweden, the stability of expenditures is further augmented by an extended budgetary planning procedure in which the organizational environment of the labor market authority is heavily involved. The establishment of a centralized and relatively independent labor market authority in Great Britain, the Manpower Services Commission, in the mid-1970s also created an administrative infrastructure with an institutional dynamic and vested interests conducive to the stabilization of active labor market policy; the ties between the labor market authority and its organizational environment in this case are, however, not as close as in the Federal Republic of Germany or especially Sweden. The functions of the British labor market authority are also more limited than in these two countries. In the United States, the lack of entitlements in active labor market policy and the weakness of organizational structures in the policy area facilitate the flexibility of expenditures in an upward or downward direction. In France, Great Britain, and Austria, one finds both factors that promote flexibility in expenditures and factors conducive to stability. How these different institutional conditions, including especially the different financing systems, affect the actual development of expenditures for active labor market policy is investigated in the next two chapters.

CHAPTER **8**

The Effects of Financing Systems on the Level and Structure of Active Labor Market Policy

This chapter investigates, analogous to our examination of the impact of unemployment insurance in Chapter 5, how the funding sources for active labor market policy have developed over time and under different labor market conditions. Our expectation is that the way resources are mobilized for active labor market policy influences the level and structure of policy in this area. We compare the actual development of expenditures in the countries included in the study and consider the extent to which differences can be explained by characteristics of their financing systems. Finally, we investigate how successful individual countries have been in substituting active labor market policy for passive response to unemployment. For this purpose, we compare national expenditures for active measures as a percentage of all labor market policy expenditures and search for factors in the various financing systems that partly explain the differences observed. In this context, we give particular attention to the institutional distribution of the fiscal costs of unemployment and of fiscal responsibility for active measures; this distribution is, we think, an important source of incentives for a more active labor market policy.

Table 17 provides an overview of the sources of financing for active labor market policy at three different points in time: in 1973, for the "normal" situation before the beginning of the labor market crisis; in 1975, at the first peak of unemployment; and in 1983, representing a point of long-term adjustment to the labor market crisis. As

Table 17
The Sources of Financing for Active Labor Market Policy (in %)

	Contributions to Unemployment Insurance[a]			Other Special-Purpose Levies			Central Government Budget		
	1973	1975	1983	1973	1975	1983	1973	1975	1983
Austria	68	75	78	15	11	8	17	14	14
F.R. Germany[b]	79	52	89	21	9	6	-	39	5
France	-	-	-	57	53	46	43	47	54
Great Britain	-	-	-	-	-	-	100[c]	100[c]	100[c]
Sweden	-	-	-	5	4	12	95	96	88
U.S.A.	7	6	13	-	-	-	93	94	87

Notes: Active labor market policy: expenditures for placement, adult training and rehabilitation, early retirement with an obligation to fill the resulting vacancy (Great Britain), direct measures to preserve employment, job creation, and placement assistance (wage subsidies).
Actual data available sometimes deviate from reference years indicated. Specifically: Austrian data are for the years 1973, 1975, 1984; French data for the years 1973, 1975, 1982; Swedish data for 1974, 1976, 1983; and U.S. data for 1973, 1976, 1983.

a) Funds drawn from the reserves of the unemployment insurance systems are also included because they are derived from contributions paid in earlier years.
b) Contributions and federal grants to the Federal Employment Institute are used to finance both active labor market policy and wage-replacement benefits. We assume here that both sources are used proportionally (i.e., corresponding to their respective shares in total expenditures) to finance active measures and wage-replacement benefits.
c) Including local government budgets (shares varying from 4 to 14%).

the table shows, the financing structure of active labor market policy is on the whole simpler than that for wage-replacement benefits. There are only two countries in which active measures are financed to a large extent through contributions to unemployment insurance: Austria and the Federal Republic of Germany. In three countries—Great Britain, Sweden, and the United States—the financing of active programs is almost exclusively through the central government budget and thus essentially from general tax revenues.[1] In the United States, only the public employment service, which is less important than in other countries, is financed through insurance contributions. The relative growth in the importance of financing through contributions in the United States is a result of the fact that expenditures for training programs and (especially) job creation measures declined at the beginning of the 1980s while expenditures for counseling and placement services remained relatively stable. In Sweden, the relative importance of special-purpose levies increased in the early 1980s;[2] a further increase can be anticipated as a result of the new temporary layoff fund introduced in 1985. Special-purpose levies are also important in the systems predominantly financed through contributions: Austria and the Federal Republic of Germany. In both cases, the programs involved are different systems of financing risks in the construction industry, that is, winter construction subsidies for firms (Germany) and bad weather benefits for short-time workers (Austria).

The sources of financing for active measures are most widely dispersed in France. About 50 percent is financed through the central government budget, and the balance from various special-purpose levies and taxes—in particular for training programs. Contributions in a strict sense also play a role but cannot be quantified: unemployment benefits used for entering self-employment and subsidies from unemployment insurance funds for training certain categories of the unemployed.

If one disregards the special case of the Federal Republic of Germany, no essential changes in financing structures can be observed over the period examined. The percentage share of financing through contributions declined considerably in the Federal Republic at the beginning of the labor market crisis because the deficit of the Federal Employment Institute was covered through funds from the central government budget. In 1983, the share of financing through contributions was again higher because the FEI's budget deficit had been reduced. The stability of the structure of financing in Austria is, on the one hand, a result of the levy-type organization of the contributions system, which requires that contributions to unemployment insurance be adjusted to reflect the level of expenditures for active and passive labor market policy;[3] on the other hand, it is also a consequence of the low level of unemployment because of active employment policy. The Austrian financing system for labor market policy has not yet been subjected to a "system-threatening" test such as has occurred in the Federal Republic.

Financing active labor market policy primarily through contributions and through an integrated (i.e., including both passive and active measures) labor market fund appears thus to be the exception rather than the rule. This is the practice only in Austria and the Federal Republic of Germany, and it is hardly possible to draw any conclusions from the Austrian case because active labor market policy plays such a very small role within economic and social policy there. France is again a special case because of the extreme fragmentation of its financing structures. It is the only country that finances active labor market policy to a considerable extent through levies paid into special-purpose funds or through special-purpose taxes. The percentage share of such financing remained relatively stable at about 50 percent over the entire period.

Table 18
Average Expenditures for Active Labor Market Policy as a Percentage of Gross
Domestic Product (GDP) and Average Unemployment Rates (1973 - 1988)

	Average Expenditures (% GDP)	Average Unemployment Rate
Austria	0.20	2.4
F.R. Germany	0.71	5.3
France	1.01	7.0
Great Britain	0.62[a]	7.3
Sweden	1.74	1.9
U.S.A.	0.27	7.1

a) 1974 - 1988.

As we shall see below, these findings with regard to structures of financing can partly explain the large national differences in the development of expenditures and in the effectiveness and in the distributional impact of active labor market policy. We now turn to a consideration of trends in expenditures.

8.2 The Effects of Financing Systems on the Level and Program Structure of Active Labor Market Policy

The six countries display major differences in the level of expenditures for active labor market policies (see Table 18 and Figure 9). If one relates expenditure levels to gross domestic product (GDP), three categories of countries can be identified: at the bottom are Austria and the United States with average expenditures for active labor market policy between 0.2 and 0.3 percent; at the top is Sweden with almost 2 percent of GDP; the average levels of expenditures for active measures in the other three countries lie between 0.6 and 1 percent of GDP and are thus relatively close together. As Table 18 shows, there is no relationship between level of expenditures and the level of unemployment. There are considerable differences in unemployment rates among countries with similar levels of expenditures (e.g., Germany, Great Britain). Conversely, countries with similar unemployment rates display quite different levels of expenditure for active labor market policy. The latter is true above all for Austria and Sweden: in Sweden, the low unemployment rate is particularly a result of the application of active labor market policy, whereas in Austria, the unemployment rate is low despite the low level of expenditures for labor

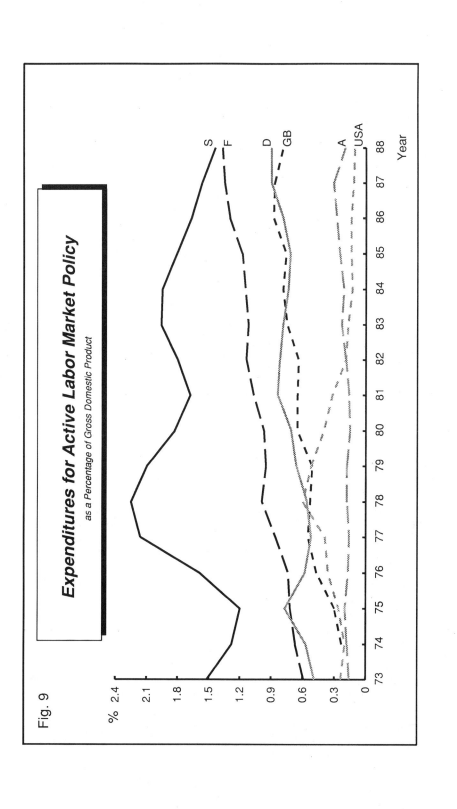

Fig. 9

Expenditures for Active Labor Market Policy

as a Percentage of Gross Domestic Product

S
F
D
GB
A
USA

Year

% 2.4
2.1
1.8
1.5
1.2
0.9
0.6
0.3
0

73 74 75 76 77 78 79 80 81 82 83 84 85 86 87 88

Table 19
Areas of Emphasis in Active Labor Market Policy (1973 - 1988)

	Adult Training Programs	Job Creation Programs	Measures to Preserve Employment	Training and Integration of Youth
Austria	XXX	X	XXX	
F.R. Germany	XXX	XX	XXX	
France	XXX	X	X	XXX
Great Britain	XX	XX	X	XXX
Sweden	XXX	XX	X	X
U.S.A.	XXX	XX		XX

XXX   =   Major area of emphasis.
XX   =   Important program area.
X   =   Program area of lesser importance.

market policy. Swedish labor market policy is thus under a great deal of pressure to act because unemployment would be high without its intervention, which is not the case in Austria.

8.2.1 The Tasks and Program Structure of Active Labor Market Policy

The considerable differences in the level of active labor market policy are primarily a consequence of the differences in the role that labor market policy plays within economic and employment policy in individual countries. In Austria, unemployment has been kept low during the period studied through an expansive countercyclical fiscal policy in combination with a series of other factors. The integration of youth in employment takes place essentially through a well-developed apprenticeship system. Up until the middle of the 1980s, active labor market policy was, therefore, not required to assume employment policy functions but was largely confined to training measures for adults, measures to assist firms in economic difficulty, and seasonal employment programs (see Table 19). Insofar as employment was created in the public sector, this took the form of regular employment. Temporary public job creation was not used at all; the first job creation programs were established in the mid-1980s.

In Sweden, active labor market policy does have an important function in regulating the level of unemployment: if full employment is threatened as a result of an economic downturn or unavoidable structural change in the economy (promoted by the solidarity wage policy), then it is the task of active labor market policy to keep open unemployment at a low level. Both training measures for adults and youth and demand-oriented programs, especially job creation measures, have been utilized for this purpose on a large scale.

The level of expenditures for active labor market policy differs little in the Federal Republic of Germany, France, and Great Britain, although there are considerable differences in program structure. During the period investigated, training programs for adults and various measures to preserve employment (short-time work, bad weather subsidies in the construction industry) predominated in the Federal Republic of Germany. Job creation measures were also at times significant; after a period of contraction, they were again greatly expanded in the mid-1980s.

In Great Britain, training and integration measures for youth clearly predominate. In France, training and integration programs for youth and adults have been most important in active labor market policy, whereas job creation programs played hardly any role there until the mid-1980s. The importance of training and integration or work-experience programs for youth, which account for large shares of expenditures for active labor market policy in France and Great Britain and which also play an important role in Sweden and the United States, seems to be a consequence of the inadequate supply of initial vocational training (apprenticeships) or its predominant locus outside of industry (i.e., classroom training). Programs for adults have correspondingly been less important in these countries, although they are, according to the conceptions developed by the OECD in the 1960s, the classical target group of active labor market policy (OECD 1964).

Measures to preserve employment were used only to a limited extent in Great Britain and the United States. This is primarily a consequence of the widespread practice of layoffs in the United States and the fact that seasonal measures to preserve employment have never played a significant role in these countries.[4] In the United States, where active labor market policy was originally largely a training program for problem groups, expenditures increased considerably from a rather low initial level in the late 1970s. With the establishment of large public service employment programs, it even came to play a central role in employment policy. At the beginning of the 1980s, labor market policy was, however, again reduced to its original function and low level of expenditures.

8.2.2 Financing Systems and the Level of Active Labor Market Policy

There is no direct and lawlike relationship between the average level of expenditures for active labor market policy and national differences in financing and budgeting systems. This does not mean, however, that active labor market policy is not influenced by financing systems. In the following discussion, we point out some relationships between financing systems and the budgeting process, on the one hand, and levels of expenditure for active labor market policy, on the other.

The particularly low initial level of expenditures for active labor market policy in Austria was certainly primarily a result of the specific division of labor between fiscal and labor market policy. The decision to finance new additional active labor market policy programs through the unemployment insurance fund at the end of the 1960s meant, however, that additional funding had become available for these discretionary programs[5] without any changes in the contribution rate. Expenditures for active labor market policy thus originated as a residual sum determined by subtracting unemployment benefit payments from total revenues of the unemployment insurance system. An essential factor that slowed the potential rise in expenditures was the limited capacity of the labor administration to implement measures; it regularly failed to fully exhaust available funding. One reason for this situation is the fact that personnel expenditures of the labor administration are financed not out of unemployment insurance funds but separately through the central government budget and are thus subject to the restraints affecting the latter. Finally, the financing of programs through the unemployment insurance system seems also to have impeded the broadening of the spectrum of activities to include disadvantaged marginal groups (who, as a rule, have not been regular contributors to unemployment insurance).

In the Federal Republic of Germany, two factors initially determined the level of active labor market policy at the end of the 1960s and beginning of the 1970s: the fact that training measures take the form of entitlements and the fact that active labor market policy is financed through the unemployment insurance fund, which was experiencing big annual surpluses and had accumulated large reserves during this period. The considerable reserves and favorable (even though false) prognoses with regard to anticipated revenues in the 1970s led to a relatively generous design of the training and retraining programs, resulting in a rapid increase in expenditures that could only be checked by (time-consuming) changes in the terms and conditions of programs. If financing from unemployment insurance contributions was initially a principal reason for the relative generosity of labor market policy, this situation reversed itself when the Federal Employment Institute's budget ran into deficit. In contrast to financing through the central government budget, where such program-specific deficits do not occur, this deficit was highly visible and consequently easily recognized by policymakers. Expenditures for active labor market policy were cut back in the mid-1970s and at the beginning of the 1980s when wage-replacement benefits absorbed an increasing share of the Federal Employment Institute's budget. The financing of active and passive measures through contributions to a common fund thus can reduce the level of expenditure for active measures during periods of economic crisis and have an expansive effect under more favorable labor market conditions.

Another important factor in the development of expenditures is the capability of the responsible administration to implement programs, to promptly make use of available funds and when necessary to articulate existing needs. This administrative capacity for implementation depends inter alia on the number and qualifications of available personnel. However, the German federal government regularly reduced planned expenditures for personnel during the FEI's annual budgeting process because the high level of unemployment was expected to be only a short-term phenomenon. This certainly also impeded an increase in the level (and probably also qualitative improvements) of active labor market policy that would have otherwise been possible.

The relatively high level of expenditures for active labor market policy in France is in part a result of the inclusion of the vocational training levy on employers, from which they can deduct their own expenses for training in firms or in joint centers. This means that expenditures that in other countries are only recorded as expenditures by private industry or, for example, in the budgets of employers' associations and chambers of commerce are included here as part of public active labor market policy. Nevertheless, the levy does provide a solid financial basis for the development of labor market training, which certainly results in considerably more collectively organized training than would be the case without the levy. Because the unemployment insurance system in France is jointly administered by the social partners and financed only to a lesser extent through the central government budget, increasing expenditures for wage-replacement benefits exert no direct pressure for cuts in active measures. Presumably, the "dispersion" of the financing sources has a generally favorable effect in promoting an increase in expenditures and hence the relatively high level of expenditures for active policy in France because it makes the mobilization of additional resources less spectacular and visible than would be the case in a "unitary" financing structure.

The relatively low level of expenditures in Great Britain up until the middle of the 1970s is essentially a consequence of political priorities. Despite already relatively high levels of unemployment at the beginning of the 1970s, active labor market policy was initially regarded as merely an instrument for narrowly defined adjustments of supply and demand on the labor market through placement activities and training programs. Only after the establishment of the labor market authority—the Manpower Services Commission— and the rise in and persistence of mass unemployment did active labor market policy come to play a role in dealing with problems of the level of unemployment and problem groups on the labor market. The growth of expenditures was facilitated by the existence of the MSC, which, as an independent organization in which interest groups were directly represented, could lobby with the Treasury more aggressively for resources than could the Department of Employment itself. The complete and separate financing of active labor market policy through the central government budget facilitated the direct implementation of changed priorities in policy after 1975 and was certainly a factor contributing to the lack of cutbacks in this area in the 1980s despite rapidly increasing expenditures for wage-replacement benefits—in contrast to the development in the Federal Republic of Germany. The cuts were instead concentrated in the area of passive benefits. The level of expenditures for active measures would have increased even more rapidly if actual expenditures had not lagged, at times considerably, behind budgeted spending levels. This was partly a consequence of deficiencies in planning but predominantly the result of bottlenecks in the capacity of the British labor market authority to implement programs.

In addition to the clear political priority given to active labor market policy and the increasing activity in the area of youth training, budgeting and finance-planning procedures also play a role in explaining the high level of expenditures in Swedish labor market policy. The extensive consultations with interest groups and the high degree of integration of regional and local labor offices in the budgeting process, flexible formulation of rules for job creation measures, the preparation of extensive stand-by plans (project banks), and a generous policy of personnel manning enable the Swedish labor market authority to quickly implement large and rapidly expanding programs. In contrast to the situation in other countries, the implementation capacity of the labor administration in Sweden is not a limiting factor in increasing expenditures. This is because the personnel and administrative costs provided in the program budget of the labor administration depend upon the size of the program: they are calculated as a percentage rate of expected program expenditures. The problem of additional programs being introduced without the necessary personnel resources to implement them does not occur in Sweden, or at least not to the same extent as in other countries.

Two additional factors seem to increase the overall level of expenditures for active labor market policy in Sweden. Because not only unemployment insurance but also unemployment assistance (KAS) are provided for a limited time period, local governments would be quickly burdened with high levels of public assistance payments in cases of long-term unemployment. The local authorities successfully ward off this threatening cost avalanche by initiating job creation programs within the decentralized planning process for active labor market policy. The high cost of training measures in state training centers may well be another reason for the expansion of expenditures for active labor market policy. This so-called AMU training was financed up until 1985 on a cost-reimbursement basis, and there was therefore little institutional incentive for an efficient use of resources.[6] A basic organizational reform has since been adopted which, as of 1986, introduced some competition into the provision of training, and it is hoped that this will result in considerable savings.

The level of U.S. labor market policy was largely determined in the 1970s and 1980s by changing political priorities and the changing tasks assigned to labor market policy. Given the almost exclusive financing of active measures through general revenues in the federal budget, changed political priorities could be relatively easily translated into changes in expenditures. An initially expansive and later contractive influence on the level of expenditures resulted from the specific role of Congress in the U.S. budgeting process. In contrast to most European fiscal systems, the U.S. Congress has the right to initiate expenditures; that is, it can institute programs even against the will of the administration and can provide existing programs with funds that were not requested in the executive budget proposal. Furthermore, the electoral prospects of individual members of Congress are more dependent than is the case in Europe on their success in having items that visibly benefit their districts included in the federal budget—because of the electoral system and the weakness of the national political parties. Both of these factors led Congress to provide increasingly more funds for job creation programs in the 1970s—in part against the will of the administration. When public criticism of abuse and substitution effects increased, eligibility requirements were so restrictively formulated at the end of the 1970s that programs lost their economic and fiscal attractiveness for local governments, and the interest of members of Congress in job creation measures declined correspondingly. It then became possible to eliminate them entirely under President Ronald Reagan without significant resistance. The absence of an independent labor market authority in the United States, which certainly would have been an obstacle to such cuts because of its own organizational rigidities and institutional interest, is also a significant factor.

As we have seen, the different levels of expenditure and program structures for active labor market policy are primarily determined by the difference in roles that active labor market policy is allocated within economic and employment policy as a whole in individual countries. The independent influence of differences in financing and budgeting systems is, however, also apparent. They determine the room for maneuver for the realization of political priorities and thus facilitate or impede the expansion of programs and expenditures. Thus, Swedish labor market policy would hardly be able to carry out the function allocated to it in employment policy if it were largely financed through contributions instead of through the central government budget; to require it to support the general goal of full employment (which is not concentrated on contributors) would be demanding too much from a system financed through contributions and based on insurance principles. Austrian labor market policy, with its financing system based on contributions, which does not allow longer-term deficits or surpluses and thus approximates a levy system, could not have been used in this way in support of a full employment policy because all increases in expenditures would have led to increases in contributions.

8.3 EXPENDITURES FOR ACTIVE LABOR MARKET POLICY AS A PERCENTAGE OF ALL LABOR MARKET POLICY EXPENDITURES

In our study, we have divided labor market policy roughly into two main areas of activity: the provision of wage-replacement benefits (passive policy measures) and the various measures to combat or prevent unemployment (active policy measures). The declared goals of labor market policy in many countries give active labor market policy

Table 20
Average Expenditures for Active Labor Market Policy as a Percentage of Total Labor Market Policy Expenditures for the Years 1973 - 1988 Compared with Active Expenditures as a Percentage of Gross Domestic Product (GDP) and Unemployment Rates

	Average Percentage of Active Measures in Total Expenditures (Degree of Activity)	Average Percentage of Expenditures for Active Measures in GDP	Average Unemployment Rates
Austria	26	0.20	2.4
F.R. Germany	42	0.71	5.3
France	44	1.01	7.0
Great Britain[a]	31	0.62	7.3
Sweden	75	1.74	1.9
U.S.A.	30	0.27	7.1

a) Columns 1 and 2 average 1974 - 1988.

precedence over passive benefits: measures and programs to prevent and combat unemployment are supposed to replace as much as possible the passive acceptance of unemployment and the mere provision of income security for the unemployed. The greater the share of active measures in total expenditures for labor market policy (degree of activity), the more labor market policy can be said to fulfill this goal. Because the ratio of active to passive measures can also be large if the level of wage-replacement benefits is low or declining, this indicator has to be interpreted with caution in comparing nations or in analyzing developments within one country over time. This measure, of course, tells us nothing about the quality of the active measures.

The six countries investigated differ considerably with respect to both their average degree of activity and its stability over time. We first consider the average values for the entire time period investigated, then the variations in the degree of activity over time, and finally the possible interrelationships between the degrees of activity and the financing systems.

8.3.1 The Average Degree of Activity

Table 20 shows the average percentage of expenditures for active labor market policy in total labor market policy expenditures, average expenditures for active labor market policy as a percentage of GDP, and the average unemployment rates for the six countries. The data show clearly that the goal of largely replacing passive benefits with active measures is only approximately realized in Sweden, where the degree of activity is almost twice as high as in any other country; the remaining countries do not differ greatly, with Austria displaying the lowest degree of activity.

If one compares the average degree of activity, the average level of expenditures (as a percentage of GDP), and the unemployment rates in individual countries (Figure 10), the degree of activity increases with the level of expenditures for active labor market policy, as might be expected. Countries with especially large expenditures for active labor market policy spend relatively less for passive benefits, and vice versa. The spectrum ranges from Austria (low level of expenditures, low degree of activity) through the United States, Great Britain, the Federal Republic of Germany, and France to Sweden (high level of expenditures, high degree of activity).

If one assumes that a high degree of activity is indicative of a successful struggle against unemployment through active labor market policy measures as opposed to the passive acceptance of unemployment, then one would expect a high degree of activity to be associated with (ceteris paribus) relatively low unemployment rates and vice versa in cross-national comparisons (even if the relationship is only crude as a result of the many other intervening variables). The data in Table 20 and Figure 10 do, in fact, appear to show the expected relationship. Austria, where a low degree of activity coincides with a low unemployment rate, is the exception. This is a result of the fact that Austrian unemployment rates have been kept low without resort to active labor market policy measures but are still high enough to cause expenditures for passive benefits to greatly exceed those for active programs.

8.3.2 Fluctuation in the Degree of Activity

As Figure 11 and Table 21 show, the degree of activity of labor market policy has declined in all countries during the period investigated—with the exception of Great Britain. The goal of preventing unemployment, instead of merely protecting the unemployed from its financial consequences, has receded farther under conditions of increasing unemployment. This is even true for Sweden, which still displays a quite high degree of activity. Only in Great Britain is the degree of activity still about as high at the end of the period studied as it was at the beginning. In the following discussion, we examine trends in the degree of activity in individual countries, taking into consideration the underlying absolute expenditure data (see Figure 12).

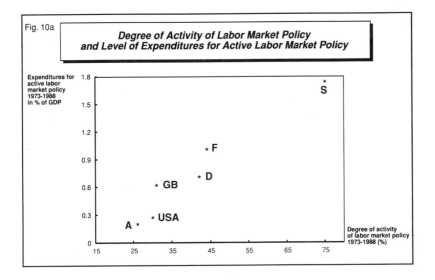

Fig. 10a

Degree of Activity of Labor Market Policy and Level of Expenditures for Active Labor Market Policy

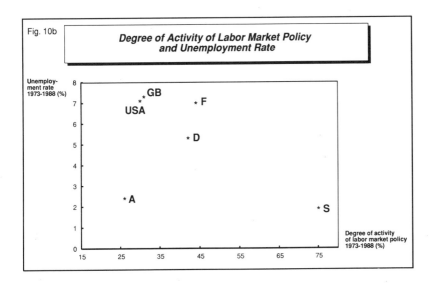

Fig. 10b

Degree of Activity of Labor Market Policy and Unemployment Rate

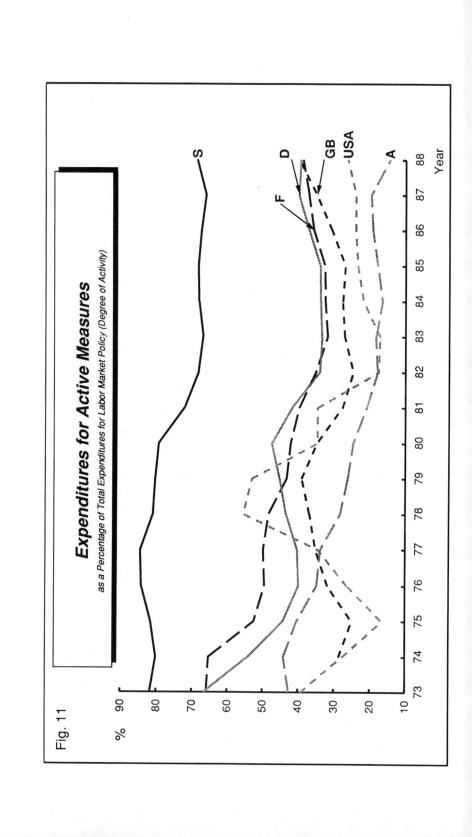

Fig. 11

Expenditures for Active Measures

as a Percentage of Total Expenditures for Labor Market Policy (Degree of Activity)

Table 21
Expenditures for Active Measures as a Percentage of Total Labor Market Policy
Expenditures (Degree of Activity)

	Austria	F.R. Germany	France	Great Britain	Sweden	U.S.A.
1973	42.6	66.6	65.9		81.8	39.2
1974	44.1	54.1	65.3	28.6	80.1	27.6
1975	40.4	44.3	52.5	25.0	81.6	16.7
1976	34.8	39.9	49.5	31.8	84.2	26.4
1977	33.8	40.3	49.9	35.2	84.5	34.5
1978	28.3	43.5	48.4	36.9	81.0	55.5
1979	26.2	45.3	43.3	39.1	80.4	53.1
1980	24.7	47.5	42.2	34.8	79.4	34.7
1981	21.0	41.8	39.8	27.7	72.2	34.6
1982	17.9	34.1	35.2	24.7	68.3	17.6
1983	18.4	33.5	31.9	27.1	67.0	17.2
1984	16.6	33.9	32.6	27.7	68.2	21.9
1985	17.9	34.0	32.7	27.0	68.4	23.5
1986	19.3	37.1	35.8	30.7	67.5	24.1
1987	19.8	40.0	37.2	35.0	66.2	24.1
1988	14.5	39.5	38.9	39.9	68.7	26.3

The declining degree of activity in Austria is a result of the fact that expenditures for passive benefits increased considerably more rapidly than did those for active measures. As mentioned above, the available financial resources of the unemployment insurance fund were primarily used to improve wage-replacement benefits for the unemployed. The declining degree of activity in Austria is thus indicative of the priority given to an "incomes policy for the unemployed" and the rather sluggish implementation of active labor market policy.

The degree of activity of German labor market policy declined very rapidly between 1973 and 1976 as expenditures for wage-replacement benefits increased considerably more rapidly than did expenditures for active measures (which also increased significantly) because of the rapid increase in unemployment (but also because of improvements in wage-replacement benefits). Between 1976 and 1980, the degree of activity stabilized, as did (at a relatively high level) the unemployment rate, increasing slightly after 1977 with expenditures for active measures rising more rapidly than those for passive benefits. Between 1980 and 1983, German labor market policy was again less successful in realizing the goal of giving priority to active measures; expenditures for unemployment benefits increased rapidly while expenditures for active labor market policy remained almost constant after 1981, which represents a reduction in real terms. Only after 1983 does the degree of activity begin to stabilize at a lower level in com-

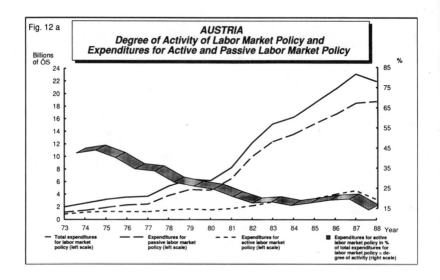

Fig. 12 a

AUSTRIA
Degree of Activity of Labor Market Policy and
Expenditures for Active and Passive Labor Market Policy

Fig. 12 b

FEDERAL REPUBLIC OF GERMANY
Degree of Activity of Labor Market Policy and
Expenditures for Active and Passive Labor Market Policy

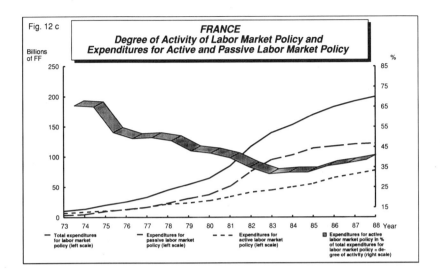

Fig. 12 c

FRANCE
Degree of Activity of Labor Market Policy and
Expenditures for Active and Passive Labor Market Policy

Billions
of FF

%

— Total expenditures
for labor market
policy (left scale)

— Expenditures for
passive labor market
policy (left scale)

– – – Expenditures for
active labor market
policy (left scale)

▨ Expenditures for active
labor market policy in %
of total expenditures for
labor market policy = de-
gree of activity (right scale)

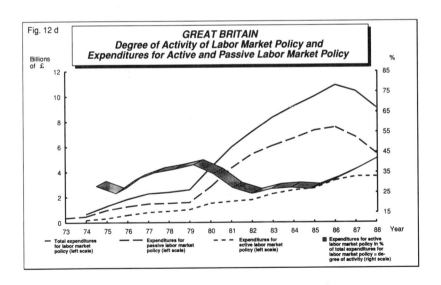

Fig. 12 d

GREAT BRITAIN
Degree of Activity of Labor Market Policy and
Expenditures for Active and Passive Labor Market Policy

Billions
of £

%

— Total expenditures
for labor market
policy (left scale)

— Expenditures for
passive labor market
policy (left scale)

– – – Expenditures for
active labor market
policy (left scale)

▨ Expenditures for active
labor market policy in %
of total expenditures for
labor market policy = de-
gree of activity (right scale)

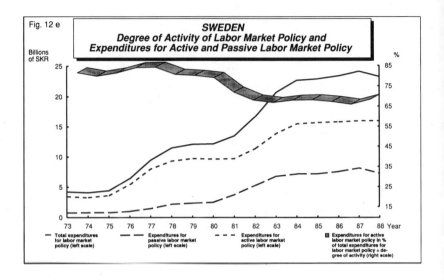

Fig. 12 e

SWEDEN
Degree of Activity of Labor Market Policy and Expenditures for Active and Passive Labor Market Policy

Billions of SKR

%

— Total expenditures for labor market policy (left scale)   — — Expenditures for passive labor market policy (left scale)   – – Expenditures for active labor market policy (left scale)   ▨ Expenditures for active labor market policy in % of total expenditures for labor market policy = degree of activity (right scale)

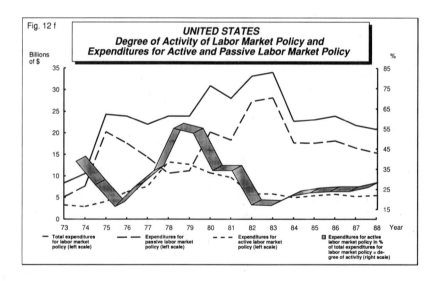

Fig. 12 f

UNITED STATES
Degree of Activity of Labor Market Policy and Expenditures for Active and Passive Labor Market Policy

Billions of $

%

— Total expenditures for labor market policy (left scale)   — — Expenditures for passive labor market policy (left scale)   – – Expenditures for active labor market policy (left scale)   ▨ Expenditures for active labor market policy in % of total expenditures for labor market policy = degree of activity (right scale) parison with earlier years because expenditures for wage-replacement benefits cease to increase. Between 1985 and 1987, there is again a modest increase in the degree of activity because expenditures for active measures rise more rapidly than those for passive benefits.

The almost continuous decline in the degree of activity of French labor market policy until the mid-1980s is a result of the fact that the steady increase in expenditures for active labor market policy, which accelerates after 1980, is offset by the even more rapid increase in expenditures for passive benefits. This pattern is especially strong in the years 1974–75 and between 1978 and 1983; only after 1985 do expenditures for active measures increase more rapidly than wage-replacement benefits. It should be recalled here that the heavy emphasis on early retirement provided by the unemployment insurance system, on the one hand, and improvements and expansions in unemployment benefits, on the other, were the predominant factors contributing to the increase in expenditures for passive measures. If one regards early retirement as less passive or defensive than financing support payments for the unemployed, then the degree of activity of French labor market policy declined less markedly than shown in Figure 12.

Great Britain is the only country in which the degree of activity of labor market policy has not declined since 1974. Until 1979, expenditures for active labor market policy increased considerably faster than did wage-replacement benefits; under the conservative government the expansion of active measures initially lagged behind the growth of unemployment benefits and then subsequently increased disproportionately under the same government. After 1986, there was another rise in the degree of activity as a result of declining expenditures for wage-replacement benefits and stable expenditures for active measures. Important factors explaining the stability of the degree of activity are the cutbacks in the unemployment benefit at the beginning of the 1980s and the displacement of benefit recipients from unemployment benefit onto supplementary benefit, which together have led to a decline in real per capita benefits and thus prevented the rapid increase in unemployment from leading to a similarly rapid growth in the expenditures for wage-replacement benefits.

The degree of activity of U.S. labor market policy[7] declined during the period investigated, although, in contrast to other countries, a large temporary increase occurred between 1975 and 1978. This was a consequence of a rapid increase in expenditures for active measures while expenditures for passive benefits were declining. In no other country during the period investigated did we find such a marked decline in expenditures for unemployment benefits. This phenomenon—which occurred again after 1983—is above all attributable to two factors: the much greater (in comparison to Europe) cyclical responsiveness of the American labor market—largely because of institutional factors (Köhler and Sengenberger 1983:288) and the short duration of unemployment benefits, which results in a rapid decline in the percentage of the unemployed receiving benefits in case of high and persistent unemployment. After 1979, there is a particularly sharp drop in the degree of activity of labor market policy, which is a result of the absolute decline in expenditures for active measures and the rapid increase in wage-replacement benefits for the unemployed in the new recession. The United States is thus the only country investigated in which the decline in the degree of activity is a result of an actual cutback in active labor market policy—and not merely a slower expansion in contrast to passive benefits. After 1983, there is again a slow increase in the degree of activity because of the drop in unemployment benefits and the stability of active expenditures.

Sweden is the only country investigated in which the programmatic goal of priority for active labor market policy has thus far been largely realized. But the very high degree of activity of Swedish labor market policy also gradually declined between 1977 and 1983. Until 1980, there was in fact hardly any increase in unemployment, and the growth in expenditures for passive benefits was only a result of the changed structure of unemployment (i.e., relatively more unemployed with a higher benefit entitlement) and to various improvements in benefits, some of which had already been introduced earlier. With the return to power of the Social Democratic Party and along with an economic upswing, the downward trend in the degree of activity was stopped in 1983.

8.3.3 The Relationship between Financing Systems and the Degree of Activity

Because the degree of activity of labor market policy is as a rule higher where the level of expenditures for active labor market policy as a whole is higher (see Figure 10), the factors suggested above as possibly explaining national differences in the level of expenditures are also applicable in explaining differences in the degree of activity. In the following discussion, we examine the extent to which the institutional-budgetary locus of active and passive expenditures may have influenced the short-term and medium-term development of the degree of activity.

In Austria, the Federal Republic of Germany, and Sweden, active and passive measures are budgeted in the same budget. In the former two countries, the basis of financing is contributions; in Sweden, the labor market budget is financed through the central government budget and through special-purpose levies. In the United States, there is completely separate budgeting of active and passive measures (which are even located at two different levels of the federal system). In France, some expenditures for passive and for active measures are financed through the central government budget and grouped together in the corresponding program budget. In Great Britain, a large proportion of wage-replacement benefits and all of active labor market policy are financed through the central government budget.

The following patterns are relevant for assessing the potential influence of these institutional systems on the degree of activity. The expansion of active measures usually leads to savings in expenditures for wage-replacement benefits by reducing unemployment, and in the case of common budgeting the resultant savings occur in the same budget as do expenditures. Common budgeting of active and passive programs may thus facilitate net cost budgeting of expenditures for active measures—that is, the deduction of related savings in wage-replacement benefits from gross program costs—and can, therefore, promote the substitution of active for passive measures. On the other hand, separate budgeting of active and passive programs may impede a strategy of replacing the passive acceptance of unemployment with active measures because expenditures for active measures cannot be directly offset by the related savings in wage-replacement benefits. The simple conclusion that common budgeting facilitates an activation of labor market policy and tends to raise the degree of activity is not, however, legitimate because there could also be other possible causal chains. For example, expenditures for wage-replacement benefits increase more or less automatically when unemployment increases and thus engender fiscal pressure. When there is common budgeting, this pressure directly affects active programs, but when there is separate budgeting, there is no such relationship, and the pressure (for cuts or increased revenues) may be directed at other areas of expenditure or at contributors. This could mean that, in contrast to the causal chain described, common budgeting of active and passive programs can lead to a declining degree of activity under conditions of rapidly increasing unemployment when active measures are crowded out in the common budget by expenditures for passive benefits.

Which of these causal chains predominates and whether they play any role at all depends on a number of additional conditions particular to each country. In Austria, common budgeting has provided neither incentives for increasing the degree of activity by strengthening active measures nor the prerequisites for a crowding out of active policy by wage-replacement benefits because unemployment was low without recourse to active labor market policy. The situation is different in the Federal Republic of Germany and Sweden. Despite having the same characteristic (common budgeting), expenditures for active labor market policy in the Federal Republic of Germany were displaced or crowded out at least in the years 1974 to 1976 and 1980 to 1983 by the growth of passive expenditures—as the rapidly sinking degree of activity shows (Bruche and Reissert 1985:125–31), while there was hardly any evidence of this trend in Sweden—even at a much higher level of activity. Two major reasons can be offered for this difference (these are surely not the only ones). In Sweden, the clear programmatic primacy of active labor market policy and the especially strong influence of trade unions on the labor market budget favor continuation of the level of active measures even in critical financial situations; in the German system, in which active measures have only partly the status of entitlements, it is rather passive benefits and not active measures that are protected. Of primary significance, however, is the fact that common budgeting of active and passive programs in the Federal Republic takes place within the narrow confines of the contribution-based fund of the Federal Employment Institute instead of in the central government budget, as is largely the case in Sweden. In Germany, the resources of the Federal Employment Institute are quickly exhausted when wage-replacement benefits increase, and the responsibility of the federal government to cover FEI deficits does not impede a crowding out of active measures (Bruche and Reissert 1985:125–31). The fiscal pressure engendered by wage-replacement benefits is less strongly felt in the large Swedish central government budget because pressure for cuts is directed not at active labor market policy alone but at government expenditures as a whole.[8] The same reasoning is also applicable to the British central government budget, through which the bulk of expenditures for wage-replacement benefits and all of active labor market policy are financed.

For the United States and largely also for France, a direct crowding out of active measures by wage-replacement benefits is not possible because they are budgeted separately; the development of expenditures for active measures is, rather, independent of the financial situation of the respective unemployment insurance fund(s). This means, however, also that the possibility of directly offsetting gross expenditures for active programs by resulting savings in wage-replacement benefits in the same budget, which in principle promotes the activation of labor market policy, is absent. Nevertheless, this institutional configuration does avoid one of the problems of such net cost incentives, namely, that the largest savings in wage-replacement benefits result when active programs are concentrated on core members of the labor force (who receive more in benefit payments) rather than on groups with a marginal labor force attachment. Separate budgeting is thus more conducive to a problem-group orientation and has certainly facilitated the heavy emphasis on youth in French labor market policy and on economically disadvantaged groups in American labor market policy.

8.4 THE FISCAL COSTS OF UNEMPLOYMENT AND THE INCENTIVES FOR ACTIVE LABOR MARKET POLICY

A more comprehensive explanation of national differences in the degree of activity of labor market policy may be achieved by transcending the narrow perspective of expenditures for labor market policy and their modes of financing. We showed above (section 5.4) that unemployment is a burden on public budgets not only as a result of expenditures for wage-replacement benefits but also because it leads to a decline in revenues from taxes and social security contributions and to increasing expenditures for other social benefits. Wage-replacement benefits constitute only one part of the fiscal costs of unemployment. Reducing unemployment through the use of active labor market policy thus not only results in savings in wage-replacement benefits but also reduces other fiscal burdens of unemployment for public budgets, which are even greater. It is therefore plausible to assume that decisions on the level of active labor market policy in individual countries are affected not only by the fiscal interrelationship between active measures and wage-replacement benefits—as was suggested in the previous section—but also by the reciprocal relationship between expenditures for active labor market policy and the total fiscal costs of unemployment.

Estimates of the fiscal costs of unemployment and evaluations of labor market policy programs in most countries emphasize that expenditures (gross costs) of public budgets for active measures lead to a reduction in the costs of unemployment so that the actual costs to public budgets (net costs) of active labor market policy are relatively small, amounting to only a fraction of gross costs (see our country studies and OECD 1984a:137 ff.; Nordisk Rad 1984; Bruche and Reissert 1985:81–124, 132–39). Such studies on the gross and net costs of active labor market policy have been widespread since the 1970s, and because they have received considerable public attention it is reasonable to assume that they have also influenced decisions on labor market policy. If this is the case, if net cost calculations have influenced the decision-making and budgeting process of labor market policy, then it can be assumed that measures and programs of active labor market policy are most likely to have replaced the passive acceptance of unemployment when the following two conditions are fulfilled:

1. The gross costs of active measures and programs have to be offset by a relatively high reduction in the fiscal costs of unemployment so that the net costs of an activation of labor market policy are, on the whole, relatively small.

2. The reduction in the fiscal costs of unemployment resulting from active labor market policy must benefit those institutions that also are responsible for expenditures for active programs. If this is not the case and the program-related budgetary relief largely benefits institutions other than those responsible for active measures, then there is no strong institutional incentive for the stabilization and expansion of active policy. Under such circumstances, active policy would largely result in positive external effects benefiting other institutional budgets and have hardly any self-financing effect for the responsible institutions. In the case of "fiscally segmented net cost calculations" (Wagner 1983:170), the incentives for a more active policy are slight.

The different degrees of activity of labor market policy in individual countries and their fluctuation over time seem to confirm the existence of the expected pattern of incentives. Although the total fiscal costs of unemployment differ only insignificantly from country to country (see section 5.4), and hence could not possibly be the source of any differential incentive for activity in labor market policy,[9] there are great differences among countries with regard to the institutional distribution of the costs of unemployment and thus with regard to the second condition described above. In some countries, the institutional incidence of the costs of unemployment, and thus of the program-related budgetary relief caused by active labor market policy, largely coincides with institutional responsibility for active labor market policy, facilitating net cost calculations and a more active policy. In other countries, net cost calculations are impeded by the institutional incongruity of the costs of unemployment and responsibility for

Table 22
Distribution of Burden on Public Budgets due to Unemployment and Spending
Responsibility for Active Labor Market Policy among Individual Types of Budgets

	Budgetary Burden of Unemployment (Fiscal Costs of Unemployment)				Responsibility for Expenditures for Active Labor Market Policy			
	Central Government	Member States/ Local Governments	Unemployment Insurance	Pension Insurance/ Health Insurance	Central Government	Member States/ Local Governments	Unemployment Insurance	Pension Insurance/ Health Insurance
Austria	X	X	XX	X				XXX
F.R. Germany	X	X	XX	X				XXX
France	XX		X	XX	XXX			
Great Britain	XXX		XX		XXX			
Sweden[a]	XXX	X		X	XXX	X		
U.S.A.[a]	XX	X	XX	X	XXX		X	

XXX = More than 60%.
XX = 30% to 60%.
X = 10% to 30%.

a) Data on the institutional distribution of the costs of unemployment for Sweden and the U.S.A. are
based on crude estimates; see table 12 above.

labor market policy expenditures. Table 22 clarifies these interrelationships and incentive patterns that at least partially explain national differences in the degree of activity of labor market policy.

In Great Britain, practically all active labor market policy measures are financed through the central government budget, which also bears the total costs of unemployment—if one includes the closely linked national insurance fund. Possible budgetary relief through active programs thus coincides with the location of responsibility for an active policy and the corresponding budgetary burdens. It is therefore not surprising that net cost calculations play a considerable role in the budgeting process for labor market policy in Great Britain, and frequent references to the low net costs of active labor market programs by the British employment ministry have contributed greatly to the introduction and expansion of these programs (Reissert 1985:126 f.; Barnett 1982:128 f.). The fact that the degree of activity of labor market policy in Great Britain has remained constant over time is at least in part a result of this factor.

In Austria, the unemployment insurance fund is responsible for all expenditures for active labor market policy but bears only about half of the fiscal burden of unemployment. Thus, only about half of the potential budgetary relief from labor market policy initiatives goes to the institution responsible for such expenditures. The budgetary relief that such measures yield for the federal government are of no significance for the unemployment insurance fund because it is completely separate from the federal budget and has to finance its expenditure increases solely through contributions. The considerable program-related budgetary relief that results for the *Länder* and local governments and for the pension and health insurance systems also does not benefit the unemployment insurance system. Under these circumstances of institutional incongruity between budgetary burdens and possible budgetary benefits, net cost calculations play hardly any role in the budgeting process for labor market policy in Austria (Wagner 1983). This is at least one reason why labor market programs have hardly replaced the financing of unemployment benefits and the degree of activity of labor market policy has declined considerably in Austria. The situation in the United States is similar. The federal budget is almost exclusively responsible for expenditures for active labor market policy; the budgetary relief that they entail goes largely to the benefit of individual state unemployment insurance systems and other public budgets. This institutional incongruity is one important reason why net cost calculations are seldom used as an argument for a stronger activation of U.S. labor market policy.

In Sweden, the costs of unemployment are borne, in addition to the central government budget, above all by the pension insurance system and—because of local income taxation and responsibility for public assistance—by the local and provincial governments (Wadensjö 1985). Responsibility for expenditures for active labor market policy lies essentially with the central government budget and with the budgets of the local and provincial governments, which have to contribute a considerable share of the cost of job creation measures. Despite the greater institutional fragmentation of the costs of unemployment in Sweden (e.g., in comparison to Great Britain), the potential budgetary relief through active labor market policy goes largely to the same institutions that bear the budgetary burden of active measures. This institutional congruity of fiscal costs and benefits has promoted the use of net cost calculations in Sweden—as in Great Britain —and has facilitated the substitution of active labor market policy measures for the financing of unemployment and, hence, a high degree of activity in Sweden.

The Federal Republic of Germany and France represent an intermediate position with regard to the above sketched incentive effects for a more active labor market policy. In the Federal Republic, about two-thirds of the costs of unemployment are borne by the tightly interrelated budgets of the federal government and the Federal Employment Institute, which is responsible for active labor market policy.

Thus, there is neither a complete institutional congruity of fiscal costs and benefits nor a complete incongruity. Net cost calculations to the benefit of a more active labor market policy play neither a particularly large role nor a small role in the Federal Republic of Germany in comparison with other countries (Bruche and Reissert 1985:132–39). In France, the fragmentation of the costs of unemployment offers in principle little incentive for active labor market policy. Because, however, a large share of active measures is financed through the training levy paid by firms that have a considerable interest in benefiting from their funds in the form of (collective) training measures, there are, in a different form, considerable financial incentives for an activation of labor market policy. This explains in part why French labor market policy has a relatively high degree of activity among the countries investigated.

CHAPTER 9

The Effects of Financing Systems on the Business Cycle and on Regional, Sectoral, and Interpersonal Redistribution

9.1 The Dynamics of Expenditures for Active Labor Market Policy in Relationship to the Business Cycle and Unemployment

Ideally, expenditures for active labor market policy would exhibit a countercyclical pattern, rising as the labor market situation deteriorates (growing problem pressure) and declining as the labor market situation improves. It is, therefore, interesting to examine the development of expenditures for labor market policy in comparison with GDP growth (as a crude indicator of the general economic situation) and the unemployment rate (as a crude indicator of the labor market situation).[1] This section examines the extent to which expenditures for active labor market policy in individual countries conform to the ideal pattern and the role therein played by financing systems.

9.1.1 Fluctuations in Expenditure for Active Labor Market Policy in Relationship to the Business Cycle

Table 23 below and Figure 9 earlier in section 8.2 provide an overview of fluctuations in the level of expenditure for active labor market policy (as a percentage of GDP) between 1973 and 1988; Table 24 summarizes data on variation in the level of expenditures. It is apparent that expenditures for active labor market policy in all countries investigated, with the exception of Austria, varied considerably over time. Two different groups of countries can be distinguished according to their coefficients of variation (which standardize the sometimes considerable differences in level of expenditures among countries): Sweden, the Federal Republic of Germany, Austria, and France with a

Table 23
Expenditures for Active Labor Market Policy (% GDP)

	Austria	F.R. Germany	France	Great Britain	Sweden	U.S.A.
1973	0.16	0.49	0.59		1.52	0.24
1974	0.18	0.57	0.67	0.23	1.28	0.20
1975	0.20	0.77	0.72	0.30	1.20	0.26
1976	0.17	0.58	0.74	0.47	1.59	0.36
1977	0.16	0.52	0.86	0.55	2.16	0.39
1978	0.18	0.56	0.99	0.53	2.25	0.60
1979	0.18	0.66	0.95	0.51	2.10	0.52
1980	0.15	0.71	0.97	0.65	1.83	0.40
1981	0.16	0.84	1.07	0.65	1.68	0.32
1982	0.19	0.82	1.14	0.64	1.80	0.19
1983	0.23	0.79	1.12	0.75	1.96	0.17
1984	0.21	0.74	1.15	0.79	1.95	0.13
1985	0.25	0.72	1.18	0.76	1.81	0.14
1986	0.28	0.79	1.30	0.88	1.67	0.14
1987	0.31	0.90	1.35	0.87	1.57	0.12
1988	0.20	0.90	1.37	0.79	1.44	0.11

Table 24
Average Level of Expenditures for Active Labor Market Policy (1973 - 1988),
Coefficient of Variation and Amplitude of Fluctuation

	Expenditures for Active Labor Market Policy as Percentage of GDP, Average 1973-1988	Coefficient of Variation for Active Expenditures, 1973-1988[a]	Difference between Highest and Lowest Year for Active Expenditures as Percentage of GDP
Austria	0.20	0.22	0.16
F.R. Germany	0.71	0.18	0.41
France	1.01	0.23	0.78
Great Britain[b]	0.62	0.30	0.65
Sweden	1.74	0.17	1.06
U.S.A.	0.27	0.54	0.48

a) Coefficient of variation = Standard deviation/Mean.
b) 1974 - 1988.

low degree of variation, and Great Britain and the United States with greater dispersion of the volume of expenditures in relationship to the median. The United States and Great Britain thus manifest—independent of the average level of expenditures—the greatest flexibility in expenditures.

If one takes the sometimes large differences in the national levels of expenditure into account by examining the amplitude of fluctuations between the highest and the lowest expenditure levels as a percentage of gross domestic product, a somewhat modified picture emerges. In Austria, the observed stability is confirmed with the maximum variation amounting only to 0.16 percent of GDP. Despite their greater dispersion, Great Britain and the United States fall in a middle group with Germany and France in which the highest levels of expenditure are 0.4 to 0.8 percentage points of GDP above the lows. Finally, the very high level of expenditures in Sweden results in a large difference of one percentage point between the highest and lowest percentage values.

The coefficients of variation and amplitudes of fluctuations as a percentage of GDP are, of course, only statistical values that can be the result of quite different developments—as Figure 9 and Table 23 demonstrate. Thus, although Great Britain and the United States have comparable coefficients of variation, the dynamic of expenditures over time is quite different. While the two countries begin the period with similar levels of expenditure for labor market policy, their levels differ greatly at the end of the period. In order to correctly interpret the quantitative measure of variation over time, it is necessary to compare the dynamic of expenditures with the development of the economy and the labor market.

Therefore, we examine in a second step the relationship between the development of expenditures for active labor market policy and changes in the state of the economy and the labor market situation. Figure 13 shows the relationship for the six countries investigated among the development of expenditures for active labor market policy, GNP growth rates, and the unemployment rate.

Figure 13 (see also Table 25) shows that only Sweden has consistently varied expenditures countercyclically in order to smooth out the curve of the unemployment rate. Expenditures for active labor market policy (as a percentage of GDP) show a negative correlation with the real rate of growth. The Federal Republic of Germany also manifests—at a lower average level of expenditures—an initially countercyclical pattern of expenditures, which, however, always culminates with a certain time lag in a clearly procyclical pattern. The variation in the volume of expenditures in Sweden is above all a result of quick changes in the scope of job creation measures. The use of training measures is also adjusted with a somewhat greater delay. In Germany, it is particularly expenditures for short-time work and in part also for training and job creation programs that account for the observed variations in expenditures.

In the other countries studied, one finds (with minor exceptions in Great Britain) no countercyclical variation in the volume of expenditures. In Austria, France, and Great Britain, expenditures for active

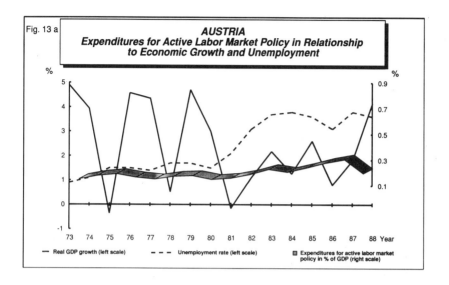

Fig. 13 a

AUSTRIA
Expenditures for Active Labor Market Policy in Relationship to Economic Growth and Unemployment

— Real GDP growth (left scale)   - - - Unemployment rate (left scale)   ▨ Expenditures for active labor market policy in % of GDP (right scale)

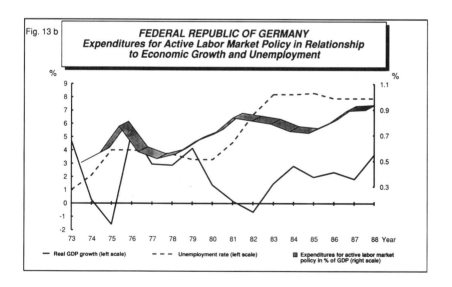

Fig. 13 b

FEDERAL REPUBLIC OF GERMANY
Expenditures for Active Labor Market Policy in Relationship to Economic Growth and Unemployment

— Real GDP growth (left scale)   - - - Unemployment rate (left scale)   ▨ Expenditures for active labor market policy in % of GDP (right scale)

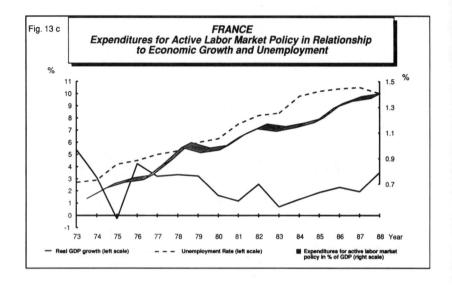

Fig. 13 c

FRANCE
*Expenditures for Active Labor Market Policy in Relationship
to Economic Growth and Unemployment*

— Real GDP growth (left scale)   - - - Unemployment Rate (left scale)   ■ Expenditures for active labor market policy in % of GDP (right scale)

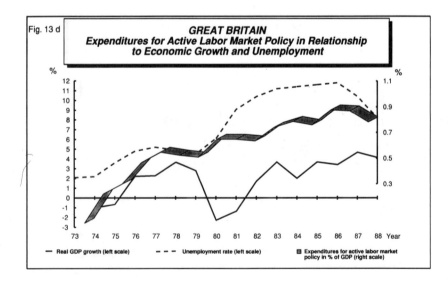

Fig. 13 d

GREAT BRITAIN
*Expenditures for Active Labor Market Policy in Relationship
to Economic Growth and Unemployment*

— Real GDP growth (left scale)   - - - Unemployment rate (left scale)   ■ Expenditures for active labor market policy in % of GDP (right scale)

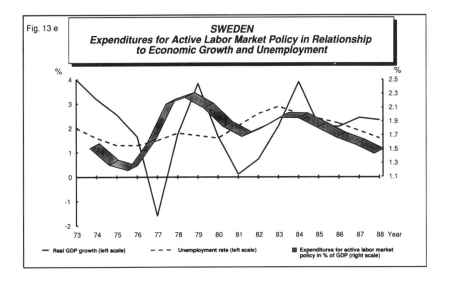

Fig. 13 e

SWEDEN
Expenditures for Active Labor Market Policy in Relationship
to Economic Growth and Unemployment

— Real GDP growth (left scale)   – – – Unemployment rate (left scale)   ▨ Expenditures for active labor market policy in % of GDP (right scale)

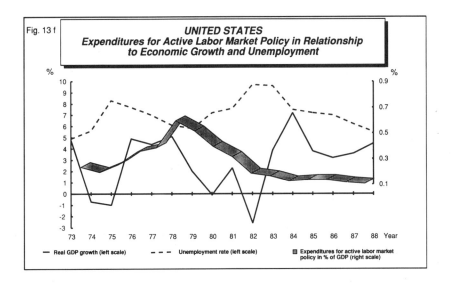

Fig. 13 f

UNITED STATES
Expenditures for Active Labor Market Policy in Relationship
to Economic Growth and Unemployment

— Real GDP growth (left scale)   – – – Unemployment rate (left scale)   ▨ Expenditures for active labor market policy in % of GDP (right scale)

Table 25
Comparative Interpretation of Figure 13

	Austria	F.R. Germany	France	Great Britain	Sweden	U.S.A
Active labor market policy as percentage of GDP (A) and GDP growth rate (G)	A constant, independent of variation in G	A variation 1974-76 and 1980-81 countercyclical, 1977-79, 1982-83 and 1986-88 procyclical	Predominantly increasing A independent of G fluctuations, A slightly countercyclical in 1977-78 and 1980-81	In part countercyclical (1975-77, 1980, 1984), in part procyclical fluctuations in A	Until 1979 and after 1985 countercyclical fluctuations in A, 1980-81 and 1983-84 procyclical fluctuations	Rise and decline in A with procyclical tendency 1975-80 and 1982. After 1984, A stable, independent of G
Active labor market policy expenditures as percentage of GDP (A) and unemployment rate (UR)	A and UR parallel, but little response to UR increase after 1981	1974-75 A and UR parallel, 1976-80 procyclical tendency (A declines when UR constant, and A increases when UR declines), 1980-81 parallel, 1982 and thereafter procyclical	Most of time A and UR vary roughly in tandem, only 1978 decline in A despite increasing UR, 1988 vice versa	A increases when UR increases (sometimes with a time lag)	UR on the whole constant as result of countercyclical variation in A, after 1981 A and UR parallel	On the whole inverse relationship between A and UR, after 1983 A und UR parallel
Summary categorization	Noncyclical use of labor market measures under slight influence of labor market developments	Countercyclical use of labor market measures at beginning of downturn. Subsequently procyclical variation in measures	Noncyclical, long-term increasing tendency under the influence of labor market developments	Sometimes countercyclical variation, mostly noncyclical increasing trend under the influence of labor market developments	Mostly countercyclical application of labor market measures	Mostly procyclical use of labor market measures often contrary to labor market trends

labor market policy developed approximately parallel to the development of the labor market situation. In France and Great Britain, there was a secular trend toward higher expenditures and rising unemployment; this trend included a large increase in the level of expenditures for measures to combat youth unemployment. In the United States, the development of expenditures for active labor market policy was usually procyclical and contrary to the trend on the labor market. Only since 1984 has active labor market policy moved parallel to labor market developments.

9.1.2 Financing Systems and the Dynamics of Active Labor Market Policy

It should be emphasized again that the characteristics of financing systems represent only one of a multiplicity of factors that influence the scope and effectiveness of active labor market policy. The complexity of the causal relationships involved—as well as the small number of cases investigated here—makes it impossible to isolate the impact of individual factors.

In Austria, the stability of expenditures for active labor market policy was facilitated by low unemployment, which was a consequence of a successful countercyclical economic policy. The unemployment insurance fund did not face the need to pay wage-replacement benefits to a rapidly increasing number of unemployed. Moreover, revenues from the contributions to unemployment insurance grew rapidly during the period investigated—more than three times as fast as did the overall economy (see Appendix). Among other reasons, this was because of the disproportionate increases in the ceiling on income subject to contributions. As a consequence, the unemployment insurance fund had considerable room for maneuvering. These resources were used primarily to improve wage-replacement benefits (including the payment of pension insurance contributions for the unemployed) rather than for the expansion of active labor market policy. This was partly a result of limitations on the capacity of the labor administration to implement active measures. A more important factor, however, was the influence of the trade unions,[2] which regarded labor market policy primarily as an instrument of incomes policy and—in contrast to, for example, the case of Sweden—showed little interest in an expansion of active labor market policy.

The countercyclical variation in expenditures at the beginning of economic downturns and the subsequent transition to a procyclical pattern of expenditures in the Federal Republic of Germany is partly attributable to the financing system and partly to the policy instruments used. The relatively generous conditions for the use of short-time work and their position as an entitlement lead to a rapid expansion of this instrument for preserving employment in the initial phase of cyclical downturn and a likewise automatic decline during a recovery. Because training programs for the unemployed are also an entitlement, this area also reacts with a certain sensitivity to changes in the number of unemployed. The repeatedly observed transition to a procyclical pattern of expenditure is to a large extent a result of the financing system. When unemployment increases at the beginning of an economic downturn, the Federal Employment Institute usually has accumulated reserve funds at its disposal sufficient to finance both the increased need for wage-replacement benefits and increased expenditures for active labor market policy. However, when a sharp economic downturn occurs, the reserves of the FEI are quickly exhausted. The federal government must cover the ensuing deficit and initiates restrictive measures to eliminate it, which primarily affect active labor market policy programs because they can be most easily reduced. In the long run, there are again surpluses caused by the cutbacks and improvements in the labor market situation, and reserves are again accumulated that also flow into active programs. The consequence of this deficit-surplus rhythm is a pattern of expenditures for active labor market policy that turns from being countercyclical to being procyclical and finally, when unemployment remains constant, again becomes expansive (Bruche and Reissert 1985:125–31).

The long-term trend toward increasing expenditures for active labor market policy, along with increasing unemployment observed in France and Great Britain, is largely determined by political priorities and the structural problem of growing youth unemployment. Expenditures for passive programs have no influence on trends in expenditures for active labor market policy or only insofar as the central government budget as a whole comes under pressure. Because active labor market policy in Great Britain is exclusively financed through the central government budget, political priorities can be relatively easily translated into expenditures. The obstacles lie primarily in the insufficient capacity for implementation, which has led to a consistent failure to spend available funds. The consistent trend and the high rates of increase observed in France can, in part, be explained by the fragmentation of the budgeting process and the partial financing of training measures through special-purpose levies. Both factors have made a broad mobilization of resources possible and have kept labor market policy from being a highly visible block of expenditures that might become the object of budget cutbacks.

The trend in expenditures for active labor market policy in the United States is unique among the countries investigated. In no other country has there been such a break in the long-term trend toward increasing expenditures; expenditures actually show a long-term decline (not only in relationship to gross domestic product but also absolutely). This development can be explained in terms of a number of political and institutional factors. Because of the almost exclusive financing of active measures from federal general revenues, changes in political priorities can be directly translated into changes in expenditures. Because of its strong position in the budgeting process, priorities are also heavily influenced by changing balances of power in Congress and by the political utility of labor market programs for members of Congress. Finally, also not without significance is the fact that labor market programs have been temporary (until 1983), not based on entitlements, and implemented not by an independent labor market authority with its own institutional self-interest but by local governments, individual states, and special-purpose organizations receiving ad hoc resource allocations from the federal government. All these factors have facilitated flexibility in expenditures in the sense of both the rapid expansion and the following radical contraction of active labor market policy.

In Sweden, there are also a number of more structural or institutional reasons that underlie and promote the massive countercyclical use of active labor market policy—in addition to the basic strategy and strong political basis of the Swedish model of active labor market policy (see Meidner and Hedborg 1984). First, the strong influence of the trade unions and local governments in the budgeting process should be emphasized. In the context of the solidaristic wage policy, trade unions regard active labor market policy as a means of avoiding loss of income for their members and support its countercyclical use particularly for this reason. Local governments regard the countercyclical use of job creation measures as an instrument for preventing long-term unemployment from becoming a financial burden on local government budgets as a result of increasing expenditures for public assistance for those who have exhausted their unemployment benefits. Moreover, since 1976, training measures (which are an entitlement program) receive two-thirds of their funding from a special levy on firms, which rises with the level of expenditures and thus makes possible a short-term expansion of training. The existence of a fixed formula linking the personnel resources available to the volume of program expenditures also facilitates rapid increases in expenditures. Finally, the availability of contingency funds, which can be expended without parliamentary approval, as well as the routinized process for submitting supplementary budget requests promote a flexible response to changing labor market situations.

9.1.3 Summary

We can observe in conclusion that the variation in and responsiveness of expenditures for active labor market policy are influenced by three factors: (1) the type and characteristics of the instruments used, which, according to their function and program conditions, react more or less (or not at all) automatically to changes in the labor market (built-in stabilizer effect); (2) the setting of political priorities, which is not necessarily influenced by the financing side (political priorities); and (3) the financing and budgeting system, which either constitutes a neutral basis for a largely unrestricted politically motivated variation in the volume of expenditures or greatly influences directly or indirectly the level and trend in expenditures through its own dynamic (impact of the financing system).

The Federal Republic of Germany and Austria illustrate how the development of expenditures in integrated systems financed through contributions is more directly dependent on trends in revenues than is the case for systems financed through general revenues in the central government budget. The decisive point is the fact that deficits occurring in a fund financed through contributions can be more easily localized than is the case for expenditures within the central government budget and that in an integrated system there is a direct competitive relationship between active measures and wage-replacement benefits. On the other hand, a direct political intervention in budget decisions and hence a highly unstable pattern of expenditures as in the United States is less likely where financing is based on contributions instead of general revenues. Financing through the central government budget thus entails a greater degree of freedom that may be utilized either for more or for less problem responsiveness. The automatic stabilizer effect, which is built into systems based on contributions and is most pronounced in the Federal Republic of Germany, can constitute a good basis for a labor market policy that is responsive (in its timing) to the labor market situation, if it is not disabled or diminished in its impact by discretionary changes in regulations caused by the localized character of the deficits that occur.

9.2 THE REGIONAL REDISTRIBUTIVE EFFECTS OF LABOR MARKET POLICY

9.2.1 Aspects of Analyzing Redistributive Effects

The financing of labor market policy can have an impact on its regional, sectoral, and individual distribution. For example, one might hypothesize that financing systems based on contributions and insurance principles have less redistributive effects than do tax-financed systems. The actuarial principles on which contribution-based systems are constructed are compatible with intertemporal redistribution of resources but hardly with interregional, intersectoral, or interpersonal redistribution, at least not as a permanent feature and systemic goal.

However, because financing systems are not in reality constructed according to a theoretical design but are rather the product of complicated compromises, historical contingencies, and particular institutional traditions,[3] the above hypothesis is difficult to test empirically. Furthermore, systems based on contributions can in practice also include solidaristic elements (redistribution), and tax-based systems can be linked to special purposes. This mixture of system principles has, moreover, an impact on the behavior of participants which is difficult to predict theoretically. Because of the small number of countries included in our study and the shortcomings in the data available, empirical examination of the above hypothesis is extremely difficult. And we cannot accept Hegel's view that "when the facts do not correspond to theory, too bad for the facts." Nevertheless, this classical idealist attitude has an accurate core: in the long run, a financing system cannot contradict its own inherent goals, or only at the price of a loss of efficiency.

We will, therefore, use our initial hypothesis only as a guiding theme in the following discussion. Our aim is merely to summarize the clearly evident redistributive effects and to consider whether they correspond to our theoretical expectations and why they sometimes deviate from or contradict them. We cannot hope to falsify or verify the initial hypothesis but merely to differentiate it in the course of the following discussion. In examining the regional and sectoral redistributive effects, we also analyze in part the effects of the financing of wage-replacement benefits that were not considered in Part II of our analysis.

In our empirical analysis, we distinguish between two types of redistributive effects:

1. Effects that result exclusively from the allocation of *expenditures* for labor market policy. Here we are concerned with the extent to which the distribution of expenditures for labor market policy to regions, sectors, and groups of persons is problem adequate, responsive to the different problem situations on the labor market.
2. Effects that result from the interrelationship of revenues and expenditures. Here we are concerned with the extent to which the intake of resources for labor market policy and their use on the expenditure side lead to redistribution among regions, sectors, or individuals.

In the following discussion, we attempt to identify these redistributive effects in the individual countries and to determine how they are related to differences in financing systems. Because of the inadequacy of the data available, we have to limit our analysis of interpersonal redistribution to the analysis of distribution of expenditures and cannot always include all countries in comparisons. In investigating the distribution of expenditures for labor market policy and its problem adequacy, we distinguish in principle among three different distributional patterns:[4]

1. The pattern of expenditures is *proportional* when the regional, sectoral, or individual distribution of expenditures for labor market policy corresponds to the percentage shares of individual regions, sectors, or groups of persons among the unemployed.
2. *Selectivity* means that expenditures go disproportionately (i.e., in excess of their percentage share of unemployment) to so-called problem regions, problem sectors, or problem groups. This can be achieved either by excluding regions, sectors, or groups of persons entirely from programs or by giving priority to particularly affected problem regions, sectors, and groups in the application of the instruments of labor market policy.
3. The third pattern can be termed *favoritism*; expenditures flow disproportionately to better-off sectors, regions, or individuals. In this case, problem areas, sectors, and groups are relatively neglected.

These distributional patterns have to be assessed in light of the different labor market and employment policy goals that they may express. For example, the proportional pattern may reflect goals of cyclical demand management, selectivity places more emphasis on goals of social and structural policy, and favoritism can probably only be justified in terms of enhanced efficiency in combination with a policy of promoting regional and occupational mobility.

9.2.2 The Regional Selectivity of Active Labor Market Policy

One of the original ideas of active labor market policy as formulated in Sweden and by the OECD in the 1960s (with a leading Swedish role) was that of regional selectivity. Pockets of unemployment were supposed to receive preferential treatment in the allocation of training and job creation measures, and their labor surplus was supposed to be channeled into more prosperous regions in order to combat both unemployment and inflation. This conception is, of course, outdated in a situation of mass unemployment. However, regional differences in unemployment have persisted and even increased absolutely. Today, as in the past, they still justify regionalized labor market policy (Garlichs, Maier, and Semlinger 1983; Schmid 1983a).

Is there any recognizable relationship between the regional distribution of expenditures for active labor market policy and their financing systems? Is it true that insurance-oriented systems based on contributions are, because of their reliance on actuarial principles, less able to engage in selectivity in the application of labor market policy than are tax-financed systems? Although the data available are limited, some indication is given by data from five of the six countries included in our study.

In the Federal Republic of Germany, a comparison of the percentage share of regional labor offices in expenditures for active measures with their percentage share of total unemployment shows that the regional distribution of active measures of the Federal Employment Institute essentially corresponds to the pattern of favoritism (Bruche and Reissert 1985:150–54; Reissert 1988). Districts with low unemployment rates (Baden-Württemberg, Hesse) receive a disproportionately high percentage of expenditures, while districts with very high levels of unemployment (Lower Saxony/ Bremen, North-Rhine Westphalia, Berlin) receive a disproportionately low share of expenditures. Expenditures for active labor market policy are clearly not concentrated in problem regions.[5] A more detailed breakdown of expenditures shows that districts with a favorable labor market situation receive a disproportionately high share of expenditures especially in those policy areas in which programs are largely provided as entitlements and in which there is little or no effort to concentrate the instruments on problem groups (training and retraining, short-time compensation, programs for the construction industry, rehabilitation). In the case of discretionary programs of labor market policy (job creation programs, mobility assistance), regions with lower unemployment are, by contrast, underrepresented while regions with particularly poor labor market situations are as a rule overrepresented. At least in the area of job creation measures, a pattern of selectivity in expenditures can be observed.

There are various possible explanations for the predominance of favoritism in important areas of active labor market policy in the Federal Republic of Germany. The concentration of active programs on persons who otherwise would have claim to unemployment benefits or unemployment assistance (benefit recipients) can result in regions with relatively few long-term unemployed, youth, or women (who often are not eligible for benefits) receiving a relatively large share of program resources. In the case of short-time compensation, the disproportionately high uptake in regions with relatively low unemployment—especially Baden-Württemberg—may be explained by the fact that their relatively favorable labor market situation makes it easier to ride out economic downturns with short-time work. In the case of training and rehabilitation measures, a superior infrastructure of schools, personnel, and so on, can be one reason for the higher uptake in areas with low unemployment. The regions with a more favorable labor market situation are better able to implement active measures because the labor offices in these regions are less tied down with the administration of unemployment, that is, the provision of unemployment benefits. Personnel reallocations among regions are rare even when there are marked regional differences in the development of unemployment.

The results for Austria, the other system of active labor market policy investigated that is based on contributions, are not as clear as in the case of the Federal Republic. In Austria, too, most provinces (*Länder*) with disproportionately high unemployment receive lower percentage shares of expenditures for active labor market policy (Burgenland, Kärnten, Niederösterreich) (according to 1984 data); the Steiermark is, however, an exception in that it has a relatively high level of unemployment and also receives a disproportionately large share of expenditures. There is thus also a pattern of favoritism in Austria—as our hypothesis anticipates. It is, however, not as strong as in the Federal Republic of Germany.

A comparison of the regional percentage shares of expenditures for active labor market policy with the regional distribution of unemployment in 1982 and 1983 in Great Britain shows a proportional pattern of distribution: the percentage share of expenditures in individual regions is practically identical with their percentage share of unemployment (for England, Scotland, and Wales; Reissert 1985:113 f.). According to budget plans—which were not fully implemented because not all available funds were expended—the regions with highest unemployment (Scotland and Wales) were even to receive a slightly larger share of expenditures; there was a weak pattern of selectivity. This corresponds to our theoretical expectation that tax-financed systems of active labor market policy are more likely to exhibit a pattern of selectivity or at least proportional expenditures than are systems based on contributions, because more prosperous regions can be expected to resist a large and persistent redistribution of contributions to crisis regions as a violation of insurance principles. Nevertheless, even Great Britain cannot be said to represent a clear example of a pattern of selectivity (at least not at the level of aggregation analyzed here), although all active labor market policy is financed through the central government budget and thus from general revenues.

Surprisingly, this is also true for Sweden. Although we were only able to compare the percentage share of participants in training measures with the percentage share of unemployment in the twenty-four provinces (*läns*) for the year 1979, there was no region with above-average unemployment that benefited disproportionately from training measures. By contrast, there were many regions with low unemployment and a disproportionately high number of participants. It should, however, be borne in mind that the regional unemployment rates varied only slightly (with one exception, Norrbotten) around the low average rate of unemployment of 2 percent. Moreover, as suggested above, the distribution of training measures has to be regarded differently from, for example, problem-group-oriented job creation measures or wage-cost subsidies to facilitate reintegration. Favoritism can be justified here in terms of efficiency criteria, that is, in terms of policy goals of growth and mobility. Finally, the extent to which already prospering regions are favored in expenditures for training is relatively slight; one can describe it as a pattern of distribution that lies between favoritism and a proportional pattern.

The findings for the United States are less ambiguous than in the case of Sweden. A comparison of expenditures for various active labor market programs in individual states in 1980–81 with their percentage share of unemployment shows that the distribution of resources in all important programs is selective—if sometimes weakly. States with higher unemployment tend to receive disproportionately more funds, and vice versa. These findings for a tax-financed system confirm our original hypothesis. The results are not surprising because federal funds for labor market policy are distributed according to formulas that are problem-group oriented (see section 7.3 above).

In summary, it can be said that in the countries investigated, systems of active labor market policy financed through contributions tend toward a regional distribution of resources that exhibits a pattern of favoritism (the Federal Republic of Germany) or at least a proportional pattern (Austria); there is no selectivity to the benefit of problem regions. By contrast, tax-financed systems permit a selective pattern (United States and, at least in budget plans, also Great Britain). There is, however, no guarantee that such a policy will be implemented. If active labor market policy is differentiated according to types of measures, clearly problem-group-oriented instruments of labor market policy—such as job creation measures—may reflect a pattern of selectivity even in systems financed through contributions.

A regional distribution of the scarce resources for active labor market policy that is problem adequate requires a deliberate and comprehensive selectivity in the targeting of resources. For this purpose, resources have to be concentrated on problem groups (and not on benefit recipients), and the regional distribution of resources should reflect the relative urgency of regional labor market problems. In contribution systems such as the Federal Republic of Germany, such an orientation of active labor market policy conflicts with the actuarial outlook derived from the unemployment insurance system, which is a consequence of the joint financing of passive and active labor market policy through a common fund financed by contributions. In this system, a stronger selective orientation of the instruments of active labor market policy is resisted by regions with more favorable labor market situations, which attempt to recoup part of their contribution payments especially through active labor market policy. A further obstacle is the distribution of infrastructural and personnel resources among the regions for the administration and implementation of labor market programs. Only a redistribution of these types of resources in favor of regions with less favorable labor market situations (or an expansion of capacity in these regions without reduction elsewhere) would make it possible to alter the distribution of the volume of programs.[6]

9.2.3 Stabilization of Regional Demand

A further interesting question for labor market policy is the extent to which patterns of revenues and expenditures lead to an interregional redistribution. If the flow of labor market policy revenues and expenditures redistributes resources to regions particularly affected by unemployment, it can partially offset the loss of purchasing power resulting from unemployment and hence contribute to the stabilization of regional demand.

The regional stabilizer effect of labor market policy and its financing can be best studied by examining the revenue and expenditure balances for individual regions. Astonishingly, no detailed regional breakdown of revenues and expenditures for labor market policy is available (at least no published data) for any of the countries investigated here. Some incomplete information can be found for Great Britain, the United States, and Germany.

In the Federal Republic of Germany, data on expenditures and on revenues from contributions of the Federal Employment Institute are available for the nine regional labor offices (Bruche and Reissert 1985:147–49; Reissert 1988). The results show a considerable interregional redistributive process. The magnitude of the redistribution between the constituent states (*Länder*) through the German labor market authority, the Federal Employment Institute, is approximately as large as that through the regular revenue-sharing system between the states. Particularly Baden-Württemberg but also Hesse and southern Bavaria are net payers of labor market policy; Lower Saxony/Bremen, Schleswig-Holstein/Hamburg, northern Bavaria, and Rhineland-Palatinate/Saarland are net recipients. This redistributive pattern largely reflects differences in regional labor market problems—although not exactly. Although the redistributive process through revenues from contributions and the payment of unemployment benefits flows in the direction of the intensity of unemployment, this is less the case for active labor market policy because a considerable share of active measures—as described above—goes disproportionately to regions with relatively favorable labor market situations (and correspondingly high payments in contributions).

An analysis available for Great Britain comes to a similar conclusion (Disney 1984; Reissert 1985:103–10). In the case of Great Britain, the regional redistributive effects of wage-replacement benefits and their financing system are even greater than those resulting from all programs of state regional policy. The regional redistributive effect of the supplementary benefit for the unemployed and its financing through taxation is greater than that of the unemployment benefit financed through social security contributions. This result is in accord with our hypothesis. It is a result particularly of the fact that the (largely progressive) taxes used to finance supplementary benefit through the central government budget take more resources from regions with relatively favorable economic and labor market situations than do (proportional) social security contributions.

The situation in the United States is quite different. Unemployment insurance is largely regulated by the individual states and financed through contributions to the individual state systems. The federal government provides special benefits which are financed in part through the federal budget. If the individual state unemployment insurance systems are no longer able to cover the costs of unemployment benefits through their own revenues from contributions (e.g., because of high unemployment), they receive loans from the federal government to finance their deficits. This limited regional redistribution is only temporary because the federal loan has to be repaid and the debtor states face financial sanctions (interest payments on the loan, an increase in the federal unemployment insurance contribution). As a result of its far-reaching decentralization, the U.S. unemployment insurance system plays practically no role in stabilizing regional demand. This is evident from the different financial situations of the individual state unemployment insurance funds. Low contribution rates and stable financing are the rule in states with more favorable labor market situations, whereas contribution rates and deficits are high in states with unfavorable labor market situations. At the end of 1983, four states with high rates of unemployment (Illinois, Michigan, Ohio, Pennsylvania) accounted for 70 percent of the outstanding loans made by the federal government to individual state unemployment insurance systems (Vroman 1986).

In summary, the financing of labor market policy not only operates as a general economic stabilizer over the course of the business cycle but can also serve to stabilize regional demand. Revenues from contributions and taxes are relatively high in regions with less unemployment, and the expenditures for wage-replacement benefits (and possibly also for active labor market policy) are relatively low. In regions with high levels of unemployment, the situation is reversed. Under the conditions of a balanced labor market budget, demand in regions with particularly high levels of unemployment (net recipients) is stabilized by the rechanneling of demand from regions with particularly low levels of unemployment (net payers). Of course, the prerequisites for this effect are a centralized system of revenues and expenditures (in contrast to the decentralized U.S. system), contributions structured according to ability to pay (or tax financing), and a pattern of expenditures that is at least proportional if not selective.

9.3 THE SECTORAL SELECTIVITY OF LABOR MARKET POLICY

Employment risks are also unequally distributed in sectoral terms, and within the same economic sector they vary from enterprise to enterprise. Depending on how this structure of risk is reflected in labor market policy and its financing, different patterns of distribution and presumably also different patterns of response by employers and employees result.

9.3.1 The Sectoral Distribution of Expenditures

In principle, distribution can be influenced either from the revenue or from the expenditure side. A sectoral targeting of expenditures is, however, seldom found in labor market policy. Interesting exceptions in the case of wage-replacement benefits are found in France and the United States. In France, the unemployed who are laid off for "economic reasons" received considerably higher wage-replacement benefits than did other unemployed persons during certain periods; because dismissals for economic reasons occur mostly in crisis sectors such as steel and mining, this special regulation (*allocation speciale*) has indirectly had an intersectoral redistributive effect. In the United States, special extended unemployment benefits—financed through federal funds—for workers who lost their jobs in sectors facing strong international competition (Trade Adjustment Assistance) have sometimes existed.

In both cases, the wage-replacement benefits were an alternative to protectionist measures and designed to facilitate structural change. This example of the instrumentalization of wage-replacement benefits for active goals illustrates that it is not always valid to identify benefits with passive labor market policy.[7] It is noteworthy that the active sectoral instrumentalization of wage-replacement benefits was entirely (United States) or largely (France) financed through the central government budget. Such a strategy would be difficult to reconcile with financing based purely on contributions.

The example of bad weather benefits in the Federal Republic of Germany, which are financed through contributions to the Federal Employment Institute, shows that financing through contributions does not exclude selectivity on the expenditure side. (We include bad weather benefits among the active instruments in labor market policy because it is a measure to preserve employment.) The financing through general contributions of an instrument limited to the construction industry represents, however, a unique exception. In Austria, bad weather benefits are largely financed through a levy paid by employers and employees in the construction industry; this instrument does not exist in other countries. Otherwise sector-specific risks are as a rule financed through levy systems organized at the sectoral level or through risk-related contribution rates (see more on this below).

Seasonal and short-term cyclical risks clearly represent borderline cases that, although not strictly confined to certain sectors, are in fact very concentrated in sectoral terms. This distribution of claims means that financing systems that do not differentiate among industries lead inevitably to intersectoral redistributive effects. The construction industry in the Federal Republic of Germany is a clear example. Because only part of the expenditures of the Federal Employment Institute that go to this industry are raised through a special levy on the construction industry (the winter construction levy), enterprises and employees in the construction industry are to a considerable extent subsidized by other branches of industry. The volume of this net transfer in favor of the construction industry amounts to between 0.5 billion and 1 billion deutsche marks annually (Bruche and Reissert 1985:155). The tourist industry as well as certain rapidly shrinking areas such as coal and steel are likely to exhibit similar positive balances.

There have also been a number of investigations dealing with the sectoral redistributive effects of labor market policy in Sweden, particularly with regard to the construction industry. The findings resemble those for Germany: the construction industry is subsidized to a considerable extent by unemployment insurance (including the large state subsidies in Sweden) (Björklund and Holmlund 1983; Edelbalk and Wadensjö 1978). Swedish agricultural and forestry workers as well as dock workers and fishermen also receive significant net subsidies (Björklund and Holmlund 1986:57). The fact that employees' contributions to the various Swedish unemployment insurance funds are in principle risk-related fails to reduce this redistributive effect, because there is only a weak relationship to the actual risk of unemployment, and contributions themselves account for only a small share of revenues for wage-replacement benefits.

Cross-subsidies between branches of industry with resulting competitive distortions are presumably less in the U.S. unemployment insurance system than in Germany or Sweden. Because contribution rates in the United States are determined by experience rating, they reflect the dismissals (or temporary layoffs) occurring in firms in past years. The essential difference to Sweden consists in the fact that contributions are paid only by employers and that contribution rates reflect the actual incidence of dismissals in *individual* enterprises and not a (hypothetical) industry-specific group risk. The goal is to internalize part of the costs of dismissals and layoffs. In this way, dismissals are supposed to be made less attractive for firms in a situation in which legal protection against dismissal is slight or nonexistent. However, contribution rates only vary between certain limits and thus fail to fully reflect risk. For example, because most firms in the U.S. construction industry already pay the highest contribution rates, further dismissals usually do not entail any additional costs.

The relationship among financing, intersectoral redistribution, and the reactions of individual firms (employment practices) has hardly been researched. For example, it would be interesting to examine whether a permanent de facto subsidy for some sectors (e.g., the construction industry) through unemployment insurance impedes competitiveness and modernization in these sectors. A study of the Swedish construction industry provides some evidence in this respect. The study was possible because of the fortunate circumstance that the Swedish construction industry was first covered by the unemployment insurance system in 1964. There was thus a clear before-and-after situation with regard to employment practices. Econometric analyses confirm the hypothesis that the inclusion of the construction industry in the unemployment insurance system functioned like a wage subsidy, maintaining employment at a higher level than it would have been under purely market conditions (Edelbalk and Wadensjö 1978). More research is necessary to determine whether this cross-subsidization is justified. The following arguments can, for example, be advanced in favor of this practice: the demand for construction work is heavily regulated, the maintenance of excess capacity may be desirable for reasons of public policy, and uncontrollable risks (weather conditions, seasonal fluctuations) should be borne collectively.

The financing of measures to maintain employment during short-term cyclical fluctuations in demand represents a similar borderline case. In the Federal Republic of Germany, this is the function of short-time benefits, which are financed by general contributions to the Federal Employment Institute (i.e., from a common pool). This program, which is an entitlement, is in a comparative perspective rather unique. Only France has a similar program, but the French employers have to bear a considerably greater share of financing than in Germany, and uptake is much lower. If financing takes place from a common pool and large sectoral differences in vulnerability to cyclical downturns exist, then considerable intersectoral redistribution can be expected to occur. There are, however, no extant analyses of this phenomenon.

In Sweden, where temporary layoffs (*permittering*) have also been partially financed through unemployment insurance, there has been a shift toward an increased reliance on risk-related levy financing. In the new system of temporary layoffs employers have to bear the full wage costs themselves on certain days (on the 1st, 2nd, 3rd, 11th, 12th, 21st, and 22nd day), and on the other days (up to a maximum of 23) the full wage costs are borne equally by the short-time work fund (financed through a levy on employers of 0.05 percent of payroll) and a state subsidy. If layoffs exceed thirty days, the employer must again bear the full cost of wages. The participation of enterprises is voluntary and regulated by collective agreements. The higher costs for firms are offset by a weakening of employees' protection against temporary layoffs and hence a greater flexibility in the use of short-time work. As a result of the built-in system of cost sharing depending on the duration and incidence of short-time work, enterprises now have an incentive to organize consecutive and, if possible, longer-term periods of short-time work (of up to twenty or thirty days) because their share of the costs declines with the duration of the layoff period (to about 50 percent) (Edelbalk and Wadensjö 1986).

Comparable programs exist in the United States only in individual states (and mostly on an experimental basis). The U.S. functional equivalent, temporary layoffs, is financed through the unemployment insurance system (insofar as its prerequisites are fulfilled). Because of the incompleteness of experience rating, enterprises that have already reached the highest contribution rate have an incentive to engage in frequent temporary layoffs. One must, therefore, assume that in the United States, as (to a lesser extent) in Sweden, seasonal and cyclical differences in the uptake of unemployment insurance benefits lead to intersectoral redistribution.

9.3.2 The Sectoral Distribution of Revenues

The revenue side of financing also contributes to sectoral selectivity in labor market policy. The central issue here (in addition to that of the risk-relatedness of contributions discussed above) is the basis for calculating unemployment insurance contributions and the fear that contributions paid as a percentage of wages will have a negative impact on employment. We have already reviewed the German discussion of this topic elsewhere (Bruche and Reissert 1985:182 ff.), and a brief summary is sufficient for our purposes here.

When contributions (to unemployment insurance) are proportional to wages and the ceiling on covered wages is high (as in the Federal Republic, France, and Austria), it is reasonable to assume that labor-intensive branches of industry have to bear a relatively greater burden of contributions than do capital-intensive ones. Insofar as the latter are industries that are rapidly declining or undergoing intensive rationalization, then their heavy payments in contributions correspond to the high expenditures for unemployment that they cause. The extent to which redistribution of the burden of unemployment takes place in the sense that labor-intensive branches of industry have to bear part of the burden of expenditures for unemployment caused by capital-intensive industries requires more detailed investigation.

There would certainly be an interindustry shift in the financial burden of unemployment insurance if contributions were not (only) paid as a percentage of wages but also, for example, of value added. Capital-intensive industries would then have to pay more and labor-intensive ones less. A review of simulations for the Federal Republic of Germany concludes, however, that the interindustry shift in financial burden would constitute only a very small fraction of the value of production in most branches of industry (Bruche and Reissert 1985:189). Whether a change in the basis of calculating contributions would be beneficial from the point of view of employment policy (see the discussion of the so-called machine tax in the Federal Republic) cannot be definitively answered. Because none of the countries examined here uses value added as a basis for contributions, our international comparison is of no assistance in answering this question. As mentioned above (Chapter 6), we consider the retention of earnings-based contributions to be justified for systemic reasons.

Table 26
Average Weekly Working Hours in Manufacturing

	1974	1978	1983	1986
Austria[a]	39.0	36.3	36.1	35.5
F.R. Germany	41.9	41.6	40.5	40.4
France	42.9	41.0	38.9	38.7
Great Britain[b]	44.0	43.5	42.6	42.7
Sweden	38.7	37.7	37.7	38.3
U.S.A.	40.0	40.4	40.1	40.7

Data source: ILO 1984, 1987, table 12A.

a) Monthly time worked divided by 4.
b) Men only.

Contributions may affect employment not only as a result of their basis (wages and salaries) and the contribution rate but also because of the relationship between the ceiling on earnings subject to contributions and average earnings. If employers' contributions become fixed nonwage labor costs as a consequence of a low ceiling—that is, they only vary per employee but not according to time worked and total pay per employee—then there is an incentive for enterprises to prefer longer working time to additional hires (see Hart 1984).

Econometric simulations for the manufacturing industry in Germany have shown that a reduction in the upper limit on earnings subject to contributions in the social security system would hardly increase the number of employees but instead significantly raise the number of hours worked per employee (Hart and Kawasaki 1985, 1986). The fact that the upper limit on earnings subject to social security contributions is low in the United States but relatively high in France and the Federal Republic of Germany, where it has also increased more rapidly than income during the last fifteen years, could lead to a significant difference between these two countries and the United States in the development of the number of hours actually worked. Table 26 appears to confirm this expectation.

While the average number of hours actually worked has declined in the Federal Republic of Germany and especially in France, it has even risen in the United States. Whether this difference can actually be explained in terms of differences in the ceiling on earnings subject to social security contributions must necessarily remain speculative given the crudeness of the data and the multiplicity of causal factors involved. It does, however, seem justified to conclude that an increase in the ceiling will be more likely to have a positive rather than a negative employment effect, if contribution rates remain constant.

9.4 INTERPERSONAL REDISTRIBUTIVE EFFECTS OF LABOR MARKET POLICY

Our initial hypothesis states that tax-financed systems of labor market policy can be expected to have greater interpersonal redistributive effects than if labor market policy is financed through contributions. Our comparison of the terms and conditions of labor market programs in Chapter 7 provides some evidence bearing on this thesis.

In systems financed through contributions, eligibility for active labor market measures is frequently limited to persons who have become entitled to wage-replacement benefits through qualifying employment. Stipends or wage subsidies during participation in such programs are regarded as the equivalent of the benefits to which they would otherwise be entitled. Frequently there is also an entitlement to participate in major programs. By their nature, systems financed through contributions give preference to those with the greatest ability to pay on the revenue side and to those who are as little at risk as possible on the expenditure side. Because the implementation of contribution-financed manpower programs is usually linked to the administration of the unemployment insurance system, a contributor bias tends to develop among administrative officials which can be formulated crudely as follows: those who have paid into the system the most and the longest are given priority in labor market programs so long as the prospects are good that they will again become reliable contributors to unemployment insurance after completion of the program. As a result of this more or less conscious adherence to insurance principles, active labor market policy in systems financed through contributions tends to exhibit a distributional pattern that is either proportional or even more favorable to those with better labor market prospects.[8]

Such considerations are foreign to tax-financed systems. In these systems, participation in active labor market policy programs is often restricted to particular groups of persons who are particularly disadvantaged or disproportionately affected by unemployment. On the other hand, this selectivity also means that the targeting of programs reflects not only social and economic criteria but also political considerations, which can change quickly. One way to test the degree of individual selectivity in systems based on contributions versus those based on taxation would be to compare the variation in selectivity over time. We would expect variation to be greater in tax-financed systems than in systems based on financing through contributions. Unfortunately, there are no long-term time-series data available that are sufficiently detailed and comparable to test this thesis. Considerations of fiscal policy can also affect selectivity in systems financed through general revenues, as when recipients of public assistance are given preference in order to relieve the welfare budgets of governments (at whatever level). In addition, redistribution does not necessarily benefit the most needy; it can also—intentionally or unintentionally—favor those who are better off. For example, during periods of economic prosperity, public job creation measures in Sweden and the United States have been used primarily to provide temporary employment opportunities for disadvantaged persons; during economic downturns, they have been used principally for countercyclical purposes (e.g., for general construction and civil engineering, reforestation, and similar projects) and thus have been more likely to benefit the relatively better labor market prospects among the unemployed.

Tables 27 and 28 summarize available data on the selective impact of two central labor market programs with regard to female participation.[9] Our expectation would be that systems financed through contributions will not show any redistribution in favor of women (a relatively disadvantaged group in the labor market and not a core group among contributors to unemployment insurance), whereas tax-financed systems could (but need not) exhibit such a pattern. The available data on female participation support our thesis. Women are underrepresented in training programs in comparison with their percentage share in total unemployment in Austria and especially in the Federal Republic of Germany (see also Weitzel 1983). By contrast, countries with tax-financed systems of labor market policy—Great Britain, Sweden, and the United States—exhibit a pattern of selectivity or at least a proportional pattern; female participation in programs is as great or greater than their share of all unemployed. In the case of job creation measures, the results are less clear, in part because these programs have only recently been established on a large scale in Austria and France. In the Federal Republic of Germany, women are also underrepresented as expected, but with a tendency toward more equal representation (see also Engelen-Kefer 1986); the same is true for the United States and especially for Sweden in the 1970s and, to a lesser extent, for Great Britain. The explanation in the case of Sweden and the United States is obvious: in both countries,

Table 27
The Financing of Training and Retraining Measures and Their Selective Impact

| | Financing | | | Average Percentage of Women | | | |
| | | | | Unemployed | | Program Participants | |
	C	E	T	1974-1979	1980-1985	1974-1979	1980-1985
Austria	XXX			50[a]	41	40[a]	37
F.R. Germany	XXX			48	46	25	29
France	X	XX	X	n.d.	48[b]	n.d.	n.d
Great Britain			XXX	24	28[c]	43[d]	35[e]
Sweden		X	XX	52	48	55	45
U.S.A.			XXX	47	43[f]	50	52[g]

Note: Includes only longer-term, usually full-time training and retraining measures for adults (basis is usually number of entrants and not average number of participants).

C = Contributions to unemployment insurance.
E = Earmarked levies.
T = Taxation (central government budget).

XXX = Financing exclusively from this source.
XX = Predominant source of financing.
X = Partial financing.

a) 1978-1979.
b) 1984.
c) 1980-1984.
d) 1977.
e) 1980-1984.
f) 1980-1982.
g) 1980-1981.

n.d. = No data available.

particularly in Sweden, job creation measures were initially designed primarily as countercyclical instruments and only subsequently reoriented more selectively toward labor market problem groups. After 1978, temporary public service employment programs in the United States were targeted on disadvantaged persons (especially low-income persons and the long-term unemployed), whereby female participation also increased rapidly. This structurally favorable effect proved, however, to be a pyrrhic victory for active labor market policy. State and local governments lost interest in the program as a result of its increasing orientation toward labor market problem groups so that it was possible to eliminate it with little opposition at the beginning of the Reagan administration.[10]

Table 28
The Financing of Job Creation Measures and Their Selective Impact

	Financing			Average Percentage of Women			
				Unemployed		Program Participants	
	C	E	T	1974-1979	1980-1985	1974-1979	1980-1985
Austria	-	-	-	50[a)]	41	-	-
F.R. Germany	XX		X	48	46	28	35
France	-	-	-	n.d.	48[b)]	-	-
Great Britain			XXX	24	28[c)]	22[d)]	21
Sweden			XXX	52	48	31	38
U.S.A.			XXX	47	43[e)]	41	50[f)]

Note: Temporary supplemental public service employment usually also organized by public sponsors.

C   = Contributions to unemployment insurance.
E   = Earmarked levies.
T   = Taxation (central government budget).

XXX   = Financing exclusively from this source.
XX   = Predominant source of financing.
X   = Partial financing.
-      = Program type little used or not at all.

a)   1978-1979.
b)   1984.
c)   1980-1984.
d)   1978-1980.
e)   1980-1982.
f)   1980-1981.

n.d. = No data available.

PART FOUR

Summary and Conclusions

CHAPTER **10**

Financing Systems as an Institutional Determinant of Labor Market Policy

Most theories have a limited life expectancy. Reality tends to render them rapidly obsolete. One decade of mass unemployment in many OECD countries has refuted widely held theses in comparative politics. Thus, it was maintained, for example, that leftist parties in government are more successful in fighting unemployment than governing parties of the right, whereas the reverse was assumed to be true with respect to fighting inflation. Evidence could be adduced in support of this claim for the 1960s (Hibbs 1977), but it has not fared well in the face of developments in the 1970s (Therborn 1986).

The favorite theme for comparative research—Does politics make a difference?—was subsequently supplemented by the corporatist thesis. According to this thesis, countries with a high degree of unionization and centralized and cooperative industrial relations combined with a leftist governing party are better able to cope with economic crises than countries without such organizational and power arrangements. Numerous studies found evidence in support of this thesis for the 1970s (Cameron 1984; Schmidt 1982; Lange and Garrett 1985), but the 1980s have demonstrated that even countries without such characteristics have been economically successful (e.g., Switzerland, Japan) whereas corporatist model countries (e.g., Austria, the Netherlands) increasingly encountered difficulties (Schmidt 1986; Therborn 1987).

Some theories of state and social expenditures in comparative politics have had a similarly short life span. The standard thesis, for example, that a high and growing level of transfer payments for social security is exclusively associated with leftist governing parties and strong centralized labor movements (Sharpe and Newton 1984) has been falsified by recent studies (Lane 1987).

241

This is not the place to reflect extensively on the short life expectancy of theories in social science. Instead, the present analysis has taken as its point of departure a frequently diagnosed shortcoming: the neglect of historically ingrained institutional arrangements influencing both the formation of political will and the effectiveness of political programs (Scharpf 1987c; Therborn 1987:279; Lane 1987:22). Such arrangements may lead conservative governments to adopt employment policies that one would generally expect only from labor governments. A typical example is the labor market policy of the conservative-liberal coalition government in Sweden that was in power from 1976 to 1982. Conversely, historically rooted traditions may induce leftist governments to adopt policies one would usually label conservative. A typical example is the labor market policy of the Social Democrats in the Federal Republic of Germany, particularly in the period leading up to their removal from office (1981–82).

It seemed to us, therefore, appropriate to modify the question that so far has guided comparative political research by asking whether institutions make a difference. Most comparative studies in this new tradition have concentrated on the systems of regulation and industrial relations. This study has taken up a much neglected aspect of labor market institutions: the system of financing labor market policy. In the following, we summarize the institutional approach from which we started and the main results of our comparative study. The final chapter will draw the policy conclusions.

10.1 INSTITUTIONS MAKE A DIFFERENCE

Institutions, in the form of norms, organizations, procedural and financing regulations, and the distribution of responsibilities and jurisdictions, as well as in the form of habits and traditions, determine which decisions are to be made in a specific situation; who is to decide what, when, and with what resources; and how conflicts between participants are to be settled. Institutions legitimize action as well as inaction. The absence of a full employment policy may therefore well be an expression of an institutional framework that relieves functionally competent organizations (or persons) from their responsibility in an orderly and thus legitimate fashion. The question arising at this point is which institutions ensure that responsibility for effective employment action is assigned in an adequate fashion with respect to its timing, relevance, and social implications.

Institutions function as filters for information and interests, as incentives for individual and collective decision makers, or as norms for individual or collective behavior, and thus immediately narrow the range of conceivable decisions and actions. They function selectively vis-à-vis possible alternatives for action by favoring some and impeding or altogether precluding others (Commons 1959; Luhmann 1964; Offe 1972; Scharpf 1983, 1987a). Institutions thus have the character of preselections or predecisions. They are not politically neutral but rather reflect specific power relations; they are congealed political will. As such, they can be changed in principle when a new political will is being formed. Once established, however, they take on a dynamic of their own and give rise to unplanned steering effects. On account of their hidden-hand function and inertia, they may clash with different decision-making situations, new power relations, or political intentions.

The effects of financing institutions on the design and effectiveness of the policy area of labor market policy has been the subject of this study. Financing institutions determine who is to suffer the consequences of unemployment or the costs of avoiding them. They determine whether those affected by unemployment will receive any wage compensation at all and, if so, the level and duration of benefits. They also determine whether, instead of financing unemployment (passive labor market policy), social resources will be used for preventive measures or the elimination of unemployment (active labor market policy). These institutional arrangements, in turn, have repercussions on the behavior of labor market actors: on the search behavior of the unemployed, on the mobility behavior of the employed, on firms' hiring practices, on wage negotiations between unions and employers, and finally on the labor market policy behavior of governments and bureaucracies at different levels.

Our attention has focused on the latter. Mass unemployment which has existed in most European countries for more than a decade, can certainly not be explained solely with reference to the financing system of labor market policy. However, as we have shown, financing institutions explain a great deal of typical and recurrent policy responses to critical situations. In the Federal Republic of Germany, the growing discontinuation of wage-replacement benefits for many unemployed, the relatively modest countermeasures against mass unemployment through active labor market policy, the temporarily procyclical instead of countercyclical responses of labor market policy, and the concentration of work promotion measures on already favored regions and groups rather than on those most severely affected are directly related to the construction of the financing system. Compared to other countries, however, we found also some advantages of the German financing system. In other countries, such as the United States, the process of discontinuation has run an even harder course; the social security of the unemployed who are still eligible for wage-replacement benefits is insured much better in Germany, France, and Sweden than in other countries, such as Britain; and active labor market policy, particularly further training for the adaptation of qualifications and temporary public work contributes more to preventing and reducing unemployment in Germany and especially in Sweden than it does in some other countries, such as Austria and the United States.

The specific characteristics on which the advantages and disadvantages of the financing systems of labor market policy are based were the subject of the foregoing analysis. How has public labor market policy developed under conditions of different financing systems, and to what extent have financing systems led to different forms of unemployment insurance and active labor market policy? In order to answer this question, an international comparison appeared to be useful because the question of whether financing institutions make a difference can be answered only empirically by observing different, actually existing financing systems.

10.2 THE ORGANIZATION AND FINANCING OF LABOR MARKET POLICY

Our point of departure was the fact that in the last two decades labor market policy in the six countries selected (Austria, Federal Republic of Germany, France, Great Britain, Sweden, United States) has been shaped under entirely different institutional conditions. The distribution of tasks and competencies, responsibilities and regulations for financing, and procedural regulations structuring revenues and expenditures differ significantly from country to country. The spectrum of forms of organizing and financing labor market policy in the six countries investigated extends from the concentration of all functions in a central organization to the dispersal of labor market policy functions among a multiplicity of organizations and from almost full financing through contributions to almost total financing through the central state budget. The current forms of organization and financing in the individual countries can be summarized as follows.

In Austria, the ministry for social administration and its subordinate regional labor offices are responsible for the design and implementation of all labor market policy. Expenditures are financed from a fund into which employers' and employees' contributions to unemployment insurance flow and which—with certain exceptions—may only experience short-term deficits or surpluses. Reserve funds may not be accumulated beyond a fixed limit, and any deficits incurred are covered only temporarily by loans from the federal budget. There are special regulations for administrative costs as well as for bad weather and bankruptcy benefits, which are (in part) financed through the federal budget or special levies on employers.

In the Federal Republic of Germany, labor market policy responsibilities are concentrated in a single organization, the Federal Employment Institute (FEI). It is an independent body whose activities are supervised in matters of law by the ministry of labor, which in certain cases may issue directions to the FEI or has to be consulted by it. Its activities are largely financed through contributions from employers and employees. In contrast to the situation in Austria, there is in Germany no requirement that revenues be immediately adjusted to reflect changes in expenditures because there are no legal obstacles to the accumulation of reserve funds and any deficits incurred (after reserves have been exhausted) must be covered by a grant from the federal budget that does not have to be repaid. Means-tested benefits for the unemployed—unemployment assistance—are normally financed from the federal budget, from taxes. The financing of bankruptcy benefits and the program to promote winter construction is through special levies on employers.

In France, the design, financing, and implementation of active and passive measures are largely separate. Unemployment insurance (UNEDIC/ASSEDIC) is responsible for most benefit expenditures for the unemployed as well as for early retirement measures. It is financed through employers' and employees' contributions and through a state subsidy that covers a certain (and changing) percentage of expenditures. However, the state assumes no blanket responsibility for covering any deficits that may arise. When the unemployment insurance system began to run deficits at the beginning of the 1980s, special state tax measures were introduced to provide additional resources to the unemployment insurance fund (an income tax surcharge and a solidarity contribution by public service employees and pensioners with additional earnings). The state budget through the employment ministry also finances unemployment assistance as well as the more recent (after April 1984) early retirement measures and the bulk of expenditures for active labor market policy measures, particularly the relatively extensive integration and training measures for unemployed youth. An exception is vocational training measures, which are largely financed through a special levy on firms; however, it only has to be paid in full when there are no other recognized expenditures for internal or external training.

In Great Britain, the Department of Health and Social Security is responsible for unemployment insurance benefits, whereas the Department of Employment and its subordinate labor market authority, the Manpower Services Commission, is responsible for active labor market policy. Unemployment benefits are paid through the national insurance fund, which is subordinate to the social security ministry and is also responsible for pensions and other social benefits. It is financed through a general social security contribution by employers and employees with a (small and variable) grant from the state budget; there is only a single social security contribution for the entire social security system. Although the amount of the contribution in Great Britain—as in other countries—varies with earnings (and the contribution rate since 1985 is even progressive, those with greater earnings paying a higher rate), the unemployment benefit is a flat-rate benefit (with family supplements). Great Britain is thus the only country among those investigated in which the equivalence principle (i.e., insurance principle) is not followed in determining the level of contributions and benefits in unemployment insurance. The means-tested supplementary benefit for the unemployed, which has become much more important than the unemployment benefit in providing income security for the unemployed, is financed through the central government budget, which is also the source of funding for active labor market policy.

In Sweden, unemployment insurance is administered by trade union unemployment insurance funds, to which members pay contributions. The contributions have, however, remained very low and have over time been increasingly supplemented with funds from the state budget. This state contribution now accounts for about 90 percent of expenditures for unemployment benefits. Unemployment assistance (KAS), which—when the general conditions are met—is not means-tested, is fully financed through the state budget. Active labor market policy is designed and implemented by the labor market authority AMS on the basis of guidelines from the labor ministry. It, too, is fully financed through the state budget, although funds for temporary layoff compensation (until 1984) and income stipends for participants in training and rehabilitation measures are—like unemployment assistance and the state contribution to the unemployment insurance funds—largely (two-thirds) refinanced from a payroll tax levied on employers. In recent years, the actual percentage refinanced in this way has, however, usually fallen short of this target figure.

In the United States, the individual states are the unemployment insurance carriers; the system of contributions and benefits is, therefore, different form state to state. In almost all individual states, contributions to unemployment insurance are only paid by the employers, whereby the contribution rate is determined by experience rating, the extent to which layoffs and redundancies in the work force of individual employers generate claims on the unemployment insurance system. In addition to the unemployment insurance programs in the individual states, there is also a national extended benefits program, which is financed equally from the unemployment insurance contributions of the individual states and from an additional uniform federal employers' contribution to unemployment insurance. (From 1982 to 1985, there was also a special temporary program of follow-on unemployment benefits financed through federal government funds.) If they incur deficits, the individual state unemployment insurance systems receive loans from the federal budget; the federal government attempts to encourage prompt repayment through sanctions including interest payments for loans. Active labor market policy programs are financed through the federal budget and implemented by individual states, local governments, and other sponsors; only the funds for the placement service are financed through a portion of the federal unemployment insurance contributions.

According to this overview, we are confronted with the situation that similar problems in the employment system are processed by different organizational and financing structures. Now, if we can ascertain that different institutional conditions give rise to different response patterns with respect to the employment problem, we will have gained important clues for answering the more ambitious question concerning the possibility of politically designing institutions (institutional engineering) in cases where they have evident and politically undesirable flaws. In the following, we summarize the evidence we have found concerning the different policy responses to the employment crisis caused by the different institutional arrangements of financing labor market policy.

10.3 EFFECTS OF FINANCING SYSTEMS ON EXPENDITURES FOR ACTIVE LABOR MARKET POLICY

An evaluation of financing institutions must start with the distinguishing characteristics of the respective systems. The focus of our study was on the source of financing. Other important characteristics include budgeting rules (who participates in preparing the labor market budget), rules for balancing the budget (procedures for dealing with deficits or surpluses), and the relationship of various functional budgets with each other as well as with the state budget as a whole (integrated versus fragmented, centralized versus decentralized budgets).

10.3.1 Sources for Financing Active Labor Market Policy

A rough distinction was made between financing from contributions and taxes. Financing sources were classified as contributions if they consisted of unemployment insurance contributions or other deductions for specific purposes (e.g., levies for winter or bankruptcy allowances). Labor market policy financed by the general state budget was classified as tax-financed because taxes constitute the principal financial source of the state budget. According to this distinction, Austria and Germany are essentially contribution systems, while Great Britain represents virtually the ideal type of a tax system; Sweden and the United States, predominantly tax systems, nevertheless contain significant contribution elements, and France may be characterized as a mixed system. Taking into account only active labor market policy, the differences become even more pronounced: Britain and the United States (the latter with the exception of the relatively insignificant placement agencies) become pure tax systems, and the Federal Republic of Germany represents an almost pure contribution system.

The distinction of financing sources is of great significance for how financing systems respond under strong pressure. With respect to taxes, the principle of nonappropriation applies; that is, tax revenues as a rule are not tied to specific purposes. Under these circumstances, budget items are competing, and policy priorities or politics will determine the behavioral response under strong fiscal pressures. Earmarked contributions, on the other hand, generally establish a claim for benefits if certain conditions are fulfilled (insurance of equivalence principle). Contributory systems generate some kind of property rights so that respective budget items are, in principle at least, not competing. Under strong fiscal restraints, such institutional arrangements will lead to protective responses either by increasing contributions or by excluding marginal claimants.

10.3.2 Volume of Expenditures for Active Labor Market Policy

The question now arising is how much the countries included in our analysis have expended on active (as opposed to passive) labor market policy, and whether any relationships can be identified between expenditure levels and financing systems. Our findings can be summarized in the following way. Sweden has by far the highest level of expenditures; Austria and the United States have the lowest. The other three countries form an intermediate group with approximately the same volume of expenditures. The average share of expenditures for active labor market policy amounts to almost 2 percent of GDP in Sweden (during the investigation period), in Austria and the United States by contrast it is between 0.2 and 0.3 percent, and in the other countries it ranges from 0.6 to 1 percent.

These different expenditure levels are primarily a result of the different roles assigned to active labor market policy in individual countries in the context of their economic and employment policies. In Sweden, active labor market policy constitutes an essential element of employment policy, whereas in Austria employment policy is based on different elements (particularly fiscal policy). However, independent effects of different financing systems can also be identified. Thus, Swedish labor market policy could not have fulfilled its assigned employment policy function if it had been primarily financed by contributions rather than the state budget. Contribution systems always presuppose an (individual or group-specific) relationship between contributions and benefits (equivalence) which is no longer given once they are put in the service of general employment policy objectives whose benefits go far beyond the circle of contributors. Especially Austrian labor market policy—which has a contribution-based financing system that in the longer term does not permit the accumulation of deficits or surpluses and is thus equivalent to a levy system—could not have been utilized for an extended and countercyclical employment policy because any increases in expenditures would have triggered higher contribution rates and induced contributors' resistance.

10.3.3 Dynamics of Expenditure Trends

The effects of different financing systems on the dynamics of expenditures are even more pronounced than they are on the volume of expenditures. In Great Britain, Sweden, and the United States, political priorities can be relatively easily translated into corresponding expenditures because active measures are financed (almost) exclusively out of the state budget. Expenditure trends therefore have corresponded to the very different political priorities in each country. In Britain, spending on active labor market policy (particularly aimed at unemployed youth) has been continuously expanded in line with political objectives; in Sweden, it has been adjusted countercyclically in accordance with its employment policy function; in the United States, following the political priorities of the administration and the Congress, there was initially a significant expansion and subsequently in the 1980s a drastic—procyclical—reduction. In the United States, a flexible spending policy responding very quickly to changing political priorities has also been facilitated by the fact that most labor market policy programs are of limited duration and not tied to individual legal entitlements as well as being administered by local governments, individual states, and special local associations rather than by an autonomous organization. Organizational rigidities and vested interests, which in countries with autonomous labor administrations create stability and prevent rapid change, in the case of the United States only play a minor role.

In those countries where the state budget is not the primary source of financing manpower programs, expenditure trends are clearly shaped by the way they are being financed. In France, the fragmentation of spending and financing responsibilities (which, among other things, spreads the burden through various deductions for special purposes) does not show labor market policy in its totality as a transparent expenditure block that could become the object of budgetary considerations; it thus favors continuous spending growth. In the Federal Republic of Germany, the Federal Employment Institute in an initial period is able to deal with rising unemployment on accounts of its reserves for financing both the growing demand for wage-replacement benefits and increased spending on active labor market policy. Extensive employment losses, however, rapidly deplete the FEI's reserves; the federal government then has to make up the resulting deficit, subsequently adopting measures (cutbacks) to eliminate the deficit. These concentrate primarily on spending for active labor market policy because it is considered the most readily disposable budget item. In the longer run, surpluses and reserves can be built up again which in turn benefit active spending programs. The outcome of a decision-making framework thus influenced by financing is a spending pattern in the area of active labor market policy that initially responds countercyclically to an increase in the unemployment rate, subsequently changes to a procyclical course, and finally may become expansionary again if the unemployment rate remains at a constant level.

Viewing expenditure trends on the premise that spending on active labor market policy should adjust itself to the labor market situation over time—that is, by increasing when the situation in the labor market is unfavorable and decreasing when it is positive—the following picture emerges. Active labor market policy systems financed by the general state budget facilitate a quickly adaptable countercyclical policy, provided the political will exists. If it does not exist, however, they also leave room for spending variations that run entirely counter to solving the problem. One example of this is the drastic cuts in the labor market budget (for active measures) in the United States in the early 1980s even though unemployment at that time was strongly on the increase. Contribution-financed systems—if, as in the Federal Republic of Germany, they allow for surplus and deficit accumulation—have a built-in stabilizing effect on the economy, which to some extent provides a good basis for a countercyclical spending policy. During severe and long-lasting recessions with their attendant financial problems, however, it is particularly in contribution-financed systems which combine active and passive policy elements that identifiable deficits may occur which are then eliminated by arbitrary cuts in active measures that do not correspond to the problem.

10.3.4 Degree of Activity of Labor Market Policy

According to the official labor market policy objectives of most countries, active labor market policy is given priority over passive labor market policy. Measures and programs of active labor market policy aimed at training, job creation, and job preservation are to take the place, as far as possible, of the passive acceptance of unemployment and the mere protection of the unemployed against the financial consequences of unemployment. This objective has not been achieved in most of the countries examined. Only in Sweden is the degree of activity of labor market policy—that is, expenditures on active measures as a share of total labor market policy spending—considerably greater than 50 percent. In almost all countries analyzed, it declined during the investigation period; only in Britain did it remain stable (though in part as a result of cuts in passive benefits).

In addition to other factors, differences in financing systems are also responsible for different activity levels of labor market policy in individual countries. To varying degrees, financing systems facilitate substituting active labor market policy for a passive acceptance of unemployment. Embarking on active labor market policy rather than accepting unemployment presupposes that active labor market policy programs can largely be financed through funds that otherwise would have to be used for maintaining the potential participants in such programs while they remain unemployed. The extent to which this precondition is fulfilled differs widely among countries. In all countries, the costs of active labor market policy measures can be put in the context of the roughly equal financial burden on public budgets that would otherwise arise as a result of the unemployment of program participants (wage-replacement and other social benefits, lost revenue from taxes and social insurance contributions). That is, the net costs (additional costs) of successful labor market programs are substantially lower than their gross costs. Yet the decreased burden on public budgets resulting from programs that reduce unemployment does not in all countries accrue to those institutions charged with the responsibility of funding active programs; frequently the budgetary relief to a considerable extent goes to institutions that have no part in active labor market policy.

The incentives and opportunities for the institutions responsible for active labor market policy to apply a net-cost calculus and substitute active labor market policy for passive acceptance of unemployment therefore differ widely from country to country. In Great Britain, on account of the far-reaching responsibility of the state budget for active and passive labor market policy and the centralization of tax and social insurance systems, the diminished budget burden resulting from a reduction in unemployment for the most part accrues to the same institution that is responsible for active policy spending and the corresponding budget burden. Much the same applies to Sweden. In other countries—particularly the United States and Austria—such an institutional congruity of budgetary burdens and potential budgetary benefits does not exist because active and passive labor market policies are either institutionally separated or to a large extent divorced from tax and social insurance systems. These diverging conditions explain at least in part why the degree of activity of labor market policy (which does not say anything about the quality of measures) is exceptionally high in Sweden, and why in Britain it has taken a more consistent course than in other countries. In countries with a low or negative incentive for substituting active for passive measures, variations in the degree of activity therefore are also significantly higher than in countries where such incentives do exist. During the observation period (1973–1988), the coefficient of variation of the degree of activity was 0.36 in Austria and 0.38 in the United States compared to 0.09 in Sweden and 0.16 in Great Britain.

So far, we have dealt with the impact of financing systems on policy behavioral responses to economic and budget balance changes. Is there also a systematic relationship between characteristics of financing systems and the allocative and distributive consequences of labor market policy? The following section summarizes the evidence with respect to this question.

10.4 Effects of Financing Systems on the Efficiency and Distributive Effects of Labor Market Policy

10.4.1 Effects of Unemployment Insurance on Social Security and Distribution

An attempt to gain a comparative view of unemployment insurance benefits in individual countries, their generosity, and their distribution effects at first glance creates a confusing picture; eligibility criteria and the differentiation of benefits according to income groups, household types, and duration of unemployment differ to such an extent that no easily comparable structures emerge. Nevertheless, some patterns can be recognized from existing studies: Sweden, the Federal Republic of Germany, and France provide a relatively high level of wage-compensation payments, whereas the corresponding levels in Great Britain and the United States are relatively low. The level of benefits does not necessarily depend on the financing system: largely contribution-financed systems of unemployment benefits can be found in countries with high wage-replacement rates as well as in those with low rates (Germany and the United States, respectively), and the same is true for largely tax-financed systems (Sweden and Great Britain, respectively).

Differences in conditions concerning entitlement, on the other hand, are related to financing systems. Contribution-financed systems predominantly characterized by insurance principles as a rule offer the longest protection while at the same time (increasingly) closely tying the benefit duration to preceding contribution periods. Largely tax-financed systems not based on insurance principles offer a generally shorter period of income protection while at the same time less closely tying benefit duration to the preceding length of employment. Instead, they tend to differentiate benefits according to social criteria (consider Great Britain).

Tax-financed benefit systems of subsistence protection for the unemployed tend to have greater redistributive effects than contribution-financed systems which are closely geared to the insurance principle. This becomes evident in both interpersonal and interregional respects: the regional redistributive effects of unemployment insurance in largely tax-financed systems tend to be greater than in contribution-based systems. The extreme case is represented by the contribution-financed unemployment insurance system in the United States, which on account of its decentralization has practically no regional equalization effects. One reason for the greater redistributive capacity of tax-financed systems is that they work under less of an obligation than contribution-financed systems to gear their benefits toward acquired claims and instead are able to differentiate their benefits according to social criteria. In addition, tax financing tends to affect individual incomes and regions progressively; that is, the wealthy contribute more to financing than the poor. Contribution financing, in contrast (particularly if income thresholds are low, as in the United States), tend to be regressive; that is, the poor pay proportionally more than the rich (Disney 1984).

Tax- and contribution-based systems also respond differently to the financial strain resulting from high and long-term unemployment. Financing systems without a close relationship between contributions and benefits in such a situation tend to reduce benefits for all recipients while not altogether excluding specific groups of unemployed. This leveling response is very clearly illustrated in the case of Great Britain, where the share of benefit recipients in the total number of unemployed has remained at a high and constant level while average benefits have drastically declined.

By contrast, countries strictly following insurance principles tend to restrict eligibility and increasingly to discontinue benefits for certain individuals (segmentation response; consider the United States as well as, to a lesser degree, the Federal Republic of Germany and France). Once again, the equivalence principle of contribution systems accounts for different responses. It provides a certain property right for insurance benefits, thus making cuts more difficult, while tending to exclude bad risks. Benefit systems not characterized by equivalence, on the other hand, are in principle open to all risk groups but are hardly protected against cuts in individual benefits. The Austrian contribution system at first glance appears to be an exception because the share of benefit recipients in the total number of unemployed has not declined. Austria's financing system, however, was not subject to any severe tests in the form of high unemployment during the observation period; if the thesis presented here is valid, a segmentation response is to be expected as a result of significant increases in the number of unemployed.

10.4.2 Unemployment Insurance and Functioning of the Labor Market

There is a dominant concern in economic theory that a high level of wage replacement granted for a long period of time may adversely affect the adjustment function of the labor market. Increased benefit claims, misuse, or extensive use of benefits in this view reduce necessary wage flexibility, increase the duration of unemployment, give individuals an incentive to register as unemployed even though they are not really available for the labor market, or even lead people to quit voluntarily (Clark and Summers 1982). On the demand side as well, according to this theory, unemployment insurance induces the adoption of production methods with higher layoff risks and lowers the employers' willingness to hire because of increased nonwage labor costs.

A survey of the empirical literature on the countries examined here shows that well-supported conclusions on the incentive effects of unemployment insurance are not yet available. While most existing studies agree that unemployment insurance tends to bring about a higher level of unemployment, they consider the total effect to be small even in generous systems.

These at best modestly negative incentive effects of unemployment insurance contrast with positive effects that are even more difficult to quantify, but which in the light of plausible theoretical considerations turn out to be no less significant. Effective social protection in the case of involuntary unemployment ensures a stabilization of demand at the macroeconomic level (not least because of the higher propensity to consume on the part of low-income earners) and strengthens the loyalty to fundamental social institutions at the macrosociological level. At an intermediate system level, where the interest representatives of capital and labor meet, a functioning unemployment insurance also encourages cooperation among interest groups, thus increasing particularly the willingness on the part of unions to participate in adapting to changing markets and technologies in an offensive rather than defensive fashion. At the micro level, reliable and generous social security benefits in case of unemployment also increase the willingness on the part of those in dependent employment for greater labor market mobility. This will be the case particularly if the preconditions for such mobility are accompanied by effective measures of active labor market policy. The opportunities provided by active labor market policy, in turn, will reduce the probability of the social security system being exploited. Given the prospect of acquiring insurance claims, unemployment insurance also enhances the desire for regular work (eligibility effect) and thus may reduce moonlighting (Hamermesh 1979; Clark and Summers 1982).

10.4.3 Regional and Individual Distributive Effects of Active Labor Market Policy

Theoretically, there are many reasons supporting the conjecture that tax-financed systems of active labor market policy—as in the case of unemployment insurance—have different distributive effects from contribution-financed systems. In particular, it can be expected that tax-financed systems are better able than contribution-financed systems to concentrate their spending on problem regions and problem groups. The reason for this is the insurance principle in contribution systems that tends to concentrate benefits on contribution payers and therefore on the core group of the labor market, thus conflicting with a more selective labor market policy.

Empirical analyses for the most part confirm these expectations. The regional distribution of active labor market policy in tax-financed systems largely responds to problem pressures; that is, the shares of individual regions in labor market policy spending roughly correspond to their respective shares in total unemployment (Great Britain); in the United States, problem regions even receive disproportionately high consideration. In the Federal Republic of Germany's contribution-financed system, on the other hand, the regions already favored by the labor market situation benefit disproportionately from active labor market policy. The concentration of labor market policy measures on contribution payers and individuals eligible for unemployment benefits according to the equivalence principle is, among other things, the reason why problem regions do not receive greater consideration.

Much the same results emerge when we turn to individual distribution effects. Tax-financed systems of active labor market policy in Great Britain, Sweden, and the United States usually succeed in concentrating benefits on problem groups or at least in giving equal consideration to problem groups among those benefiting from the measures. In the Federal Republic of Germany, by contrast, the disadvantaged groups in the labor market—as a result of the equivalence principle—tend to be underrepresented in active labor market policy.

CHAPTER 11

Lessons from the International Comparison

Our study has indicated that different political responses to mass unemployment can be explained in part with reference to different financing systems of labor market policy. Moreover, relationships between financing systems and the allocative and distributive effects of labor market policy could be identified. Institutions, we conclude, do make a difference.

This result, however, should not be misunderstood in the sense of representing a scientific regularity. Financing rules and the organizational structures within which they are embedded do not have any direct effects. Rather, their effect is dependent upon objective and subjective configurations: technological, economic, and demographic initial conditions as well as the cognitive and normative orientations of individuals dealing with these institutions, experiences passed on over generations, and learning processes. The same formal structure may give rise to different effects under different configurations. Financing institutions are filters, and it is easier to predict what will not go through than what will actually come out at the end. Financing institutions thus share the ambivalent status of other institutions: they are necessary but by no means sufficient conditions for the realization of certain societal goals.

With these caveats in mind, the results of our international comparison may be used to explain failures or achievements of labor market policy in the context of specific institutional and political configurations. In this concluding chapter, we shall therefore summarize our policy conclusions in two different ways. First, we will focus, for illustrative purposes, on the West German case from a comparative perspective and use our results in order to look for clues with respect to a question for which political research in the Federal Republic of Germany so far had not found any satisfactory solution: Why have responsible politicians in the Federal Republic of Germany not decided in favor of a more consistent full employment strategy through

258

the greater use of active labor market policy, even though so much good will (at least in programmatic statements) has existed and active labor market policy, as various analyses have confirmed (e.g., Haveman and Saks 1985; Kühl 1987; Schmid 1988), has been relatively efficient? These clues will be summed up in two theses: (1) the thesis concerning an institutional incongruity in the German financing system and (2) the thesis of institutionally restricted room of maneuver for changing party policies.

Second, we will try to generalize the outcome of our comparative study under the perspective of designing proper financing institutions of labor market policy with respect to certain policy objectives. Taking into account the nondeterministic feature of institutional arrangements mentioned above, these conclusions shall not be interpreted as cooking recipes; they can only serve as rough guidelines which have to be transformed into the specific historical and institutional context of each country.

11.1 CONSEQUENCES OF INSTITUTIONAL INCONGRUITY: THE WEST GERMAN CASE IN COMPARATIVE PERSPECTIVE

The fiscal incongruity thesis has two distinct though related aspects. On the one hand, the largely contribution-based financing of active labor market policy does not correspond with the external effects going beyond the circle of contribution payers that a greater use of this policy would entail. On the other hand, the diminished budget burden resulting from a reduction in unemployment does not entirely accrue to those institutions that are responsible for active policy spending and the corresponding budget burden.

Among the countries included in our comparative study, Sweden illustrates the institutional conditions for an offensive use of active labor market policy. Swedish labor market policy could not have fulfilled its employment policy function had it been financed essentially through contributions rather than the state budget. Contribution systems always presuppose an (individual or group-specific) relationship between contributions and benefits (equivalence) that is no longer given once it is made to serve general (not concentrated on contribution payers) employment policy objectives.

This is confirmed by Austrian labor market policy. With its contribution-supported financing system which permits neither long-term deficits nor surpluses and is in effect much like a levy system, labor market policy could have hardly served employment policy purposes because any spending growth would have led to rate increases and met with the resistance of contribution payers.

In the Federal Republic of Germany, labor market policy is also financed in principle through contributions to the Federal Employment Institute. However, this financing system is somewhat more flexible than Austria's. Surpluses, for example, may be used to build up reserves to be depleted again in bad times. The federal government is legally responsible for deficits. The creators of the Employment Promotion Act (*Arbeitsförderungsgesetz*) had assumed that this situation would arise only under exceptional circumstances and on a modest scale. But since 1974, this assumption no longer corresponds to reality. The huge gaps in the FEI's budget during both recessions resulted in budget cuts at the expense of active labor market policy. Because most measures of active labor market policy are of the public good type—that is, they result in external effects that go far beyond the circle of contribution payers—partial funding by the central government budget, such as through regulated federal subsidies to the FEI, could help to avoid the crowding out of active labor market policy by unemployment benefits (Schmid 1986).

By the same token, the vertical and horizontal fragmentation of financing institutions may impede or at least slow down an offensive labor market policy if spending responsibility and the financial repercussions of measures are disjointed. Active labor market policy instead of an acceptance of unemployment presupposes that labor market programs can largely be financed through funds that otherwise would have to be expended on income maintenance of the unemployed. In the Federal Republic of Germany, however, this precondition is fulfilled only in part. Expenditures on active labor market policy measures are, to a large extent, outweighed by the fiscal costs of unemployment that would otherwise arise as a result of program participants being unemployed (wage-replacement and other social benefits, revenue losses on taxes and social insurance contributions) so that net costs (additional costs) of successful labor market programs are significantly lower than their gross costs. The reduced budget strain as a result of such programs successfully lowering unemployment, however, does not in all cases benefit those institutions responsible for active program spending; frequently, the benefit accrues in large part to institutions not involved in active labor market policy.

Whereas in Sweden, for example, positive and negative budget effects largely occur in the same fiscal institutions, this does not apply particularly in the cases of Austria and the United States. In the Federal Republic of Germany, an obvious incongruity between negative and positive budget effects can be seen particularly with respect to temporary public job creation measures. Program expenditures by municipalities which are the most important agencies for such measures and on whose initiative their success depends are offset only to a relatively modest extent by positive budget effects; at the same time, other institutions that do not shoulder any (or hardly any) share of program costs realize a financial benefit (i.e., the federal government, the *Länder*, pension and health insurance funds). The institutional incongruity between positive and negative financial effects, on the other hand, is less pronounced with respect to further training and retraining measures as well as short-time working. Both positive and negative budget effects for the most part arise for the same institutions (and in roughly the same proportion); only in the case of the FEI does the (significant) reduction in its budget burden not fully make up for its gross expenditures (Bruche and Reissert 1985:132–35).

The institutional barriers for offensive, active labor market policy described above conversely do not only represent obstacles for a politically motivated sudden freeze on promotion measures, as in the case of the United States. Paradoxically, they also constitute levers for a certain expansion of active policy when by reduced spending on unemployment benefits (whether as a result of restrictive regulations on eligibility for wage compensation or unexpected positive developments on the labor market) the financial situation of the FEI proves to be favorable. Such a situation existed, for example, in 1968–69 when the Employment Promotion Act came into being, as well as in 1982–84 when the Christian Democratic-Liberal coalition succeeded the Social Democratic-Liberal coalition. The political turning point, therefore, did not mean a structural break. On the contrary, the new government embarked on a renewed expansion of active labor market policy—especially for the financing of temporary public job creation measures and the "qualification offensive"—of course, less so (though certainly in part) for programmatic reasons than for reasons of fiscal expediency.

The great structural break occurred not in the area of labor market policy operating through financial instruments but rather in the area of labor law, in the regulation of the labor market. The Christian Democratic-Liberal labor market policy is distinguished in part by intending to support especially small and medium-sized business (*Mittelstand*). Provisions contained in the Act concerning the Severely Handicapped as well as a relaxing of regulations for the protection of young employees benefited indeed particularly small and medium-sized firms or ensured that the burden on those firms was limited. The labor market policy demands of the organized *Mittel-stand*, however, were not fully met. The interest associations of the *Mittelstand* would have preferred a more significant lowering of con-tributions to the FEI, no further expansion in public job creation mea-sures, and a Law on Parental Leave not containing any job guarantee. Policy change revealed itself most clearly in areas where the *Mittel-stand* and big industry combined their lobbying efforts, namely, in various measures for a more flexible labor market along the U.S. model. The core element of this policy for greater labor market flexibility is a provision according to which employers—without any justification—may conclude fixed-term contracts for a period of up to eighteen months. This provision went beyond previous decisions of labor courts and supported the already existing trend to a significant increase in contractually limited hiring (Webber 1987:81; Büchte-mann 1989).

Thus, with respect to labor market policy, the verbal and pro-grammatic differences between the major political parties are significantly greater than is their actual practice. This discrepancy may be accounted for by the fact that politicians (like the rest of us) in one sense are prisoners of institutions whose Janus-faced character has be-come evident. On the one hand, they save us from imprudent experi-ments and ensure the development of stable mutual expectations and of continuous and gradual learning processes; on the other hand, they disqualify—both in practice and in theory—alternative conceptions, which in a situation of fundamental change is problematic. What are the changes—to conclude with a thought experiment—of achieving a political breakthrough by increasing the importance of labor market policy in creating and maintaining full employment in the future (Schmid 1987)? From the Conservative-Liberal side, one should for programmatic reasons probably not expect any efforts to expand ac-tive labor market policy—such as (roughly) following the Swedish model—beyond the cyclically constrained financial scope of the FEI. Could such a change be expected from the Social Democrats if they were in power and were not restrained by a small but effective Liberal partner?

In Fritz Scharpf's view, the above-mentioned institutional bar-riers are not so high as to prevent the government and a parliamentary majority from making such changes if only they wanted to. That this road was not followed when the Social Democratic-Liberal govern-ment was in power "was surely related to the fixation of all employ-ment policy thinking on the instruments of economic and financial policy. Even labor market policy actors considered the 1967 Stability and Growth Act rather than the 1969 Employment Promotion Act to be the 'relevant' legislation in the fight against mass unemployment (Kühl 1982), and particularly those Social Democrats and union officials who were especially committed to employment policy saw labor market instruments at best as sociopolitical relief, but not as an instrument for fighting unemployment" (Scharpf 1987b:289). What was missing, therefore, was the political will because the responsible politicians were not convinced by the model of active labor market policy.

This is certainly a crucial factor. But is it only persuasion that is needed to create the requisite political will? The present analysis suggests that the institutional barriers for a full employment policy that is more strongly supported by labor market policy are more serious. As long as the establishment of an active labor market policy with independent employment policy functions can be financed only through the contributions to the FEI (which, for example, does not include the self-employed and tenured civil servants), the necessary broad support from the unions and those who are employed can probably not be secured because they would be assuming the major burden without being the sole beneficiaries. An offensive turn in active labor market policy, therefore, would require reforms in the financing system that would eliminate the financial incongruities discussed above, such as through regular federal subsidies for the FEI (Schmid 1986), systems of earmarked funds (Bosch 1986), and granting local governments a greater role in income taxation in order to create financial incentives for a decentralized labor market and employment policy (Scharpf 1984; Reissert 1986). Moreover, government would have to assume a greater and more specifically regulated share in the financing of labor market policy as a precondition for improving its distributional effect, for an adequate financial minimum protection of all unemployed as well as for a more specific use of the instruments of active labor market policy for the benefit of the disadvantaged or most strongly affected groups and regions because contribution systems are inherently ill suited for redistributive policy functions.

To what extent can the German case be generalized? This is the question to which we turn now in the final section.

11.2 INSTITUTIONAL GUIDELINES FOR DESIGNING FINANCING SYSTEMS OF LABOR MARKET POLICY

Before presenting our suggestions concerning institutional guidelines, another caveat has to be stated in order to avoid misunder-

standing. Our suggestions take up only one line of institutional analysis, although we are aware of other dimensions that are involved in
the complex issue of institutional arrangements and their change.
    There are at least four traditions of institutional analysis. The
first dates at least as far back as Hobbes, who derived the necessity of a
central power from the self-destructive nature of human beings, from
the "natural state of war" (Hobbes 1973:90). In modern theory, the
Hobbesian tradition has been taken up, for instance, by the sociologi-
cal anthropologist Arnold Gehlen (1956). Gehlen defines social institutions as "artificial instincts" which are necessary because human
beings lack "good" natural or animal-like instincts. This theory was
extended by structural-functional systems theory, such as by Talcott
Parsons (1969) and Niklas Luhmann (1982). Both emphasize the requirement of maintaining a sense of orientation in a world of complex
interrelationships through the establishment of social institutions.
    The function of these institutions is to relieve human beings
from the overload of complexity, from the ever-changing and uncertain environment, by habitualized rules or standards of behavior. According to this view, institutions of the labor market could be defined
as predecisions that determine, for example, who has to pay for the
necessary costs of adjusting to ongoing economic and technological
change. Without such institutions, human systems will not be able to
cope with unexpected events occurring inside or outside the system.
With increasing standardization of behavioral rules, there is a growing
need for a specialized institution that is able to guarantee that people
will follow the rules. This institution is the state which has a monopoly of political power, the authority to establish binding rules and to
sanction deviating behavior. The problem with this approach is that it
hardly delivers operational criteria for the design or assessment of social and economic institutions. The approach tends to legitimize existing institutions simply because they have proved successful in a
Darwinistic selection process. It tends to value the order function of
institutions as such rather than evaluating them in terms of rational
efficiency criteria or principles of social equity. The state is basically
restricted to its police function, which hardly fits the historical facts.
    The second tradition could be labeled the constitutionalist or
contractual approach (e.g., Madison 1970), according to which people
voluntarily choose institutions in order to be able to enjoy the fruits of
cooperation and the division of labor. The modern version of this approach is rational choice theory. This theory is, more than anything
else, a normative theory. It tells us what we ought to do in order to
achieve our aims to the greatest possible extent. It does not, however,

tell us what our aims ought to be. Unlike moral theory, rational choice theory offers conditional imperatives, pertaining to means rather than to ends (Elster 1986:1). According to this approach, labor market institutions can be defined as tools aimed at supporting certain ends under specified behavioral conditions. An example would be determining which type of revenues and which level of unemployment benefits (replacement rates) ensure social security and redistribution in favor of low-income earners without negatively affecting the willingness to pay and the incentive to work. In the following, we will rely to a large extent on the contractual tradition. However, some caveats or limits of this approach should be recalled. First, rational choice theory runs into difficulties when contradicting aims within or between social systems are involved. Second, the specification of behavioral conditions relies on the assumption of rational behavior. Unless we fall into the positivistic trap that all observed behavior is rational, we have to develop criteria by which to differentiate between actual and rational behavior. However, such criteria hardly exist. We cannot avoid making value judgments, and these judgments have to be made explicit. Third—as we have emphasized above—the relationship between institutions and behavioral outcome is not a deterministic one. Institutions are, at best, necessary but not sufficient conditions. The outcomes are in principle indeterminate insofar as they depend on individual perceptions and skills in handling the existing institutional tools. Finally, even if we were able to design ideal institutional arrangements in theory, their implementation in practice depends on power relationships. It is at this point that the third institutional tradition should be considered.

Institutions have never been established on the basis of unanimous decisions, as the pure theory of rational choice assumes. They often have been imposed by more or less dictatorial decisions or, at best, by democratic majority rules. They thus already reflect interests and are used by vested interests to defend social and economic positions, privileges, or strategic advantages. Veblen's view that the dominant (leisure) class impedes structural change not only by property rights or authority relations (enforced by the state) but also by the diffusion of their life-style (e.g., conspicuous consumption) and instinctive conservative attitudes (Veblen 1934) has been taken up (in the context of labor market issues) especially by radical economists (Edwards 1979; Reich 1984). Employers maximize not only the production function (maximum output related to input) but also the labor extraction function (maximum work effort), whereas the success of the latter might overrule the success of the former—at least in the aggregate. Strategic power is exercised according to the principle of divide et impera, which leads to a polarization within the ruled class between insiders and outsiders. An obvious example is labor-interest associations at the professional or occupational level which regulate and limit especially the entry to professional or occupational labor markets (closed shop, etc.). But even in those cases where institutions were established by purposeful and interest-motivated actions and/or were legitimized by majority decisions, they usually have been introduced under conditions of poor or at least incomplete knowledge about the consequences of the established institutional rules. Spontaneous actions or resistance against established rules will ultimately change outdated institutions. It is here that the fourth institutional approach has something to contribute.

Modern systems theory emphasizes the ordering function of spontaneous actions in living systems (an analogue to Darwin's theory of mutation and selection) by self-reinforcing feedback loops. Institutional economics based on game theory has observed comparable ordering processes in recurring games (see the seminal article by Schelling 1971). Andrew Schotter, for example, approvingly quotes Hayek: "It is the contention that, by tracing the combined effects of individual actions, we discover that many of the institutions on which human achievements rest have arisen and are functioning without a designing and directing mind; that, as Adam Ferguson expressed it, 'nations stumble upon establishments which are indeed the result of human action but not the result of human design,' and that the spontaneous collaboration of free men often creates things which are greater than their individual minds can fully comprehend" (Schotter 1985:6; Hayek 1960).

Indeed, the rise of such spontaneous orders for two reasons cannot be denied: lack of complete knowledge and spontaneous actions of individuals. Acknowledging spontaneous ordering processes as an empirical fact, however, does not entail the normative conclusion—as especially Hayek maintains—that institutions resulting from such processes are generally preferable to and more efficient than institutions established by purposeful design. The rational tradition meets the spontaneous tradition at the point where the spontaneists need metainstitutional rules that rationalize the superiority of spontaneous ordering processes, telling us under which institutional conditions spontaneous ordering processes will not violate commonly shared human values and will not lead to spontaneous disordering or to the neglect of basic human needs. So far, at least, no one has proposed to start from the natural state of complete disorder, or to deny the needs of human beings, such as for water, air, food, and shelter (Hodgson 1988:246 ff.).

When in this final section we thus follow the rational choice approach, we are well aware of its limitations and of the three other dimensions of institutions which should not be dismissed. The Hobbesian tradition can explain the necessity of institutions (to avoid the loss of orientation in a world of complex interrelationships). The power tradition can contribute to an explanation of the persistence of old institutions or the emergence of new institutions. And the libertarian tradition reminds us of the possibility of spontaneous ordering processes as well as of the metainstitutional question of to what extent we should allow this type of institutional process to occur.

We now turn to the question of what assumptions and empirical evidence will enable us to improve financing institutions of labor market policy, given specified objectives and behavioral constraints.

11.2.1 Favorable Institutional Conditions for a Desired Increase in the General Level of Active Labor Market Policy

The amount of resources a country will commit to active labor market policy for solving the problem of unemployment to a large extent depends on how highly a culture values the goal of full employment, as well as on the role labor market policy is assigned in the framework of economic and employment policy. As a thought experiment, it will be assumed that full employment has been given high priority and that active labor market policy, because of altered economic, technological, and social conditions (Schmid 1987), will be of greater significance in the future than it has been in the past. How should financing systems be designed that would promote the objective of an organizational and financial expansion of active labor market policy?

Our own studies indicate that financing institutions play a secondary, albeit not insignificant, role with respect to the level of active labor market policy. Thus, a purely contribution-financed system would hardly be compatible with a labor market policy that plays a greater role in employment policy, as is presupposed in our thought experiment. The reason is that contribution systems ultimately always imply an identifiable link between contributions and benefits. This, however, is not the case with a labor market policy that functions selectively according to changing economic, regional, sectoral, and individual conditions. An expansion of the functions of active labor market policy would seem to call for mixed financing through contributions and taxes, and perhaps a separation between the financing of active and passive labor market policy.

Closer examination reveals that most productive employment promotion measures have effects transcending both the group of participating individuals and contribution payers. In addition to their stabilizing function for the economy, public job creation measures, for example, also have sociopolitical and public good functions. The capacity of the unemployed to work is preserved, and productive activities related to such measures for the most part benefit the general public. Measures for occupational rehabilitation as well serve general sociopolitical goals and, if successful, reduce the burden for other social insurance agencies or social assistance. Career counseling for youth and measures for reintegrating women into the labor market also extend beyond the circle of insurable contribution payers. Further training and retraining not only serve to improve the individual's opportunities in the labor market but also facilitate the invariably necessary structural changes in the economy. Increases in productivity because of human capital are beneficial for the economy as a whole.

In view of the increasing external effects of active labor market policy, its costs should not be borne exclusively by dependent workers in the private sector. Rather, they should be more widely shared by taxpayers as a whole. Such a mixed form of financing may have the added advantage of assigning the financial responsibility for active labor market policy increasingly to those institutions that financially benefit from a reduction in unemployment. Such an institutional congruity of positive and negative budgetary effects through active labor market policy forms an effective incentive for a more active policy. The technical design of a mixed financing scheme is a secondary question and will depend on the existing institutional structures. Both earmarked taxes (a general labor market deduction) and regular state subsidies for contribution-financed labor market funds are suitable means of financing such extended functions of labor market policy.

If active and passive labor market policy have common sources of revenue, integrated budgeting, and joint implementation, there is a danger that active labor market policy will be crowded out by wage-replacement benefits, both in a financial and in an operative sense. In the Federal Republic of Germany, this danger has become a reality at certain times. Regulated state subsidies or the central state's general liability for deficits favor an expansion of active labor market policy, particularly if positive and negative budgetary effects of active labor market policy affect the same institutions. General levy systems as a rule slow down expansions of active labor market policy (Austria).

With large and permanent surpluses, however, even these systems tend to widen their scope and increase expenditures (Austria, Federal Republic of Germany). Levy systems for special purposes have an inherent tendency toward expenditure growth. This is unproblematic as long as beneficiaries and contributors are in principle identical. Examples for this are levy systems providing benefits for the construction industry (Austria, Federal Republic of Germany), for vocational further training, especially in the workplace (Sweden, France), and—most recently—for short-time worker funds (Sweden).

An indispensable precondition for a labor market policy with significant employment effects is a well-developed administrative infrastructure for its implementation. This includes a system of labor administration with regional branches, modern information technologies, a sufficiently large and qualified staff, and close coordination with enterprises, municipalities, unions, and other important decision makers at the local level.

11.2.2 Favorable Institutional Conditions for a Labor Market Policy with Positive Effects on Economic Stability

The economy is subject to cycles that are always in danger of running out of control and degenerating into deflation or inflation. How should financing systems be designed if labor market policy is assigned a more significant role in the context of a policy for general economic stability?

Only in Sweden and—during short periods of time—in the Federal Republic of Germany has active labor market policy played a stabilizing (countercyclical) role. Although in the United States there have been short countercyclical periods, for the most part policies have been procyclical. The institutional preconditions for a countercyclical use of active labor market policy are, in the case of contribution systems, the accumulation of reserves and the generally unlimited liability of the central state for deficits (Federal Republic of Germany). In the case of tax-financed systems, special reserve funds and institutionally facilitated forms of supplementary budgets (Sweden) are helpful. If contributions are determined on the levy principle (i.e., if contributions and expenditures have to be directly matched) and deficit liability is in principle limited, as is the case, for example, in Austria, active labor market policy can have virtually no stabilizing effects.

With respect to expenditure control, the responsiveness of active labor market policy to cyclical changes in unemployment is insured (in the Federal Republic of Germany) by entitlements of receiving relatively generous benefits during short-time work for firms facing demand shortages, as well as (in the Federal Republic of Germany and Sweden) by entitlements of participation in labor market training programs for the unemployed or people in danger of unemployment. A well-developed personnel and material infrastructure of labor administration also seems to be a precondition for an anticyclical approach to work promotion measures. If it is necessary to largely entrust established regional or local authorities with the implementation of countercyclical programs, there is a danger of significant windfalls and substitution effects (e.g., United States, in part also Sweden and, to a lesser degree, Federal Republic of Germany).

Sweden demonstrates how the economic flexibility of active labor market policy can be further improved. There, the administrative costs of programs from the start are prorated and tied to the respective program expenditures so that (at least in principle) the implementation of programs cannot fail on account of personnel or other infrastructural shortages. Systematically tying infrastructure costs to program expenditures prevents the potential operative squeezing out of active labor market policy by passive labor market policy, as could be observed in the Federal Republic of Germany.

Wage-replacement benefits also have a stabilizing function. They stabilize overall economic demand by preserving the purchasing power particularly of lower- and middle-income groups, who tend to be relatively more strongly affected by unemployment, and by taking into account their greater propensity to consume. This relates to a function of social security to be discussed below. The better a financing system can stabilize the income of the unemployed, the more adequately it will fulfill its function as a built-in economic stabilizer.

11.2.3 Favorable Institutional Conditions for Improving the Social Security of the Unemployed

In the short and medium term, contribution-financed wage-compensation systems provide more effective social security in case of unemployment than tax-financed or only quasi-contribution-financed systems. This is related to the more effective property protection of contribution systems and the greater willingness to pay on the part of contributors because of this protection. Correspondingly, it applies only to the limited group of the insured. The most generous systems in terms of benefit level and duration are contribution systems where the state is fully liable for deficits (Federal Republic of Germany) or where regular state subsidies exist (Sweden, France until 1984). With more permanent high levels of unemployment, however, contribution-oriented systems tend to eliminate bad risks (segmentation response), and they will do so increasingly rapidly the more directly these systems are governed by the levy principle (United States, Austria). Tax-financed systems under these conditions tend to reduce benefits in a way that affects all unemployed; that is, they produce a leveling response (Great Britain).

Contribution-financed systems of social security are premised on a functioning division of labor between microlevel and macrolevel control. They cannot guarantee social security during long periods of mass unemployment, nor can they offer adequate protection for bad risks even during short periods of high unemployment. It would, therefore, only be consistent to introduce a tax-financed minimum level of social security for all unemployed and to encumber the general state budget with financing long-term unemployment, specifically the agency that is in a position to make financial policy with positive employment effects. Otherwise, certain groups in society who are selected in a one-sided and arbitrary fashion (precisely those who happen to become unemployed) have to pay the costs of adapting to collectively caused employment crises.

With respect to the question of allocation, there frequently is concern that generous wage-replacement benefits reduce the flexibility of the labor market, being primarily understood as mobility of the unemployed and downward adjustment of the wage level. However, this thesis is theoretically controversial and far from empirically substantiated (see Chapter 6). In any case, this is a very complex problem. The impact of generous benefits depends entirely on the specific conditions. In a system with a coordinated interplay among micro, meso, and macro policy, generosity may even be the precondition for a willingness on the part of workers to be mobile and adaptable. In a system that essentially relies (or has to rely) on market forces for balancing supply and demand because effective institutions for mesolevel and macrolevel control do not exist, generosity will probably have the negative incentive functions ascribed to it.

Sweden is an example where the interplay among the three levels discussed above is fairly successful. In the Swedish culture of solidarity in wage policy, labor market flexibility can only be attained by socializing the costs of an adaptation that ultimately is made by the individual (principle of individualization of programs, socialization of costs). Because in this system flexibility can never be attained through

individual financial incentives (more explicitly, financial rewards and
punishment through market-determined wage differences), different
institutional mechanisms have to be present to fulfill this function: at
the micro level, loyalty, among other things evident in a strong willingness to be organized in unions and a readiness for mobility (in exchange for this, as it were, generous unemployment benefits for lower-
and middle-income groups); at the meso level, social control by the
union organization and the labor administration (in exchange for this,
various public services in support of labor mobility); at the macro
level, wage moderation through a wage policy of solidarity and, if necessary, acceptance of collective restrictions on real wages through
monetary policy measures, such as devaluation (in exchange for this,
stimulation of demand through tax policy or expansion of public services).

We have mentioned this example only to illustrate that incentive and allocation effects of wage-replacement benefits cannot be
viewed in isolation but have to be seen in their overall institutional
context. And our thesis, in a nutshell, is that generous insurance
benefits in one context may have positive allocative effects while in
another context they may be negative. A transfer of such institutional
contexts is neither possible nor is it being recommended in this concrete case.

11.2.4 Favorable Institutional Conditions for Redistributive Effects of Labor Market Policy

To the extent that labor market policy is to serve redistributive
functions, tax-financed systems and mixed-financing systems are more
suitable than pure contribution systems. Taking on extensive redistributive functions contradicts the logic of contribution systems which
ultimately rests on the principle of equivalence. As empirical analyses
have indicated, only tax-financed systems or mixed-financing systems
show more extensive and politically uncontroversial redistributive
effects. Where contribution systems have redistributive effects—for
example, in the Federal Republic of Germany, certain sectoral redistributive effects because of seasonal unemployment (favoring the construction industry) or benefits for short-time workers (favoring sectors
or supplier firms subject to economic fluctuations and strong competitive pressure)—they are the object of political criticism.

The necessity for redistributive functions very much depends
on the structure of the unemployment risk. If regional, sectoral, or individual risks were randomly distributed, there would be no need for

redistribution. However, across national borders, there seems to be a trend toward an increasingly unequal distribution of risks. But this conjecture, for which a number of reasons can be adduced (increasing international division of labor with increasing specialization, economic fluctuations in specific sectors or for specific raw materials, etc.), is still in need of further theoretical and empirical examination.

Among countries, there are at any rate significant differences, such as in the individual structure of unemployment, which to a large degree are dependent upon institutional factors outside of financing systems. The structure of the vocational training system deserves particular emphasis. The concentration of labor market policy programs on youth in many countries is a reaction to shortcomings in the system of initial vocational training (United States, Great Britain, France, Sweden). It is no accident that this emphasis on youth corresponds to a largely tax-financed labor market policy. Contribution systems would not be capable of concentrating their funds for such redistributive effects. Tax-financed systems and mixed-financing systems as a rule also achieve better results with respect to the integration and reintegration of women into the labor market.

As far as income security through wage-replacement benefits is concerned, contribution systems tend toward the proportionality principle (Federal Republic of Germany). In combination with tax effects, they sometimes even tend to favor higher-income groups (Austria). The proportionality principle is distribution-neutral and reflects existing income structures. However, the principle is unproblematic only as long as the risk of unemployment has a normal distribution across income groups. But this is usually not the case, and with permanent mass unemployment, the burden further shifts to the disadvantage of the lower-income strata. To provide a basic income protection for risks that cannot be insured or are difficult to insure, as well as for a differentiation of wage-replacement benefits according to redistributive effects, it would be an institutional advantage to have a tax share in the financing of wage-compensation benefits. On the other hand, the advantages of contribution financing, particularly with respect to income security, are so evident (relative property protection, greater willingness to pay, stabilization effect) that it should not be sacrificed for the sake of redistributive flexibility. It follows that, taking into account the whole range of labor market policy functions, a mixed-financing scheme is institutionally advantageous for both active and passive labor market policy.

11.2.5 Favorable Institutional Conditions for Greater Individual Freedom through Labor Market Policy

In the past, when unemployment insurance did not yet exist, let alone labor market policy, there were no alternatives. Any job had to be accepted merely in order to secure subsistence. Today we have moved beyond this state of affairs. A legal entitlement to unemployment insurance, which—as mentioned above—ought to be expanded into a right to minimum security for all, provides a chance to look around, to check carefully, and to consider alternatives. Occasionally, the labor administration may be able to assist, provide support in the form of information, improve qualifications, or offer temporary work. Institutionalized labor market policy, however, cannot eliminate the intensive individual job search, psychological stress, and the inevitable disappointment stemming from justified or unjustified expectations during this difficult transition period.

The question is whether individual alternatives within the unemployment insurance system can be expanded without replacing the system as a whole. Concretely, are there institutional provisions that would allow a more decentralized, individual approach to resolving employment crises? Could we have, as it were, in addition to the huge rescue ship of unemployment insurance and the large and somewhat awkward rowing boats of labor administration, speedy small sailboats that individuals or a small number of people could sail even against the wind (i.e., taking precautions against unemployment)?

We are using these metaphors to refer to enterprise, sectoral, or regional special funds that could be utilized for specific labor market policy objectives. Empirically, we believe, a tendency can be observed toward a further differentiation of such earmarked special funds. Examples are collectively negotiated fund systems for training, further training, and early retirement; short-time working funds negotiated at the sectoral level with regular subsidies from tax revenues or the general labor market budget; funds for wage-compensation benefits in case of bankruptcy; winter construction funds. The advantage of such special funds consists in the fact that contributions and benefits can be more accurately differentiated according to the principle of cause. The correspondingly greater visibility of a quid pro quo also promotes the political legitimization of such financing systems.

The impetus for such fund systems and their implementation must come from the micro and meso levels, specifically from enterprises, municipalities, regional authorities, unions, employers' associations, and other economic associations. However, public labor market policy along the lines of our thought experiment can assist with its revenues and expenditures, such as through nonrecurring infrastructural assistance (e.g., building additional training centers for specific vocational programs), regular state subsidies, tax exemptions, or rules and regulations. Why not replace a portion of the enterprises' profit taxes with rules committing profits to development or innovation funds at the enterprise level which, with the appropriate participation by employees, could then serve labor market policy objectives? Why not vary the level of the employers' unemployment insurance contributions with the effective working time per employee so that higher contribution rates would apply for overtime and lower rates for effective working time below the collectively and legally set regular hours? Why not replace part of income tax on wages by establishing special-purpose individual savings accounts with public interest and premium aid—comparable to home-ownership plans—which could then serve labor market and employment policy objectives, such as for financial assistance during extended sabbaticals, for the financing of further training courses, for temporary reductions in working time during parenting, for the flexible transition to retirement, or for starting one's own enterprise? It is time for economic democracy, but that is another story.

Basic Labor Market and
Labor Market Policy Data

Appendix
Basic Labor Market and Labor Market Policy Data

	Definition	Measurement Unit	Source
Economic and Labor Market Data			
Nominal GDP	Gross domestic product at current prices	Millions of national currency	OECD 1989a, part 3; OECD 1990a, table 1
Real GDP	Gross domestic product at 1980 prices	Millions of national currency	OECD 1989a, part 3; OECD 1990a, table 1
Central Government Expenditures	Central (federal) government expenditures (outlays)	Billions of national currency	BMF 1973 - 1990[a]
Budget Surplus (Deficit)	Surplus (+) or deficit (-) of central (federal) government budget	Billions of national currency	BMF 1973 - 1990[a]
Compensation of Employees	Wage and salary payments to employees plus employers' contributions for social security and private pension or welfare plans	Millions of national currency	OECD 1986a, table 8; OECD 1990a, table 8
Civilian Employment	Persons in civilian employment, average data for the year	Thousands	OECD 1990b, part II, table II[b]
Dependent Employment	Wage earners and salaried employees, average data for the year (Great Britain: midyear data)	Thousands	OECD 1990b, part II, table IIIA[b]
Unemployed	Persons registered as unemployed, average data for the year	Thousands	OECD 1990b, part II, table II
Unemployment Rate	Unemployment rates, average data for the year	Percent	OECD 1989b: 183

Labor Market Policy Data

	Definition	Measurement Unit	Source
Contributions to Unemployment Insurance	Employers' and employees' contributions to unemployment insurance funds (Great Britain: to the National Insurance Fund)	Millions of national currency	Bruche 1984a, 1984b; Bruche and Reissert 1985; DoL 1987; Reissert 1985; Schmid 1984[a) c)]
Expenditures for Passive Labor Market Policy	Public expenditures for unemployment benefits, unemployment assistance, bankruptcy wage benefits, early retirement schemes without a replacement condition, and related administrative costs (if available)	Millions of national currency	Bruche 1984a, 1984b; Bruche and Reissert 1985; DoL 1987; OMB 1983b-1989b; Reissert 1985; Schmid 1984[a) c) d) e)]
Unemployment Benefit	Public expenditures for unemployment benefit (see Table 3)	Millions of national currency	Bruche 1984a, 1984b; Bruche and Reissert 1985; DoL 1987; Reissert 1985; Schmid 1984[a) c) f)]
Unemployment Assistance	Public expenditures for unemployment assistance (see Table 3)	Millions of national currency	Bruche 1984a, 1984b; Bruche and Reissert 1985; DoL 1987; Reissert 1985; Schmid 1984[a) c) f)]
Expenditures for Active Labor Market Policy	Public expenditures for placement services and vocational counseling, adult training and retraining, rehabilitation, early retirement schemes with a replacement condition, wage-cost subsidies for job creation, preservation of employment and recruitment, and related administrative costs (if available)	Millions of national currency	Bruche 1984a, 1984b; Bruche and Reissert 1985; OMB 1989a: 5-104; OMB 1983b-1989 b, table G-2; OMB 1989c; Reissert 1985; Schmid 1984[a) c) d) e)]
Training and Retraining	Public expenditures for adult training and retraining	Millions of national currency	Bruche 1984a, 1984b; Bruche and Reissert 1985; DoL 1976-1982; OMB 1983a-1989a; Reissert 1985; Schmid 1984[a) c) g)]
Job Creation	Public expenditures for wage-cost subsidies to create additional temporary jobs for the unemployed in the public sector	Millions of national currency	Bruche 1984a, 1984b; Bruche and Reissert 1985; DoL 1976-1982; OMB 1983a-1989a; Reissert 1985; Schmid 1984[a) c) g)]

Definition	Measurement Unit	Source
Preservation of Employment	Public expenditures for wage-cost subsidies to preserve private employment (in particular, short-time work benefits)	Millions of national currency	Bruche 1984a, 1984b; Bruche and Reissert 1985; DoL 1976-1982; OMB 1983a-1989a; Reissert 1985; Schmid 1984[a] c)
Hiring Subsidies	Public expenditures for subsidy programs to recruit unemployed persons (including work experience programs for youth)	Millions of national currency	Bruche 1984a, 1984b; Bruche and Reissert 1985; DoL 1976-1982; OMB 1983a-1989a; Reissert 1985; Schmid 1984[a] c) g)

a) Because the Swedish fiscal year runs from July to June, public expenditure data for fiscal years have been transformed into calendar-year data by computing the averages of two consecutive fiscal years. Fiscal-year data for Great Britain and the United States have not been transformed into calendar-year data. In the United States, data on unemployment insurance contributions and passive labor market policy are on a calendar-year basis whereas data on active labor market policy are on a fiscal-year basis.

b) For the Federal Republic of Germany, 1980-1988 employment data are from a revised time series provided by the Federal Statistical Office.

c) In addition to our country studies, which are quoted here, the original data sources for these studies have also been used to update or supplement labor market policy data. Additional data for the United States have been provided by the U.S. Department of Labor (DoL) and the Office of Management and Budget (OMB).

d) In Austria and the Federal Republic of Germany, the administrative costs of the labor market administration cannot be split into costs for the administration of active measures and passive measures. It is assumed here that half of the administrative costs is incurred for active measures and the other half for passive measures.

e) In France, expenditure data for early retirement cannot be split into expenditures for schemes with a replacement condition (which, according to our definition, are part of active labor market policy) and expenditures for schemes without a replacement condition (which are part of passive labor market policy). All expenditures for French early retirement schemes are therefore classified under passive labor market policy spending.

f) In France, expenditures for unemployment benefits and unemployment assistance cannot be differentiated because elements of unemployment assistance are partly integrated into unemployment benefit schemes. Expenditures for all French wage-replacement benefits are therefore classified under unemployment benefits.

g) In Great Britain, job creation measures were merged into the new Employment Training program in 1988. The division between expenditures for training and expenditures for job creation in Britain after 1987 is therefore based on estimates (planning figures). In the United States, CETA titles IIB, IIC and III as well as the JTPA block grant and some federally administered JTPA programs are classified under training expenditures; CETA and JTPA Summer Youth and Job Corps programs as well as revenue losses from job tax credit programs are classified under hiring subsidies. Other programs offering mainly job search assistance (e.g., JTPA title III and the WIN program) are not included in either of these categories.

Austria

Economic and Labor Market Data

Year	Nominal GDP (millions of ÖS)	Real GDP (millions of ÖS)	Central Government Expenditures (billions of ÖS)	Budget Surplus (Deficit) (billions of ÖS)	Compensation of Employees (millions of ÖS)	Civilian Employment (thousands)	Dependent Employment (thousands)	Unemployed (thousands)	Unemployment Rate (%)
1973	543,460	811,724	109.6	1.5	270,380	3,010	2,271	33	0.9
1974	618,560	843,736	130.2	0.8	315,030	3,010	2,409	41	1.1
1975	656,110	840,679	157.5	-29.7	353,600	2,942	2,368	53	1.5
1976	724,750	879,157	177.5	-34.3	389,470	2,947	2,380	54	1.5
1977	796,190	917,477	186.7	-29.9	431,450	2,989	2,420	49	1.4
1978	842,330	922,232	208.2	-35.0	472,420	3,015	2,470	64	1.7
1979	918,540	965,647	225.1	-32.4	504,520	3,051	2,524	65	1.7
1980	994,700	994,700	239.5	-29.3	545,630	3,070	2,545	58	1.5
1981	1,055,970	993,220	261.9	-27.5	589,010	3,090	2,575	80	2.1
1982	1,133,530	1,004,259	291.7	-46.6	616,850	3,186	2,677	116	3.1
1983	1,201,230	1,026,154	324.1	-65.6	642,440	3,159	2,654	135	3.7
1984	1,276,770	1,039,195	339.7	-57.4	676,330	3,235	2,740	128	3.8
1985	1,348,420	1,066,305	367.0	-60.1	717,090	3,234	2,751	121	3.6
1986	1,415,500	1,074,851	394.1	-73.0	761,170	3,282	2,795	106	3.1
1987	1,477,770	1,094,359	402.9	-74.6	792,650	3,300	2,809	130	3.8
1988	1,570,640	1,139,928	434.7	-71.1	821,860	3,311	2,822	122	3.6

Labor Market Policy Data

Year	Contributions to Unemployment Insurance (millions of ÖS)	Expenditures for Passive Labor Market Policy			Expenditures for Active Labor Market Policy				
		Total (millions of ÖS)	Unemp. Benefit (millions of ÖS)	Unemp. Assistance (millions of ÖS)	Total (millions of ÖS)	Training and Retraining (millions of ÖS)	Job Creation (millions of ÖS)	Preservation of Employment (millions of ÖS)	Hiring Subsidies (millions of ÖS)
1973	2,325	1,138.3	840.0	106.4	844.2				
1974	2,907	1,433.7	1,070.3	152.6	1,129.3	554.5	44.3	292.6	5.7
1975	3,239	1,889.5	1,417.6	232.5	1,281.4	583.5	31.3	404.8	6.7
1976	3,741	2,298.8	1,656.3	346.0	1,226.1	537.3	19.3	388.5	5.3
1977	4,332	2,435.2	1,737.9	365.3	1,240.6	491.0	30.7	414.2	8.1
1978	5,182	3,787.1	2,326.1	435.0	1,495.7	636.6	19.7	491.7	13.7
1979	5,739	4,746.4	2,697.1	559.7	1,683.1	690.7	33.8	588.8	14.3
1980	6,123	4,661.6	2,563.6	607.9	1,528.3	579.4	35.4	527.7	19.1
1981	7,802	6,546.4	3,537.3	739.8	1,739.5	562.2	18.1	737.1	21.7
1982	9,836	10,027.2	5,709.7	1,185.6	2,184.3	623.7	148.4	934.0	25.9
1983	12,842	12,410.3	6,683.7	2,053.6	2,802.9	1,261.7	211.9	742.8	34.6
1984	16,840	13,572.0	6,508.1	2,726.2	2,705.1	1,385.3	62.5	602.6	51.6
1985	18,375	15,194.2	7,014.3	2,959.6	3,314.3	1,735.2	208.1	570.9	106.7
1986	19,595	16,725.0	7,811.4	3,307.7	4,008.8	2,175.3	455.8	504.7	135.0
1987	20,366	18,554.0	8,744.4	3,914.1	4,591.5	2,510.6	600.6	537.0	144.0
1988	24,408	18,803.9	8,261.1	4,206.7	3,197.8	1,520.6	385.8	388.1	98.3

Federal Republic of Germany

Economic and Labor Market Data

	Nominal GDP (millions of DM)	Real GDP (millions of DM)	Central Government Expenditures (billions of DM)	Budget Surplus (Deficit) (billions of DM)	Compensation of Employees (millions of DM)	Civilian Employment (thousands)	Dependent Employment (thousands)	Unemployed (thousands)	Unemployment Rate (%)
1973	917,270	1,271,650	121.8	-3.4	510,930	26,411	22,395	273	1.0
1974	984,580	1,275,100	133.3	-10.3	563,120	26,038	22,113	582	2.1
1975	1,026,900	1,254,830	156.3	-33.1	587,200	25,285	21,489	1,074	4.0
1976	1,121,720	1,322,740	162.5	-25.9	631,290	25,059	21,407	1,060	4.0
1977	1,197,820	1,361,790	172.0	-22.2	676,030	25,014	21,496	1,030	4.0
1978	1,285,320	1,400,900	189.5	-26.3	721,640	25,169	21,734	993	3.9
1979	1,392,300	1,459,040	203.4	-26.1	777,850	25,516	22,132	876	3.7
1980	1,478,940	1,478,940	215.7	-27.6	844,410	26,528	23,366	889	3.3
1981	1,540,930	1,481,390	233.0	-37.9	882,950	26,498	23,372	1,272	4.6
1982	1,597,920	1,471,830	244.6	-37.7	902,520	26,193	23,108	1,833	6.7
1983	1,674,840	1,493,920	246.7	-31.9	920,910	25,809	22,755	2,258	8.2
1984	1,755,840	1,535,990	251.8	-28.6	954,000	25,869	22,827	2,266	8.2
1985	1,830,490	1,566,480	257.1	-22.7	991,000	26,062	23,028	2,304	8.3
1986	1,931,420	1,603,210	261.5	-23.3	1,041,350	26,431	23,381	2,228	7.9
1987	2,006,350	1,632,680	269.0	-27.9	1,084,140	26,626	23,610	2,229	7.9
1988	2,110,560	1,692,930	275.4	-36.0	1,126,360	26,840	23,835	2,242	7.9

Labor Market Policy Data

	Contributions to Unemployment Insurance (millions of DM)	Expenditures for Passive Labor Market Policy			Expenditures for Active Labor Market Policy				
		Total (millions of DM)	Unemp. Benefit (millions of DM)	Unemp. Assistance (millions of DM)	Total (millions of DM)	Training and Retraining (millions of DM)	Job Creation (millions of DM)	Preservation of Employment (millions of DM)	Hiring Subsidies (millions of DM)
1973	5,829	2,261	1,397	144	4,515	1,820	24	1,494	9
1974	6,444	4,761	3,554	302	5,605	2,128	41	2,086	17
1975	7,786	10,011	7,768	979	7,952	2,865	138	3,327	100
1976	12,497	9,740	6,910	1,542	6,463	2,286	179	2,252	186
1977	13,773	9,257	6,290	1,595	6,257	1,513	647	1,961	266
1978	14,740	9,363	6,276	1,657	7,196	1,626	1,005	2,083	459
1979	15,926	10,996	7,471	1,974	9,120	2,260	1,171	2,539	616
1980	17,321	11,676	8,112	1,903	10,568	3,209	1,083	2,445	574
1981	18,140	18,076	13,297	2,850	12,958	3,946	1,088	3,813	454
1982	24,287	25,224	18,030	5,015	13,058	3,801	988	4,434	199
1983	28,672	26,407	17,107	7,124	13,299	3,556	1,253	4,635	158
1984	30,446	25,171	14,146	8,719	12,929	3,738	1,801	3,405	203
1985	29,492	25,613	14,088	9,126	13,222	4,089	2,863	2,670	210
1986	29,122	25,791	14,050	9,160	15,241	5,155	3,413	2,227	306
1987	32,265	27,022	15,295	9,030	17,979	6,431	3,718	2,480	323
1988	33,716	29,191	18,054	8,450	19,072	7,049		1,999	213

France

Economic and Labor Market Data

	Nominal GDP (millions of FF)	Real GDP (millions of FF)	Central Government Expenditures (billions of FF)	Budget Surplus (Deficit) (billions of FF)	Compensation of Employees (millions of FF)	Civilian Employment (thousands)	Dependent Employment (thousands)	Unemployed (thousands)	Unemployment Rate (%)
1973	1,129,835	2,340,927	226.0	4.8	557,271	20,863	16,879	593	2.7
1974	1,302,978	2,413,721	272.6	5.8	664,687	21,058	17,166	632	2.9
1975	1,467,884	2,407,001	332.0	-37.8	801,596	20,863	17,060	901	4.2
1976	1,700,553	2,509,149	374.5	-17.2	932,474	21,016	17,274	997	4.5
1977	1,917,803	2,589,881	415.0	-19.5	1,061,000	21,188	17,497	1,134	5.0
1978	2,182,588	2,676,646	482.0	-38.0	1,201,792	21,262	17,610	1,201	5.3
1979	2,481,097	2,763,409	553.8	-38.9	1,362,074	21,305	17,686	1,361	6.0
1980	2,808,295	2,808,295	637.1	-23.8	1,573,880	21,333	17,752	1,467	6.3
1981	3,164,804	2,841,328	764.3	-64.3	1,791,188	21,203	17,663	1,750	7.5
1982	3,626,021	2,913,662	837.9	-91.8	2,052,955	21,240	17,752	1,923	8.2
1983	4,006,498	2,933,904	882.4	-115.1	2,255,615	21,168	17,737	1,974	8.4
1984	4,361,913	2,972,464	1,005.6	-146.2	2,419,226	20,981	17,605	2,323	9.8
1985	4,700,143	3,028,379	1,071.8	-153.3	2,573,107	20,955	17,578	2,442	10.2
1986	5,052,519	3,098,109	1,133.4	-141.1	2,694,990	20,955	17,649	2,490	10.4
1987	5,301,320	3,158,249	1,164.7	-120.1	2,802,005	21,018	17,733	2,532	10.5
1988	5,658,620	3,269,603	1,179.9	-114.8	2,938,386	21,179	17,915	2,410	10.0

Labor Market Policy Data

	Contributions to Unemployment Insurance (millions of FF)	Expenditures for Passive Labor Market Policy			Expenditures for Active Labor Market Policy				
		Total (millions of FF)	Unemp. Benefit (millions of FF)	Unemp. Assistance (millions of FF)	Total (millions of FF)	Training and Retraining (millions of FF)	Job Creation (millions of FF)	Preservation of Employment (millions of FF)	Hiring Subsidies (millions of FF)
1973	1,747	3,467.2	1,890.3	-	6,701.6	5,718.5	-	138.9	78.6
1974	2,442	4,658.2	2,636.3	-	8,771.5	7,243.2	-	469.4	95.3
1975	6,979	9,563.1	6,867.3	-	10,548.8	8,552.4	-	792.5	136.6
1976	10,228	12,858.2	9,577.3	-	12,584.9	10,087.1	-	993.5	178.2
1977	10,930	16,488.4	12,500.1	-	16,452.3	12,629.7	-	1,079.2	896.8
1978	14,985	23,144.7	17,231.9	-	21,678.9	16,612.7	-	1,461.2	1,530.3
1979	21,025	30,840.1	22,875.3	-	23,578.4	17,302.9	-	2,348.7	1,889.7
1980	25,827	37,378.4	26,412.1	-	27,298.0	19,812.9	-	2,361.1	2,622.3
1981	29,174	51,098.7	31,489.6	-	33,826.4	23,681.4	-	3,880.3	2,955.2
1982	34,003	75,939.6	48,526.4	-	41,222.8	28,088.9	-	5,095.7	3,330.4
1983	51,322	95,496.9	44,760.6	-	44,777.0	30,740.3	-	4,678.2	3,753.3
1984	64,566	103,270.3	50,227.4	-	50,024.0	34,001.0	1.7	5,301.8	4,465.3
1985	71,513	114,422.7	56,366.6	-	55,682.5	37,304.3	2,102.3	3,937.1	3,877.6
1986	80,900	117,729.8	63,297.3	-	65,554.0	43,387.6	3,546.0	3,638.0	6,500.6
1987	84,721	120,978.8	71,641.2	-	71,630.2	47,641.3	3,600.0	2,825.2	9,182.1
1988	93,258	122,307.6	77,161.8	-	77,746.5	55,881.4	3,400.0	2,814.1	7,178.1

Great Britain

Economic and Labor Market Data

	Nominal GDP (millions of £)	Real GDP (millions of £)	Central Government Expenditures (billions of £)	Budget Surplus (Deficit) (billions of £)	Compensation of Employees (million of £)	Civilian Employment (thousands)	Dependent Employment (thousands)	Unemployed (thousands)	Unemployment Rate (%)
1973	73,750	215,469	23.4	-3.7	43,877	24,715	22,679	557	2.1
1974	84,032	213,306	31.1	-5.5	52,379	24,803	22,804	528	2.2
1975	106,114	211,879	37.8	-8.8	68,494	24,719	22,723	838	3.6
1976	124,726	216,611	44.0	-6.8	78,005	24,509	22,557	1,266	4.8
1977	145,373	221,564	47.7	-6.2	86,572	24,538	22,631	1,359	5.2
1978	167,740	229,691	54.9	-8.6	98,843	24,696	22,790	1,343	4.9
1979	197,436	236,105	66.7	-8.2	115,866	25,080	23,173	1,234	4.5
1980	230,733	230,733	84.9	-13.8	137,639	25,004	22,991	1,513	6.1
1981	253,639	227,594	90.1	-8.8	149,584	24,011	21,892	2,395	9.1
1982	277,606	231,552	99.9	-11.2	158,621	23,584	21,414	2,770	10.4
1983	302,695	240,105	107.5	-13.4	169,580	23,304	21,067	2,984	11.2
1984	323,430	244,958	135.4	-10.1	180,096	23,909	21,238	3,030	11.4
1985	354,157	254,006	146.2	-10.9	194,573	24,210	21,423	3,179	11.6
1986	379,412	262,690	152.0	-10.5	209,542	24,240	21,387	3,229	11.8
1987	416,561	274,963	156.2	-0.9	226,343	24,755	21,584	2,905	10.4
1988	462,564	286,343	162.5	6.9	249,775	25,555	22,226	2,341	8.2

Labor Market Policy Data

	Contributions to Unemployment Insurance (millions of £)	Expenditures for Passive Labor Market Policy			Expenditures for Active Labor Market Policy				
		Total (millions of £)	Unemp. Benefit (millions of £)	Unemp. Assistance (millions of £)	Total (millions of £)	Training and Retraining (millions of £)	Job Creation (millions of £)	Preservation of Employment (millions of £)	Hiring Subsidies (millions of £)
1973	3,816	364	182	150					
1974	5,123	475	227	200	190	82	3	–	–
1975	6,327	968	473	388	322	171	4	–	1
1976	7,902	1,261	582	578	587	260	37	3	4
1977	8,742	1,479	655	729	803	293	81	92	22
1978	9,188	1,516	660	755	886	311	98	174	79
1979	10,644	1,579	681	770	1,013	329	73	134	168
1980	12,813	2,823	1,328	1,182	1,505	348	65	65	225
1981	14,354	4,313	1,758	2,091	1,653	355	108	366	396
1982	16,664	5,411	1,550	3,422	1,775	326	200	260	586
1983	18,167	6,083	1,545	4,100	2,257	269	424	72	864
1984	19,422	6,664	1,578	4,742	2,557	303	558	27	963
1985	21,223	7,298	1,589	5,351	2,706	380	708	6	1,017
1986	22,778	7,546	1,734	5,556	3,341	534	1,068	–	1,082
1987	26,051	6,762	1,468	5,202	3,639	588	1,091	–	1,200
1988	30,708	5,472	1,107	4,283	3,635	1,142	467	–	1,205

Sweden

Economic and Labor Market Data

	Nominal GDP (millions of SKR)	Real GDP (millions of SKR)	Central Government Expenditures (billions of SKR)	Budget Surplus (Deficit) (billions of SKR)	Compensation of Employees (millions of SKR)	Civilian Employment (thousands)	Dependent Employment (thousands)	Unemployed (thousands)	Unemployment Rate (%)
1973	226,744	464,456	64.9	-8.3	132,687	3,879	3,521	98	2.0
1974	256,127	479,310	75.9	-10.0	153,465	3,962	3,609	80	1.6
1975	300,785	491,546	91.5	-10.8	183,786	4,062	3,715	67	1.3
1976	342,242	499,733	107.3	-10.8	218,048	4,088	3,752	66	1.3
1977	372,240	491,756	126.1	-17.8	245,217	4,099	3,770	75	1.5
1978	414,929	500,369	147.8	-31.9	273,100	4,115	3,783	94	1.8
1979	465,086	519,584	171.6	-43.8	300,130	4,180	3,843	88	1.7
1980	528,255	528,255	200.1	-54.5	338,440	4,232	3,895	86	1.6
1981	578,913	528,878	225.2	-64.0	370,353	4,224	3,890	108	2.1
1982	633,682	532,781	256.5	-77.3	391,342	4,220	3,877	137	2.6
1983	709,852	543,970	288.1	-81.8	423,525	4,224	3,891	151	2.9
1984	794,298	565,238	313.6	-72.6	463,594	4,255	3,931	136	2.6
1985	865,788	577,167	327.5	-59.0	505,417	4,299	3,986	125	2.4
1986	946,183	589,114	329.0	-31.0	553,471	4,269	3,989	117	2.2
1987	1,020,886	603,477	336.0	-9.7	597,974	4,337	3,940	84	1.9
1988	1,113,966	617,591	345.8	2.2	653,177	4,399	4,005	72	1.6

Labor Market Policy Data

	Contributions to Unemployment Insurance (millions of SKR)	Expenditures for Passive Labor Market Policy — Total (millions of SKR)	Unemp. Benefit (millions of SKR)	Unemp. Assistance (millions of SKR)	Expenditures for Active Labor Market Policy — Total (millions of SKR)	Training and Retraining (millions of SKR)	Job Creation (millions of SKR)	Preservation of Employment (millions of SKR)	Hiring Subsidies (millions of SKR)
1973	694	768.1	678.0	64.3	3,441.3	744.6	1,669.9	89.8	469.0
1974	765	812.8	653.1	67.2	3,268.5	834.6	1,315.7	37.3	615.0
1975	1,473	810.3	762.5	105.4	3,596.6	799.0	1,179.0	136.6	820.0
1976	1,578	1,017.9	1,014.8	180.6	5,435.9	829.1	1,625.5	654.0	1,054.0
1977	1,687	1,468.4	1,541.6	255.3	8,028.7	1,632.2	2,745.6	919.2	1,278.0
1978	1,834	2,192.4	1,690.0	283.2	9,339.1	2,862.9	3,381.9	537.4	1,434.0
1979	2,027	2,370.7	1,730.0	321.4	9,755.3	3,511.9	3,281.9	172.2	1,564.3
1980	2,204	2,514.1	2,595.2	408.8	9,671.5	3,367.9	3,074.1	63.1	1,586.4
1981	2,373	3,748.2	3,879.5	521.2	9,747.8	3,179.5	2,950.2	86.7	1,686.8
1982	3,869	5,297.2	5,327.4	797.0	11,402.4	3,463.6	3,887.0	134.2	1,925.5
1983	4,576	6,829.4	5,863.1	557.3	13,895.8	3,751.1	5,429.1	145.0	2,210.5
1984	6,622	7,220.4	6,066.6	388.8	15,500.6	3,823.6	4,988.3	118.5	3,889.9
1985	7,289	7,251.4	6,760.3	340.0	15,701.3	4,028.0	3,369.7	180.6	5,292.1
1986	8,878	7,612.3	7,454.7	347.4	15,827.5	4,385.5	2,676.0	351.6	5,227.9
1987	10,552	8,179.6	6,713.2	270.3	16,010.3	4,826.5	2,127.4	482.3	5,138.7
1988		7,300.0			16,021.6	5,300.7	1,809.2	523.2	4,828.5

United States

Economic and Labor Market Data

	Nominal GDP (millions of $)	Real GDP (millions of $)	Central Government Expenditures (billions of $)	Budget Surplus (Deficit) (billions of $)	Compensation of Employees (millions of $)	Civilian Employment (thousands)	Dependent Employment (thousands)	Unemployed (thousands)	Unemployment Rate (%)
1973	1,344,963	2,331,966	249.8	-17.6	807,793	85,064	76,847	4,365	4.9
1974	1,456,411	2,315,089	268.4	-3.5	885,654	86,794	78,460	5,156	5.6
1975	1,583,918	2,291,725	324.6	-43.6	952,048	85,846	77,551	7,929	8.3
1976	1,764,805	2,403,263	366.5	-66.5	1,061,846	88,752	80,519	7,406	7.7
1977	1,967,489	2,509,970	402.8	-45.0	1,181,080	92,017	83,481	6,991	7.0
1978	2,218,908	2,638,253	450.8	-48.8	1,334,485	96,048	87,205	6,202	6.1
1979	2,464,805	2,690,414	491.0	-27.7	1,497,580	98,824	89,674	6,137	5.8
1980	2,688,467	2,688,467	576.7	-59.6	1,646,254	99,303	89,950	7,637	7.2
1981	3,009,474	2,749,339	657.2	-57.9	1,817,441	100,397	91,007	8,273	7.6
1982	3,121,397	2,678,582	745.7	-127.9	1,917,904	99,526	89,967	10,678	9.7
1983	3,353,473	2,783,643	808.3	-207.7	2,032,252	100,834	91,075	10,717	9.6
1984	3,722,337	2,982,984	851.8	-185.3	2,224,438	105,005	95,120	8,539	7.5
1985	3,967,472	3,095,556	946.3	-212.2	2,379,668	107,150	97,406	8,312	7.2
1986	4,181,703	3,194,145	990.3	-221.2	2,523,912	109,597	99,847	8,237	7.0
1987	4,463,167	3,310,723	1004.6	-150.4	2,703,755	112,440	102,403	7,425	6.2
1988	4,817,775	3,459,414	1055.9	-146.7	2,922,419	114,968	104,642	6,701	5.5

Labor Market Policy Data

	Contributions to Unemployment Insurance (millions of $)	Expenditures for Passive Labor Market Policy			Expenditures for Active Labor Market Policy				
		Total (millions of $)	Unemp. Benefit (millions of $)	Unemp. Assistance (millions of $)	Total (millions of $)	Training and Retraining (millions of $)	Job Creation (millions of $)	Preservation of Employment (millions of $)	Hiring Subsidies (millions of $)
1973	6,400	5,099	4,665	—	3,283	1,021	552	—	438
1974	6,613	7,654	7,110	—	2,915	1,501	1,264	—	590
1975	6,614	20,248	19,499	—	4,073	1,947	2,448	—	665
1976	9,140	17,586	16,714	—	6,298	2,018	2,917	—	1,482
1977	11,227	14,392	13,481	—	7,582	2,294	5,781	—	3,811
1978	13,889	10,650	9,741	—	13,259	2,345	5,041	—	3,645
1979	15,081	11,229	10,253	—	12,703	2,647	3,697	—	2,491
1980	14,747	20,174	19,013	—	10,740	2,667	2,387	—	1,604
1981	15,225	18,328	17,022	—	9,691	2,699	203	—	1,853
1982	15,892	27,297	25,856	—	5,819	2,585	45	—	1,514
1983	19,114	28,151	26,593	—	5,835	1,423	—	—	1,811
1984	24,559	17,695	16,226	—	4,974	1,787	—	—	1,851
1985	24,667	17,628	16,113	—	5,412	2,008	—	—	1,498
1986	23,395	18,154	16,637	—	5,767	1,980	—	—	1,656
1987	23,528	16,496	14,923	—	5,229	2,163	—	—	—
1988	22,878	15,326	13,704	—	5,475	—	—	—	—

Notes

NOTES TO CHAPTER 1

1. In those cases in which the provision of public benefits for early retirement is coupled with requirements that the job be filled again, we categorized such benefits as being active—otherwise, passive—labor market policy (see Appendix).

NOTES TO CHAPTER 2

1. Countries are described in alphabetical order of the usual international abbreviations for automobile license plates: *A* (Austria), *D* (Federal Republic of Germany), *F* (France), *GB* (Great Britain), *S* (Sweden), *USA* (United States).

NOTES TO CHAPTER 3

1. The exception is speculative risks that are a threat to subsistence, which are dealt with usually not by the social insurance system but by prohibitions (prohibition of gambling for minors, etc.) or by systems of means-tested public assistance.
2. Not, of course, in the case of fictitious damage claims. The possibility of willfully inflicted damages is also incompatible with the pure type of

risk, but it exists de facto for all types of risks—its role in unemployment insurance is discussed below.

3. This situation naturally also presumes the existence of a market imperfection, namely, the incomplete adjustment of preferences for paid employment and for free time as a result of inflexible systems of working time.

4. For the case of short-time work, see Schmid and Semlinger 1980; Flechsenhar 1980; on layoffs see Feldstein 1975.

5. On the constraints on voluntary saving, see Matzner 1982:105. When we concentrate in the following discussion on the problem of insurance, we do not mean thereby to slight the significance of private welfare and above all private or state risk reduction (prevention). On the contrary, incentive systems for private preventive measures and state preventive policies (an essential task of active labor market policy) are preferable to mere income security for the unemployed (see Preface and Chapter 1).

NOTES TO CHAPTER 4

1. Sources: Bruche 1984b:7; Alber 1982:239, 254 ff.; Lederer 1927:362.
2. Sources: Alber 1982:239, 254 ff.; Leibfried 1977; Adamy and Steffen 1982; Wilke and Götz 1980:13 ff.
3. Sources: Alber 1982:239, 254 ff.; Bruche 1984a:4; Blaustein and Craig 1977:176; OECD 1979:110 ff.
4. Sources: Alber 1982:239, 254 ff.; Blaustein and Craig 1977:244 f.; Reissert 1985:5 ff.
5. Sources: Lederer 1927:363; Alber 1982:253.
6. Sources: Albeck and Blum 1984:234 ff.; Blaustein and Craig 1977:236 ff.
7. Not all insured persons are included in the general unemployment insurance system described here. There are special programs for some occupational groups, such as railroad employees and federal government employees.
8. This was not always the case. Until 1961, Great Britain also had a system of uniform lump-sum contributions.
9. Great Britain is again an exception.
10. For details, see Reissert 1985:24 ff.
11. For earnings between £35.50 and 55 per week, employers and employees now pay only 5 percent each; for incomes between £55 and 90, 7 percent; and for incomes between £90 and 130, 9 percent. For incomes in excess of £130 per week, employees pay 9 percent up to the upper limit on earnings subject to contributions, and employers pay 10.45 percent, also on earnings above this limit (Reissert 1985:37 ff.).
12. The federal Social Security Act also permits in principle contribution rates in the individual states below the uniform federal minimum rate.

In such a case, however, employers in the state would have to pay a correspondingly higher federal unemployment insurance contribution without being entitled to any additional benefits. See also the account of the origins of the U.S. unemployment insurance system above.

13. Not identical with the actual burden, because employer contributions can be more or less shifted forward or passed on.

14. These are Alabama, Alaska, New Jersey, and Pennsylvania.

15. In the Federal Republic of Germany called "contributions to the Federal Employment Institute" because the contributions also are used to finance active employment measures.

16. See our country reports (Bruche 1984a, 1984b; Schmid 1984; Bruche and Reissert 1985; Reissert 1985) and the literature cited therein, as well as the following comparative works: Albeck and Blum 1984; Blaustein and Craig 1977; CERC 1982, 1984; MacLennan and Weitzel 1984; OECD 1979, 1984a.

17. After a year of unemployment, the unemployment benefit is reduced by 15 percent (in comparison with that received during the first six months) and after a further six months by an additional 15 percent, and so on. At times, too, public policy in France has differentiated according to the reason for unemployment: those who lost their jobs for economic reasons (displaced workers) received 90 percent of their previous gross salary.

18. The United States has, however, made use of temporary special programs extending the period of eligibility for unemployment compensation for those who have exhausted regular benefits. However, these benefits were neither means-tested nor less than the original entitlement.

NOTES TO CHAPTER 5

1. The shifting of the financing burden back onto contributors in the Federal Republic of Germany evident in the table is particularly noteworthy in light of the fact that financial responsibility for most unemployment assistance was transferred from the Federal Employment Institute to the federal government in 1981. Without this contrary development, the shifting of the burden of financing onto contributors would have been even greater.

2. As a result of the reform of financing of unemployment insurance in 1984, which strengthened the insurance principle, the government share of financing has probably now declined.

3. According to column 4 in Table 5, Great Britain and the Federal Republic of Germany would have had the most generous benefit systems in 1975, France and the United States the least generous; in 1982, the Federal Republic and Sweden would top the generosity scale, and the United States and Great Britain would be at the bottom.

4. Because the income categories used here are not based on the actual income distribution of the unemployed, it is not representative for them.
5. The authors themselves express doubts about this procedure (Albeck and Blum 1984:7 ff.). In the United States, basic protection in case of illness is provided through the Medicare and Medicaid social programs. It is, therefore, probable that given the low wage-replacement rates, only very few unemployed purchase (private) health insurance. This is not a problem in the other countries investigated here because recipients of unemployment benefits continue to be insured in the other branches of the social security system.
6. This is particularly caused by the definition of the upper-income group, which is defined in terms of the upper limit on covered earnings in the Federal Republic of Germany. Beyond this upper limit degressive effects will also be observed in the Federal Republic of Germany; see also the studies described below.
7. When duration of unemployment is shorter than assumed by Albeck and Blum, this effect is even more apparent.
8. A certain amount of variation according to household type would also be found in the Federal Republic of Germany after 1983, when the benefit rates for single individuals and married couples without children were reduced.
9. The head of household is assigned a weight of 1, all other family members 0.5.
10. The data refer to annual income. This means that the various social benefits are not necessarily provided simultaneously. As a rule, the unemployed are only eligible for welfare payments after exhausting unemployment benefits.
11. In addition to the studies discussed here, two further ones have been conducted by the OECD (OECD 1982:56 ff.; 1984b:92 ff.). We do not consider them here because the first study is less differentiated than the two already discussed and the second study includes only three of the six countries examined here.
12. In addition, there are also *indirect* budgetary burdens as a result of unemployment that are difficult or impossible to measure. An example is the costs to the health insurance system of the health impairments resulting from the social and psychological problems of unemployment (for an overview, see Kieselbach and Wacker 1985; Land 1985); the costs of criminality (particularly youth crime) should also be included here insofar as they are a consequence of unemployment. Reductions in tax revenues as a result of the dequalification process experienced by the unemployed and the related long-term decline in the international competitiveness of individual countries, as well as the second-round effects resulting from the multiplier effect of lower individual income and consumption expenditures should also be included (Junankar 1985).

13. Only for the United States is there—to our knowledge—no roughly comparable study available. The only existing study (CBO 1982:87–92) estimates only the effects of a marginal change in unemployment (and not total unemployment), and only with regard to the federal budget (and not public budgets as a whole); on the other hand, this study also attempts to estimate second-round effects, so that the estimated budgetary burdens are relatively high. We do not, therefore, report any data for the United States and attempt only roughly to estimate the institutional distribution of the budgetary burdens of unemployment (see also the explanations in Table 12).

NOTES TO CHAPTER 6

1. The orthodox neoclassical view begins by assuming a relatively unchangeable demand function; an increase in demand can, therefore, only be induced through changes in supply prices. For a textbook on economic theory for noneconomists, see, for example, Streissler and Streissler 1984:43 f. For an example of this perspective, see Soltwedel: for the Federal Republic of Germany, he recommends that "the level of unemployment benefits should be reduced and decline with the duration of unemployment, or the duration of benefits should be reduced" as a measure to combat unemployment (Soltwedel 1984:161).
2. For an overview of unemployment insurance from the viewpoint of search theory, see, for example, Fleisher and Kniesner 1984:497–505 and the works cited therein.
3. For the Federal Republic of Germany, see the summary discussion in Bruche and Reissert 1985:182 ff.; and for other countries, Euzeby and Euzeby 1984:66 ff.
4. For a discussion of this point in greater detail, see Chapter 9.
5. Aside from orthodox, neoclassical economists who regard the existence of collective agreements themselves as a significant diminution of labor market efficiency (e.g., Soltwedel 1984).
6. Which is not very practical anyway, because the elaborate decision-making processes in a corporatist system are very costly for all parties involved. Under such institutional conditions, regulatory regimes tend to be more stable than in noncorporatist countries.
7. See, for example, the impressive statement of Bertil Rehnberg—the former head of the Swedish labor market board—on the wage-replacement rate calculations of the OECD: "Abuse can be restrained because employment offices regularly consider the possibility of active placement measures for the individual or else, for example, offer him or her vocational education. This makes it difficult for people to obtain compensation for any length of time if they are not genuinely available for employment" (Rehnberg 1984:97).

8. Because of the weakness of the relationships found in the simple two-variable model, no multiple regression analysis was carried out. The assumption that the unemployed are always aware of their net wage-replacement rate is also problematic (see Junankar 1985:59).

9. A reference to summaries must suffice here: Hamermesh 1977; Topel and Welch 1980; Danziger, Haveman, and Plotnick 1981; Gustman 1982; and Burtless 1986.

10. Further structural, particularly sectoral economic incentive effects of unemployment insurance are discussed in Chapter 9.

NOTES TO CHAPTER 7

1. The percentage of the long-term unemployed (unemployment of at least twelve months at a given point in time) as a percentage of all unemployed.

2. We do not consider here the various forms of redistribution of work through working time policy (promotion of part-time employment, regulation of overtime, flexible working time, etc.), because they are not usually included under the heading of active labor market policy.

3. For a more detailed historical and comparative analysis of the development of the instruments of labor market policy, see Schmid 1975 (for France, Great Britain, Sweden, the German Democratic Republic, and the Soviet Union); Bruche and Casey 1982 (for Austria, Belgium, West Germany, France, Great Britain, the Netherlands, Sweden, and the United States); see also *WZB* 10/1982.

4. For a comprehensive comparison of measures to combat youth unemployment in Italy, France, Great Britain, and Sweden, see *WZB* 25/1986.

5. Unemployed persons who were fifty-nine years of age could enter early retirement after a one-year period of unemployment, which in many cases led to a more or less voluntary withdrawal from work life.

6. For a comparative study of the exclusion of older employees from the work force (for France, Great Britain, the Netherlands, Sweden, and the United States), see Casey and Bruche 1983. For a comparison of early retirement programs with a replacement condition in Belgium, France, Great Britain, and the Federal Republic of Germany, see *WZB* 21/1985 and Casey 1985. The above-mentioned early retirement legislation in the Federal Republic (1984) had little impact. It is financed essentially by enterprises, which receive a grant financed through contributions from the Federal Employment Institute if the vacancy is filled again.

7. See Wildavsky 1979 for the standard work on incremental budgeting.

8. Why the principle of incrementalism does not in practice result in decrementalism in the opposite decision-making situation is described vividly by Behn 1985 with regard to the American budget process.

9. An exception is the levy system of the Industrial Training Boards which are exclusively used for the financing of apprenticeship training and are, therefore, not included here under the heading of labor market policy. See Reissert 1985:78–82 for an account of the eventful history of this levy system.

10. Very rapid increases in budget authority cannot necessarily be rapidly translated into actual increases in expenditures by these institutions. This is illustrated by the almost regular failure to exhaust budgeted funds in Great Britain (and at times also in Austria).

11. In Great Britain, the idea that an independent organization with interest groups directly represented in its administration would best be able to mobilize resources for active labor market policy was even a major consideration in the establishment of the national labor market authority, the Manpower Services Commission.

12. See Bruche 1983 for a comparative analysis of the administration of labor market programs in France, the Netherlands, Austria, Sweden, the United States—and in part the Federal Republic of Germany.

13. A particularly spectacular case of first-come-first-served was the 1979–80 program for regions with special employment problems in the Federal Republic of Germany (Scharpf et al. 1982; Peters and Schmid 1982a, 1982b). This procedure was intended inter alia to stimulate competition among labor offices and promote a rapid implementation of the program.

NOTES TO CHAPTER 8

1. For the United States, the widespread practice of layoffs (temporary redundancies), which is comparable with short-time work in Germany, is financed through unemployment insurance and hence through unemployment insurance contributions; however, it has been classified as a passive measure in this study. There are, of course, two decisive qualitative differences between layoffs and short-time work. In the case of short-time work, the employment relationship continues to exist and the uptake of this program is determined by public policy, which is not the case in the United States—except for some experiments. It therefore seems justified to classify short-time compensation as an active measure and the financing of layoffs through unemployment insurance as a passive measure.

2. Temporary layoff (*permittering*) is an exception in Sweden, which has hitherto been financed, if only to a very small extent, through the trade union unemployment insurance funds.

3. This also prevents the labor market budget from functioning as an economic stabilizer during economic downturns—at least to any great extent.

4. Seasonal unemployment is, therefore, financed to a greater extent through unemployment insurance benefits and thus through the unemployment insurance system.

5. Training measures are in Austria, as in most other countries—with the exception of the Federal Republic of Germany—purely discretionary programs. The level of program activity in each case is thus determined by the financial resources made available in the budget.

6. The state organization of vocational training in France (AFPA) has frequently been the target of similar criticism.

7. For Great Britain and the United States, the degree of activity is only an analytic construct because there is hardly any institutional relationship between active and passive labor market policies.

8. We presuppose here that although expenditures for active labor market policy lead to savings in wage-replacement benefits, these savings are not so large that no additional costs result.

9. There still may be national differences in the fiscal relief resulting from individual programs and measures of active labor market policy because they may have different types of effects on the labor market and be directed at different groups of persons in each case.

NOTES TO CHAPTER 9

1. In comparing expenditures for labor market policy with unemployment rates, it must, however, be borne in mind that as the level of active labor market policy increases, it has an increasing impact on the unemployment rate; this is especially the case in Sweden (see Figure 10). In order to get at the potential labor market situation that would have to be the point of reference for judging the appropriateness of the volume of expenditures, it is the potential total unemployment rate, what it would be without the use of labor market measures, that has to be used as a basis for comparison. This is, however, not possible because of the incompleteness of the data available on the average annual impact of active measures on the labor market. Because changes in the unemployment rate are only slightly influenced by active measures in all countries with the exception of Sweden, this indicator is still useful.

2. The unions greatly influence labor market policy in Austria inter alia by occupying key positions. The minister of social affairs is normally also simultaneously a high-level trade union official.

3. Alber (1978, 1982) offers impressive evidence for the gap between the theoretical principles and the actually established systems of unemployment insurance in European countries.

4. See on this point Hardes 1983:57–62. Instead of the concept of selectivity, Hardes uses the concept of the "concentration principle."

5. For additional evidence, see Peters and Schmid 1982a.

6. See Scharpf et al. 1982; Schmid 1983b, on the significance of personnel and organizational infrastructure for the implementation of labor market programs. The emergency program for regions with special labor market problems in 1979 analyzed by Scharpf et al. was a special case in labor market policy because it was essentially financed through the central government budget and not from contribution revenues of the Federal Employment Institute. Only under these conditions was a strong regional concentration possible (see section 7.3 above).

7. Another example is the policy of early retirement in France, which is largely financed through the unemployment insurance system and, among its other goals, also is designed to support a process of accelerated structural change. Analogously, generous wage-replacement benefits for the unemployed (e.g., in Sweden) can also be interpreted as providing active support for necessary structural change.

8. On the placement service in the Federal Republic of Germany, see the very differentiated discussion by Eberwein and Tholen 1986:162 ff., where a tendency toward favoritism is identified despite the high degree of professionalism and social consciousness of German placement officials.

9. No data are available for other possibly relevant individual characteristics such as age, duration of unemployment, entitlement to unemployment benefits, level of qualifications, and income.

10. For more details on the interpersonal redistributive effects of the U.S. CETA programs, see Mirengoff et al. 1982.

Bibliography

Adamy, Wilhelm, and Johannes Steffen. 1982. "Arbeitsmarktpolitik" in der Depression, Sanierungsstrategien in der Arbeitslosenversicherung 1927–1933. *Mitteilungen aus der Arbeitsmarkt- und Berufsforschung* 15, no. 3, pp. 276–91.

Albeck, Hermann, and Julius Blum. 1984. *Soziale Sicherung von Arbeitslosen. Ein internationaler Vergleich.* Köln.

Alber, Jens. 1978. Regierungen, Arbeitslosigkeit und Arbeitslosenschutz. *Kölner Zeitschrift für Soziologie und Sozialpsychologie* 30, no. 4, pp. 726–60.

———. 1982. *Vom Armenhaus zum Wohlfahrtsstaat. Analysen zur Entwicklung der Sozialversicherung in Westeuropa.* Frankfurt–New York: Campus.

Arrow, Kenneth J. 1971. The Organization of Economic Activity: Issues Pertinent to the Choice of Market versus Nonmarket Allocation. In: R. H. Haveman and J. Margolis (eds.), *Public Expenditures and Policy Analysis.* Chicago, pp. 59–73.

Atkinson, Anthony B., J. Gomulka, J. Micklewright, and N. Rau. 1984. Unemployment Benefit, Duration and Incentives in Britain: How Robust Is the Evidence? *Journal of Public Economics* 23, pp. 3–26.

Bach, Hans-Uwe, Hans Kohler, and Eugen Spitznagel. 1986. Arbeitsmarktpolitische Massnahmen: Entlastungswirkung und Kostenvergleiche. *Mitteilungen aus der Arbeitsmarkt- und Berufsforschung* 19, no. 3, pp. 370–75.

Barnett, Joel. 1982. *Inside the Treasury.* London: A. Deutsch.

297

Behn, Robert D. 1985. Cutback Budgeting. *Journal of Policy Analysis and Management* 4, no. 2, pp. 155–77.

Björklund, Anders. 1981. *Studies in the Dynamics of Unemployment.* Stockholm: EFI.

Björklund, Anders, and Bertil Holmlund. 1983. *Arbetslöshetsersättningen i Sverige—Motiv, regler och effekter.* Stockholm: Industrial Institute for Economic and Social Research, no. 151.

———. 1986. *The Economics of Unemployment Insurance—The Case of Sweden.* Stockholm: Industrial Institute for Economic and Social Research, no. 167.

Blaustein, Saul J., and Isabel Craig. 1977. *An International Review of Unemployment Insurance Schemes.* Kalamazoo, Mich.: W. E. Upjohn Institute for Employment Research.

BMF (Bundesministerium der Finanzen). 1973–1990. *Finanzbericht* (yearly). Bonn.

Bosch, Gerhard. 1986. Perspektiven der Finanzierung der Arbeitsmarktpolitik. In: K. J. Bieback (ed.), *Die Sozialversicherung und ihre Finanzierung.* Frankfurt–New York: Campus, pp. 320–47.

Bruche, Gert. 1983. Die Administration arbeitsmarktpolitischer Programme. Ein internationaler Vergleich (Frankreich, Niederlande, Österreich, Schweden, USA). Discussion Paper IIM/LMP 83-10. Wissenschaftszentrum Berlin.

———. 1984a. Die Finanzierung der Arbeitsmarktpolitik: Frankreich. Discussion Paper IIM/LMP 84-21b. Wissenschaftszentrum Berlin.

———. 1984b. Die Finanzierung der Arbeitsmarktpolitik: Österreich. Discussion Paper IIM/LMP 84-21d. Wissenschaftszentrum Berlin.

Bruche, Gert, and Bernard Casey. 1982. Arbeitsmarktpolitik unter Stagflationsbedingungen—ein internationaler Überblick über die wichtigsten Massnahmen seit der Weltwirtschaftskrise 1974–75. *Mitteilungen aus der Arbeitsmarkt- und Berufsforschung* 15, no. 3, pp. 232–50.

Bruche, Gert, and Bernd Reissert. 1985. *Die Finanzierung der Arbeitsmarktpolitik. System, Effektivität, Reformansätze.* Frankfurt–New York: Campus.

Büchtemann, Christoph F. 1989. *Befristete Arbeitsverträge nach dem Beschäftigungsförderungsgesetz.* Bonn.

Büchtemann, Christoph F., and Ulrich Brasche. 1985. *Recurrent Unemployment. Longitudinal Evidence for the Federal Republic of Germany.* Paderborn: Arbeitskreis Sozialwissenschaftliche Arbeitsmarktforschung, SAMF, Arbeitspapier 1985-3.

Burtless, Gary. 1983. Why Is Insured Unemployment So Low? *Brookings Papers on Economic Activity* 1, pp. 225–49.

———. 1986. Unemployment Insurance and Labor Supply: A Survey. Manuscript. Washington, D.C.: Brookings Institution.

Cameron, David R. 1984. Social Democracy, Corporatism, Labor Quiescence, and the Representation of Economic Interest in Advanced Capitalist Society. In: J. H. Goldthorpe (ed.), *Order and Conflict in Contemporary Capitalism.* Oxford: Clarendon Press, pp. 143–78.

Casey, Bernard. 1985. Early Retirement Schemes with a Replacement Condition: Programes and Experiences in Belgium, France, Great Britain, and the Federal Republic of Germany. Discussion Paper IIM/LMP 85-6a. Wissenschaftszentrum Berlin.

Casey, Bernard, and Gert Bruche. 1983. *Work or Retirement? Labour Market and Social Policy for Older Workers in France, Great Britain, the Netherlands, Sweden and the USA.* Aldershot: Gower.

CBO (Congressional Budget Office). 1982. *The Economic and Budget Outlook: An Update.* Washington, D.C.

CERC (Centre d'Etude des Revenus et des Coûts). 1982. *L'Indemnisation du chômage en France et à l'étranger.* Paris.

———. 1984. *Changements intervenus depuis 1982 dans les systèmes d'indemnisation du chômage en France et dans quatre pays étrangers.* Paris.

Clark, Kim B., and Lawrence H. Summers. 1982. Unemployment Insurance and Labor Market Transitions. In: M. N. Baily (ed.), *Workers, Jobs and Inflation.* Washington, D.C.: Brookings, pp. 279–323.

Colin, Jean François, and Jocelyne Gaudin. 1983. Le financement de la politique de l'emploi en France. Manuscript. Paris.

Commons, John R. 1959 (1934). *Institutional Economics: Its Place in Political Economy.* Madison, Wis.

CRESGE (Centre de Recherches Economiques Sociologiques et de Gestion). 1986. Comparaison internationale de l'évolution des systèmes d'indemnisation du chômage et de leurs performances au regard des objectifs de la politique économique et sociale. Manuscript. Lille.

Danziger, Sheldon, Robert Haveman, and Robert Plotnick. 1981. How Income Transfer Programs Affect Work, Savings, and the Income Distribution: A Critical Review. *Journal of Economic Literature* 19, no. 3, pp. 975–1028.

Disney, R. 1984. The Regional Impact of Unemployment Insurance in the United Kingdom. *Oxford Bulletin of Economics and Statistics* 46, pp. 241–54.

DoL (U.S. Department of Labor). 1976–1982. *Employment and Training Report of the President.* Washington, D.C.

———. 1987. *Unemployment Insurance Financial Data Handbook (ET Handbook 394).* Washington, D.C.

Eberwein, Wilhelm, and Jochen Tholen. 1986. Öffentliche Arbeitsvermittlung als politisch-sozialer Prozess. Über die Möglichkeiten und Grenzen staatlicher Arbeitsmarktpolitik am Beispiel der Region Bremen. Bremen: Universität Bremen, Zentrale wissenschaftliche Einrichtung "Arbeit und Betrieb."

Edelbalk, P. G., and Eskil Wadensjö. 1978. Unemployment Insurance and Seasonal Unemployment. *Economy and History* 21, no. 1, pp. 3–12.

———. 1986. Temporary Layoff Compensation and Unemployment—The Case of Sweden. Manuscript. Stockholm: Institute for Social Research.

Edwards, Richard. 1979. *Contested Terrain*. New York: Basic Books.

EGI (Europäisches Gewerkschaftsinstitut). 1984. *Die wirtschaftlichen Kosten der Arbeitslosigkeit in Westeuropa*. Brussels: EGI-Info 7.

Eisen, Roland. 1976. Unsicherheit und Information—Unkontrollierbares Verhalten und das Problem des moralischen Risikos. *Jahrbücher für Nationalökonomie und Statistik* 191, no. 3, pp. 193–211.

Elster, Jon. 1979. *Ulysses and the Sirens: Studies in Rationality and Irrationality*. Cambridge, Mass.

Elster, Jon, ed. 1986. *Rational Choice*. Oxford.

Engelen-Kefer, Ursula. 1986. Die Bedeutung der Arbeitsmarktsituation für die Beschäftigungslage der Frauen. *Arbeit und Beruf* 37, no. 9, pp. 269–70.

Euzeby, Alain, and Chantal Euzeby. 1984. Social Security Financing Methods, Labour Costs and Employment in Industrialised Market Economy Countries. In: ILO, *Financing Social Security: An International Analysis*. Geneva, pp. 51–85.

Feldstein, Martin S. 1975. The Importance of Temporary Layoffs: An Empirical Analysis. *Brookings Papers on Economic Activity* 3, pp. 725–45.

Fischer, Georg, and Michael Wagner. 1985. Gestaffelte Einkommenstransfers. Die Verteilungswirkung der österreichischen Arbeitslosenversicherung. *Wirtschaft und Gesellschaft* 11, no. 2, pp. 231–42.

———. 1986. *Entmutigung durch Unterstützung? Der Einfluss des Arbeitslosengeldes auf die Dauer der Arbeitslosigkeit*. Vienna: Institut für Wirtschafts- und Sozialforschung, IV 3.1.

Flechsenhar, Hans Rolf. 1980. *Kurzarbeit als Massnahme der betrieblichen Anpassung*. Frankfurt: H. Deutsch.

Fleisher, Belton M., and Thomas J. Kniesner. 1984. *Labor Economics: Theory, Evidence, and Policy*. Englewood Cliffs, N.J.

Franz, Wolfgang. 1982. The Reservation Wage of Unemployed Persons in the Federal Republic of Germany: Theory and Empirical Tests. *Zeitschrift für Wirtschafts- und Sozialwissenschaften* 102, no. 1, pp. 29–51.

Friedman, M., and L. J. Savage. 1948. The Utility Analysis of Choices Involving Risk. *Journal of Political Economy* 56, pp. 279–304.

Frühstück, Erich, and Martin Laschitz. 1985. Verluste der Sozialversicherungsträger und des Bundesbudgets durch Arbeitslosigkeit. Vienna: Institut für Wirtschafts- und Sozialforschung, IV 1.0.5.

Garlichs, Dietrich, Friederike Maier, and Klaus Semlinger, eds. 1983. *Regionalisierte Arbeitsmarkt- und Beschäftigungspolitik*. Frankfurt–New York: Campus.

Gehlen, Arnold. 1956. *Urmensch und Spätkultur. Philosophische Ergebnisse und Aussagen*. Bonn.

Gustman, Alan L. 1982. Analyzing the Relation of Unemployment Insurance to Unemployment. In: R. G. Ehrenberg (ed.), *Research in Labor Economics* 5. Greenwich-London, pp. 69–114.

Hamermesh, Daniel S. 1977. *Jobless Pay and the Economy*. Baltimore.

———. 1979. Entitlement Effects, Unemployment Insurance, and Employment Decisions. *Economic Inquiry* 17, no. 3, pp. 317–32.

Hardes, Heinz-Dieter. 1983. Ausgaben für operative Leistungen der Arbeitsmarktpolitik. In: H. Winterstein (ed.), *Selbstverwaltung als ordnungspolitisches Problem des Sozialstaates* I. Berlin: Duncker und Humblot, Schriften des Vereins für Socialpolitik N.F. 133/I, pp. 45–87.

Hart, Robert A. 1984. *The Economics of Non-Wage Labour Costs*. London.

Hart, Robert A., and Seiichi Kawasaki. 1985. Payroll Taxes and Factor Demand. Discussion Paper IIM/IP 85-1. Wissenschaftszentrum Berlin.

———. 1986. *Payroll Taxes and Factor Demand*. Stirling: University of Stirling, Discussion Papers in Economics, Finance and Investment 125. Also in: R. G. Ehrenberg (ed.), *Research in Labor Economics* 9. Greenwich–London.

Haveman, Robert H., and Daniel H. Saks. 1985. Transatlantic Lessons for Employment and Training Policy. *Industrial Relations* 24, no. 1, pp. 20–35.

Hayek, Friedrich A. von. 1960. *The Constitution of Liberty*. Chicago and London.

Heikensten, Lars. 1984. *Studies in Structural Change and Labour Market Adjustment*. Stockholm: EDI.

Hibbs, Douglas A. 1977. Political Parties and Macroeconomic Policy. *American Political Science Review* 71, no. 4, pp. 1467–87.

Hobbes, Thomas. 1973 (1651). *Leviathan*. London–New York: Dent/Dutton.

Hodgson, Geoffrey M. 1988. *Economics and Institutions: A Manifesto for a Modern Institutional Economics*. Oxford: Polity Press.

Holmlund, Bertil. 1986. Vägar ut ur arbetslöshet—Stockholmsungdomars erfarenheter. Stockholm: FIEF Working Paper 4.

Hujer, Reinhard, and Hilmar Schneider. 1986. Determinanten der Arbeitslosigkeitsdauer in der Bundesrepublik Deutschland. Manuscript. Frankfurt–Mannheim: Sonderforschungsbereich 3.

ILO. 1984. *Year Book of Labour Statistics*. Geneva.

———. 1987. *Year Book of Labour Statistics*. Geneva.

Jallade, Jean-Pierre. 1984. Protection sociale et distribution du revenu en France. Manuscript. Paris: Institut Européen d'Education et de Politique Sociale.

Junankar, P. N. 1985. *Costs of Unemployment*. Colchester: main report for Commission of the European Communities, University of Essex.

Jungk, Wolfgang. 1984. Die Einkommensposition von Arbeitslosen im internationalen Vergleich. *Sozialer Fortschritt* 33, no. 8, pp. 182-87.

Kahn, Alfred J., and Sheila B. Kamerman. 1983. *Income Transfers for Families with Children: An Eight-Country Study*. Philadelphia.

Karr, Werner. 1983. Anmerkungen zur Arbeitslosigkeit in der nunmehr 10 Jahre dauernden Beschäftigungskrise. *Mitteilungen aus der Arbeitsmarkt- und Berufsforschung* 16, no. 3, pp. 276–79.

Kieselbach, Thomas, and Ali Wacker, eds. 1985. *Individuelle und gesellschaftliche Kosten der Massenarbeitslosigkeit.* Weinheim–Basel: Beltz.

Köhler, Christoph, and Werner Sengenberger. 1983. *Konjunktur und Personalanpassung. Betriebliche Beschäftigungspolitik in der deutschen und amerikanischen Automobilindustrie.* Frankfurt–New York: Campus.

König, Heinz. 1978. Zur Dauer der Arbeitslosigkeit. Ein Markov-Modell. *Kyklos* 31, no. 1, pp. 36–52.

Kühl, Jürgen. 1982. Das Arbeitsförderungsgesetz (AFG) von 1969. Grundzüge seiner arbeitsmarkt- und beschäftigungspolitischen Konzeption. *Mitteilungen aus der Arbeitsmarkt- und Berufsforschung* 15, no. 3, pp. 251–60.

———. 1987. Wirkungsanalyse der Arbeitsmarktpolitik. In: G. Bombach et al. (eds.), *Arbeitsmärkte und Beschäftigung.* Tübingen: J. C. B. Mohr, pp. 355–83.

Lampman, Robert J. 1984. *Social Welfare Spending: Accounting for Changes from 1950 to 1978.* Orlando.

Lancaster, Tony. 1979. Econometric Methods for the Duration of Unemployment. *Econometrica* 47, no. 4, pp. 939-56.

Land, Franz-J. 1985. Sozialmedizinische Aspekte von ökonomischer Krise und Massenarbeitslosigkeit. *Sozialer Fortschritt* 34, no. 3, pp. 62–68.

Lane, J.-E. 1987. Balancing Theory and Data in Comparative Politics. *European Political Data Newsletter* 62, pp. 4–28.

Lange, Peter, and Geoffrey Garrett. 1985. The Politics of Growth: Strategic Interaction and Economic Performance in the Advanced Industrial Democracies, 1974–1980. *Journal of Politics* 47, pp. 792–827.

Lederer, Emil. 1927. Sozialversicherung. In: *Grundriss der Sozialökonomik,* IX. Abteilung, *Das soziale System des Kapitalismus,* II. Teil. Tübingen, pp. 320–67.

Leibfried, Stephan. 1977. Die Institutionalisierung der Arbeitslosenversicherung in Deutschland. *Kritische Justiz* 10, no. 3, pp. 289–301.

Leigh, Paul J. 1986. Unemployment Insurance and the Duration of Unemployment: The Case for Reciprocal Effects. *Journal of Post Keynesian Economics* 8, no. 3, pp. 387–99.

Lester, Richard A. 1962. *The Economics of Unemployment Compensation.* Princeton, N.J.

Luhmann, Niklas. 1964. *Funktionen und Folgen formaler Organisation.* Berlin.

———. 1982. *The Differentiation of Society.* New York: Columbia University Press.

MacLennan, Emma, and Renate Weitzel. 1984. Labour Market Policy in Four Countries: Are Women Adequately Represented? In: G. Schmid and R. Weitzel (eds.), *Sex Discrimination and Equal Opportunity.* Aldershot: Gower, pp. 202–48.

Madison, James. 1970 (1840). *Journal of the Federal Convention*, E. H. Scott (ed.). Freeport, N.Y.: Books for Libraries Press.

Malinvaud, Edmond. 1977. *The Theory of Unemployment Reconsidered*. New York.

——. 1984. Unemployment Insurance. Eighth Annual Lecture of the Geneva Association. Manuscript. Oslo.

Matzner, Egon. 1982. *Der Wohlfahrtsstaat von morgen. Entwurf eines zeitgemässen Musters staatlicher Interventionen*. Frankfurt–New York: Campus.

Meidner, Rudolf, and Anna Hedborg. 1984. *Modell Schweden. Erfahrungen einer Wohlfahrtsgesellschaft*. Frankfurt–New York: Campus.

Mertens, Dieter. 1981. Haushaltsprobleme und Arbeitsmarktpolitik. *Aus Politik und Zeitgeschichte (Beilage zur Wochenzeitung Das Parlament)* 38, pp. 25–31.

Mirengoff, W. E., et al. 1982. *CETA: Accomplishments, Problems, Solutions: A Report by the Bureau of Social Science Research, Inc.* Kalamazoo, Mich.: W. E. Upjohn Institute for Employment Research.

Morgenstern, Oskar. 1966. *Spieltheorie und Wirtschaftswissenschaft*. Vienna–Munich.

Narendranathan, W., S. Nickell, and J. Stern. 1985. Unemployment Benefits Revisited. *Economic Journal* 95, pp. 307–29.

Nickell, Stephen. 1979a. The Effect of Unemployment and Related Benefits on the Duration of Unemployment. *Economic Journal* 89, pp. 34–49.

——. 1979b. Estimating the Probability of Leaving Unemployment. *Econometrica* 47, no. 5, pp. 1249–66.

Niskanen, W. A. 1971. *Bureaucracy and Representative Government*. Chicago–New York.

Nordisk Rad. 1983. *Arbejdsloshedens Omkostninger i Norden—Costs of Unemployment in Scandinavia* 1. Delrapport, Stockholm.

——. 1984. *Arbejdsloshedens Omkostninger i Norden—Costs of Unemployment in Scandinavia* 2. Delrapport, Stockholm.

OECD (Organization for Economic Co-operation and Development). 1964. *Manpower and Social Affairs Committee, Recommendation on an Active Manpower Policy*. Paris.

——. 1979. *Unemployment Compensation and Related Employment Policy Measures*. Paris.

——. 1982. *The Challenge of Unemployment: A Report to Labour Ministers*. Paris.

——. 1984a. *High Unemployment: A Challenge for Income Support Policies*. Paris.

——. 1984b. *OECD Employment Outlook 1984*. Paris.

——. 1985. *OECD Employment Outlook 1985*. Paris.

——. 1986a. *National Accounts 1972–1984*. Vol. II, Detailed Tables. Paris.

——. 1986b. *Labour Force Statistics 1964–1984*. Paris.

——. 1989a. *National Accounts 1960–1987*. Vol. I, Main Aggregates. Paris.

——. 1989b. *OECD Economic Outlook 46.* Paris.

——. 1990a. *National Accounts 1976–1988.* Vol. II, Detailed Tables. Paris.

——. 1990b. *Labour Force Statistics 1968–1988.* Paris.

Offe, Claus. 1972. Klassenherrschaft und politisches System. Die Selektivität politischer Institutionen. In: C. Offe, *Strukturprobleme des kapitalistischen Staates.* Frankfurt: Suhrkamp, pp. 65–105.

OMB (Office of Management and Budget, Executive Office of the President). 1983a–1989a. *Budget of the United States Government, Fiscal Years 1984–1990.* Washington, D.C.

——. 1983b–1989b. *Budget of the United States Government, Fiscal Years 1984–1990, Special Analyses.* Washington, D.C.

——. 1989c. *Budget of the United States Government, Fiscal Year 1990, Historical Tables.* Washington, D.C.

Parsons, Talcott. 1969. *Politics and Social Structure.* New York.

Pedersen, Peder J., and Niels Westergard-Nielsen. 1984. *A Longitudinal Study of Unemployment: History Dependence and Insurance Effects.* Aarhus: Aarhus University, Working Paper 84-4.

Peters, Aribert B., and Günther Schmid. 1982a. Aggregierte Wirkungsanalyse des arbeitsmarktpolitischen Programms der Bundesregierung für Regionen mit besonderen Beschäftigungsproblemen—Zwischenbericht. Discussion Paper IIM/LMP 82-1. Wissenschaftszentrum Berlin.

——. 1982b. Aggregierte Wirkungsanalyse des arbeitsmarktpolitischen Programms der Bundesregierung für Regionen mit besonderen Beschäftigungsproblemen—Analyse der Beschäftigungswirkungen. Discussion Paper IIM/LMP 82-32. Wissenschaftszentrum Berlin.

Rehnberg, Bertil. 1984. Labour Market Conditions: Past Trends and Outlook —Policy Issues for Unemployment Insurance Programmes. In: OECD 1984a:93–97.

Reich, M. 1984. *Capitalist Development, Class Relations and Labor History.* Berkeley.

Reissert, Bernd. 1985. Die Finanzierung der Arbeitsmarktpolitik: Grossbritannien. Discussion Paper IIM/LMP 84-21c. Wissenschaftszentrum Berlin.

——. 1986. Finanzielle Spielräume für kommunale Beschäftigungspolitik? In: H. E. Maier and H. Wollmann (eds.), *Lokale Beschäftigungspolitik.* Basel–Boston–Stuttgart: Birkhäuser, pp. 35–63.

——. 1988. Regionale Inzidenz der Arbeitsmarktpolitik und ihrer Finanzierung. Discussion Paper FS I 88-18. Wissenschaftszentrum Berlin für Sozialforschung.

Scharpf, Fritz W. 1983. Zur Bedeutung institutioneller Forschungsansätze. In: Scharpf and Brockmann 1983:9–20.

——. 1984. Plädoyer für ein kommunales Hebesatzrecht bei der Einkommensteuer. *Demokratische Gemeinde* 8, pp. 36–37.

——. 1987a. Grenzen der institutionellen Reform. In: T. Ellwein et al. (eds.), *Jahrbuch zur Staats- und Verwaltungswissenschaft,* Vol. 1. Baden-Baden: Nomos, pp. 111–51.

———. 1987b. *Sozialdemokratische Krisenpolitik in Europa. Das "Modell Deutschland" im Vergleich.* Frankfurt–New York: Campus.

———. 1987c. A Game-Theoretical Interpretation of Inflation and Unemployment in Western Europe. *Journal of Public Policy* 7, pp. 227–57.

Scharpf, Fritz W., and Marlene Brockmann, eds. 1983. *Institutionelle Bedingungen der Arbeitsmarkt- und Beschäftigungspolitik.* Frankfurt–New York: Campus.

Scharpf, Fritz W., Bernd Reissert, and Fritz Schnabel. 1976. *Politikverflechtung.* Kronberg: Scriptor.

Scharpf, Fritz W., et al. 1982. *Implementationsprobleme offensiver Arbeitsmarktpolitik. Das Sonderprogramm der Bundesregierung für Regionen mit besonderen Beschäftigungsproblemen.* Frankfurt–New York: Campus.

Schelling, Thomas C. 1971. On the Ecology of Micromotives. *The Public Interest* 22, pp. 61–98.

Schmähl, Winfried. 1986. Finanzierung sozialer Sicherung. *Deutsche Rentenversicherung* 9–10, pp. 541–70.

Schmid, Günther. 1975. *Steuerungssysteme des Arbeitsmarktes. Vergleich von Frankreich, Grossbritannien, Schweden, DDR und Sowjetunion mit der Bundesrepublik Deutschland.* Göttingen: O. Schwartz.

———. 1979. The Impact of Selective Employment Policy: The Case of a Wage-Cost Subsidy Scheme in Germany 1974–75. *Journal of Industrial Economics* 27, no. 4, pp. 339–58.

———. 1983a. Regionale Arbeitsmarktstrukturen und regionalisierte Arbeitsmarktpolitik. Das Beispiel des Sonderprogramms der Bundesregierung vom 16. Mai 1979. In: Garlichs, Maier, and Semlinger 1983:14–37.

———. 1983b. Handlungsspielräume der Arbeitsämter beim Einsatz aktiver Arbeitsmarktpolitik. In: Scharpf and Brockmann 1983:135–65.

———. 1984. Die Finanzierung der Arbeitsmarktpolitik: Schweden. Discussion Paper IIM/LMP 84-21a. Wissenschaftszentrum Berlin.

———. 1986. Finanzierung der Arbeitsmarktpolitik—Plädoyer für einen regelgebundenen Bundeszuschuss an die Bundesanstalt für Arbeit. In: K. J. Bieback (ed.), *Die Sozialversicherung und ihre Finanzierung.* Frankfurt–New York: Campus, pp. 256–82.

———. 1987. Zur politisch-institutionellen Theorie des Arbeitsmarkts. Die Rolle der Arbeitsmarktpolitik bei der Wiederherstellung der Vollbeschäftigung. *Politische Vierteljahresschrift* 28, pp. 133–61.

———. 1988. *Labor Market Policy in Transition: Trends and Effectiveness in the Federal Republic of Germany.* Stockholm: EFA Report 17.

Schmid, Günther, and Klaus Semlinger. 1980. *Instrumente gezielter Arbeitsmarktpolitik. Kurzarbeit, Einarbeitungszuschüsse, Eingliederungsbeihilfen.* Königstein: A. Hain.

Schmid, Günther, and Hubert Treiber. 1975. *Bürokratie und Politik.* Munich.

Schmidt, Manfred G. 1982. Does Corporatism Matter? Economic Crisis, Politics and Rates of Unemployment in Capitalist Democracies in the

1970s. In: G. Lehmbruch and P. Schmitter (eds.), *Patterns of Corporatist Policy-Making*. London: Sage, pp. 237–58.
———. 1986. Politische Bedingungen erfolgreicher Wirtschaftspolitik. Eine vergleichende Analyse westlicher Industrieländer (1960–1985). *Journal für Sozialforschung* 26, no. 3, pp. 251–73.
Schönbäck, Wilfried. 1980. *Subjektive Unsicherheit als Gegenstand staatlicher Intervention*. Frankfurt–New York: Campus.
Schotter, Andrew. 1985. *Free Market Economics: A Critical Appraisal*. New York.
Semlinger, Klaus, and Günther Schmid. 1985. *Arbeitsmarktpolitik für Behinderte*. Basel–Boston–Stuttgart: Birkhäuser.
Sharpe, L. J., and K. Newton. 1984. *Does Politics Matter? The Determinants of Public Policy*. Oxford: Clarendon.
Soltwedel, Rüdiger. 1984. *Mehr Markt am Arbeitsmarkt. Ein Plädoyer für weniger Arbeitsmarktpolitik*. Munich–Vienna.
Stahl, Ingmar. 1978. Unemployment Insurance: The Swedish Case. *Unemployment Insurance: Global Evidence of Its Effects on Unemployment*, proceedings of conference in Vancouver.
Steiner, Viktor. 1986. Empirische Analyse des Abgangsverhaltens aus der Arbeitslosigkeit auf einem lokalen Arbeitsmarkt mittels individualisierter Verlaufsdaten. Manuscript. Linz: Forschungsschwerpunkt S44 der Universität Linz.
Streissler, Erich, and Monika Streissler. 1984. *Grundzüge der Volkswirtschaftslehre für Juristen*. Vienna.
Therborn, Göran. 1986. *Why Some Peoples Are More Unemployed Than Others*. London: Verso.
———. 1987. Does Corporatism Really Matter? The Economic Crisis and Issues of Political Theory. *Journal of Public Policy* 7, pp. 259–84.
Topel, Robert, and Finis Welch. 1980. Unemployment Insurance: Survey and Extensions. *Economica* 47, no. 187, pp. 351–79.
Veblen, Thorsten. 1934 (1899). *The Theory of the Leisure Class: An Economic Study of Institutions*. New York: Modern Library.
Vroman, Wayne. 1986. *The Funding Crisis in State Unemployment Insurance*. Kalamazoo, Mich.
Wadensjö, Eskil. 1985. The Financial Effects of Unemployment and Labour Market Policy Programs for Public Authorities in Sweden. Discussion Paper IIM/LMP 85-7. Wissenschaftszentrum Berlin.
Wagner, Michael. 1983. Beschäftigungsgarantie oder Existenzsicherung durch Sozialtransfers? *Das öffentliche Haushaltswesen in Österreich* 24, no. 4, pp. 161–77.
Webber, Douglas. 1987. Eine Wende in der deutschen Arbeitsmarktpolitik? Sozial-liberale und christlich-liberale Antworten auf die Beschäftigungskrise. In: H. Abromeit and B. Blanke (eds.), *Arbeitsmarkt, Arbeitsbeziehungen und Politik in den 80er Jahren, Leviathan*, Special Issue 8, pp. 74–85.

Weitzel, Renate. 1983. *Berufliche Bildung nach dem Arbeitsförderungsgesetz. Rechtliche und institutionelle Bedingungen der Teilnahme von Frauen im Vergleich zu Männern.* Discussion Paper IIM/LMP 83-12. Wissenschaftszentrum Berlin.

Wildavsky, Aaron. 1979. *The Politics of the Budgetary Process.* Boston–Toronto.

Wilke, Gerhard, and Gerhard Götz. 1980. *Die Finanzen der Bundesanstalt für Arbeit.* Stuttgart: Kohlhammer.

WZB (Wissenschaftszentrum Berlin). 1980–. *Internationale Chronik zur Arbeitsmarktpolitik* (quarterly). Berlin.

Index

Active labor market policy:
administration costs, 34, 53–54;
administration of, 174–75, 180;
definition, 11, 22, 29–30; financing
sources of, 163–67, 181–84;
instruments of, 163–64; level of
expenditure, 267–69; substituted for
passive labor market policy, 192–209,
252
Aid to Families with Dependent Children
(AFDC), 54, 131, 170
Albeck, Hermann, 126–30
Alber, Jens, 71
Allocation spéciale, 40, 43, 126, 133–35,
144, 229
AMI centers, 50
AMU centers, 50
Apprenticeship training, 166, 187
Arbeitsmarktverwaltung, 32–33
Association pour l'Emploi dans
l'Industrie et le Commerce
(ASSEDIC), 41–43, 74
Atkinson, Anthony, 157
Austria, 29, 32–35, 71–72, 89–90, 244–54;
effects of unemployment benefits, 155;
factors influencing expenditure levels,
188; factors influencing expenditure
variations, 217; regional distribution

of labor market policy, 224–25; role of
active labor market policy, 186
Austrian labor market authority, 33
Availability for work as requirement for
unemployment benefits, 103
Average benefit expenditures per
recipient, 121–22
Average benefit for individual recipients,
121, 254, 271

Bad weather benefits, 34, 230; bad
weather contributions, 34
Balancing budgets, 171–74
Balancing of the unemployment
insurance fund budget: Austria, 33–34,
89; Germany, 38, 89
Bankruptcy wage benefits, 34, 38
Beveridge, 75, 86
Bismarck, Otto von, 70, 79
Björklund, Anders, 157
Blaustein, Saul J., 123–24
Blum, Julius, 126–30
Budget ceilings, 170–71
Budget for labor market policy:
integrated, 169–70; separate, 169–70
Budgeting, 34, 55
Budgeting process for active labor market

309